Rebuilding Shattered Lives

Rebuilding Shattered Lives

THE RESPONSIBLE TREATMENT OF COMPLEX POST-TRAUMATIC AND DISSOCIATIVE DISORDERS

JAMES A. CHU, M.D.

JOHN WILEY & SONS, INC.

New York • Chichester • Weinheim • Brisbane • Singapore • Toronto

Library of Congress Cataloging-in-Publication Data
Chu, James A.
    Rebuilding shattered lives : treating complex post-traumatic and dissociative disorders / James A. Chu ; foreword by Christine A. Courtois.
        p.   cm.
    Includes bibliographical references and index.
    ISBN 0-471-24732-4 (cloth : alk. paper)
    1. Adult child abuse victims—Rehabilitation. 2. Dissociative disorders—Treatment. 3. Post-traumatic stress disorder—Treatment.
    I. Title.
    RC569.5.C55C48   1998
    616.85'8223906—dc21   97-32847
                                                                                        CIP

Printed in the United States of America

10 9 8 7 6

This book is dedicated to the many fine clinicians and individuals who have been a part of the Trauma and Dissociative Disorders Program at McLean Hospital, whose efforts, compassion, and expertise have contributed to the healing and growth of the patients they have served.

Contents

PART ONE:

PART TWO:

PART THREE:

Chapter 14

Foreword

I HAVE BEEN waiting for this book since 1988, when I read a clinical article by Dr. James Chu. His article, which appeared in the journal *Dissociation* was called *"Ten Traps for Therapists in the Treatment of Trauma Survivors"* and it spoke to me! It provided insight about the psychotherapy I was engaged in with abused patients, who manifested an array of symptoms and relational challenges. It simultaneously provided guidance and reassurance. Since that time, I have made it a point to seek out and read Dr. Chu's articles as they have been published and have had the pleasure of meeting him, attending his workshops, and co-lecturing with him. These experiences continued to do what the original article did: They at once reassured, educated, and offered sound counsel about the treatment of severely traumatized individuals. Dr. Chu seems always to be ahead of the curve. He has articulated issues before many of us knew they were issues, and he has offered new and broader ways to conceptualize patient dynamics and treatment approaches.

Several years ago, I began asking Dr. Chu when he was going to expand and consolidate his articles into a book and expressed my belief that, in doing so, he would make a major contribution to the literature. It was with surprise and pleasure that I learned his book was in the works. I am honored to have been asked to provide the Foreword to *Rebuilding Shattered Lives*. As I predicted, it is a significant addition to the clinical literature on the treatment of complex post-traumatic and dissociative disorders associated with past abuse. It continues Dr. Chu's tradition of explaining and demystifying the challenges presented by patients with these diagnoses, and it articulates a structured treatment process that is at once rational, responsible, and responsive.

In recent years, the treatment of adults traumatized by child abuse has been heavily scrutinized. Critics have been concerned about treatment they consider to be overly abuse-focused and have challenged the notion of recovered memories of past abuse, especially in cases where no memory was previously available. Many have also expressed concern about suggestive therapeutic techniques used to stimulate recall and about overfascination with and overdiagnosis of the dissociative disorders, particularly dissociative identity disorder. Therapists have been castigated for using misguided practices that resulted in therapeutic mishaps, the reinforcement of dissociative process, and/or the production of so-called false memories of abuse that never occurred.

The publication of *Rebuilding Shattered Lives* in the midst of this contentious debate is an important milestone. The book stakes out a middle-ground position that is very much needed. It details the continued evolution of the abuse-responsive treatment model, thereby assuring that those who have been traumatized by abuse are not again denied or abandoned. It provides strategic and technical assistance to therapists treating this population, who feel significantly under seige. It also provides an updated model that incorporates emerging research findings and attends to the most legitimate of the memory commentaries, thus reassuring the critics that their concerns have been taken seriously.

Dr. Chu's articulation of his redefined treatment model reviews its development over the course of the past two decades. He describes the importance of society's rediscovery of child abuse and other forms of interpersonal trauma along with the gains that have been made in documenting their effects and in formulating new diagnostic conceptualizations. These, in turn, have provided a foundation for the development of an abuse- and trauma-focused treatment model, designed as a corrective to traditional approaches that rarely acknowledged (let alone treated) these issues. Dr. Chu discusses the advances made by this model but also chronicles its weaknesses and how these became apparent in relatively short order, even before the false memory controversy emerged. Clinicians learned that a treatment too narrowly focused on abuse, its reconstruction, and abreaction to the exclusion of issues of safety, stabilization, and personal functioning proved to be naïve at best, damaging at worst. In the worse case, such treatment resulted in regression and an exacerbation of symptoms rather than any relief and healing. Clinicians also gained an appreciation of the extraordinary difficulties inherent in treating these patients due to their comorbid diagnoses, their complicated symptom pictures, their high degree of acuity and risk, and the intense interpersonal demands and challenges they routinely brought to psychotherapy.

It is obvious that Dr. Chu has reflected deeply upon these issues and that he has had experience in "in the trenches." He calls upon his considerable inpatient and outpatient experience with these patients and his familiarity with the pertinent literature to elucidate the treatment model and guidelines presented in this book. The model helps the clinician steer a reasonable course in providing treatment to traumatized and dissociative patients, a treatment that does not overwhelm the patient or the therapist and that manages the various risks associated with the treatment. It is a research- and training-based model, calling for caution and reason regarding all strategies and techniques, those having to do with memory recovery in par- ticular. It is also a stage-oriented treatment that, using the mnemonic SAFER for the work of the first stage, underscores self-care and symptom control, acknowledgment, functioning, expression, and relationship issues as essential preliminary tasks to be undertaken long before any directed focus is placed on abuse issues per se. Dr. Chu discusses the rationale be- hind the reworking and abreaction of traumatic material and emphasizes the importance of addressing and resolving the core abuse-related issues and beliefs that so often plague adult survivors. He shows how for the truly traumatized this treatment is far from a search for the missing memories; in- stead, it is a process of life reconstruction and enhancement.

Dr. Chu is very effective in conveying the difficulties and challenges posed by these patients (especially early in the treatment process) and cogently discusses ways to manage these challenges. I find especially in- sightful and useful his discussions on the shift of therapeutic responsibility and chronic disempowerment, empathic confrontation, and relational issues and the therapeutic dance, as well as his sound advice regarding the treat- ment of dissociative identity disorder. Clinical examples provide realistic, graphic, and compelling illustration of the points under discussion and help familiarize and desensitize the reader to their appearance and management.

I highly recommend this book. I learned a lot reading it and I felt comforted by its clinical wisdom and commonsense approach. I regard *Re- building Shattered Lives* as "must-reading" for all clinicians who treat post- traumatic and dissociative disorders.

Christine A. Courtois, Ph.D.
Author, *Healing the Incest Wound*
and *Adult Survivors of Child Sexual Abuse*
Clinical Director, The CENTER: Post-traumatic
Disorders Program, The Psychiatric Institute of Washington
and Psychologist, Independent Practice
Washington, DC

Introduction

THE PAST two decades have seen extraordinary changes in views about the traumatization of children. Attitudes of both mental health professionals and the public moved from virtual denial of the existence and effects of child abuse in the 1970s to the almost fervid preoccupation with these issues in the 1980s. In the heady excitement of those days, at least three central tenets were put forth: The abuse of children was an epidemic with untold human consequences; abuse was the hidden root of innumerable societal ills and mental illness; and recognition and uncovering of abuse memories were the keys to both individual and societal health. New ways of recognizing and treating childhood abuse were invented, and specialized treatment programs emerged across the United States and throughout the world.

However, in the late 1980s and early 1990s, the pendulum began to swing in the opposite direction. Although there were many successful treatments of adults who had survived various kinds of childhood abuse, the treatment of those with particularly severe childhood traumatization proved far from simple. Aggressive attempts to help some severely traumatized patients explore and abreact their childhood abuse resulted in profound regression and lengthy, intensive, and expensive treatment. It slowly became clear that there were pitfalls in a simplistic focus on the childhood traumatic events. In addition to experiencing the traumatic events, many survivors of abuse grew up in extraordinarily chaotic and disrupted environments that led to massive disabilities. Their lives, their relationships, and often even their identities were shattered. They developed fundamental assumptions about the world as malevolent and themselves as defective and powerless, leaving them poorly equipped to cope with even basic human functioning. Perhaps most important, they also learned to approach others with deep mistrust, making all relationships—including therapeutic relationships—tenuous and potentially explosive. In retrospect, it is easy to see how severely trau-

1

matized persons failed to benefit from a type of exploratory therapy that assumes basic trust and the ability to tolerate intense and dependent therapeutic relationships. In addition to sometimes painful and unsuccessful treatment, a premature emphasis on childhood abuse resulted in a fixation on the trauma as the central theme of the lives of some patients, with their identities becoming organized around their traumatization. Thus, rather than seeing the abuse as events to be overcome, these patients essentially began to see themselves as chronically victimized and disabled, sometimes with an expectation of compensation for their early experiences.

The early 1990s brought further difficulties. Compounding the complexities of treating survivors of extensive early trauma, the mental health community slowly began to understand that some patients' reports of their childhood abuse were inaccurate. Some patients—especially those who became fixated on their abuse—began to unconsciously embellish what they recalled, leading to ever more lurid accounts of childhood events. Other patients—especially those with impaired reality testing or who were extremely vulnerable to suggestion—began to believe that they had been abused despite all evidence to the contrary. In addition, a number of patients and other persons began to falsely allege that they had been abused as children as means of meeting needs such as avoiding legal responsibility, obtaining compensation, or resolving their internal emptiness and a compulsion to get attention.

A backlash began to develop. As often occurs in situations where human ills cannot be easily solved, childhood abuse survivors were either disbelieved or characterized as being part of a "culture of blame." Even more devastating, a coalition of parents who had been alienated from their children or who had been sued for allegedly abusing their children joined with skeptical academics in the psychiatric and psychological community to form the False Memory Syndrome Foundation (FMSF). The FMSF has pursued a well-funded and highly publicized agenda to discredit many patients who report childhood abuse and the professionals who treat them; as a result, many professionals have been targets of lawsuits and had their reputations destroyed, and many of those who work with adult survivors of childhood abuse have lived in an atmosphere of fear and defensiveness.

What will be the result of these changes in how traumatized patients are viewed? Will the legacy of abuse be once again buried in denial and blaming? There is some room for optimism despite ongoing acrimony between clinicians who treat abuse survivors and those who view abuse memories as inherently flawed and unreliable. In 1996 there were two important meetings—one in Paris under the auspices of NATO, and an international research conference sponsored by the Family Research Laboratory of the University of New Hampshire under the direction of Linda Meyer-Williams and David Finkelhor—where clinicians and investigators involved with treating traumatized patients and researchers involved with understanding memory and memory distortion gathered to find common ground. Proponents on both sides of the memory debate presented research findings and clinical evidence, resulting in a distinct abatement of the intensity of the debate on both sides. Perhaps this kind of dialogue will result in greater sophistication in the understanding of the effects of traumatization, and committed professionals will be tempered by the strife to become even more effective in their work with traumatized patients.

This book traces the advances of the past two decades in understanding the nature of childhood abuse and the treatment of its effects. The main emphasis is on some of the most severely traumatized patients and the need to develop a sophisticated understanding of their difficulties, and how to implement a responsible, rational, and balanced treatment. The book is divided into three parts. Part I traces the history of recent findings about child abuse and its effects on psychological functioning and provides an overview of the nature of traumatic memory. Part II describes the basic principles of the treatment of adults who have complex trauma-related difficulties, including detailed discussions of self-care, symptom control, and relational issues. Part III covers special topics, including the treatment of dissociative identity disorder, chronic disability, acute care treatment, and controversies in the field of dissociation. Throughout this volume, there are many clinical vignettes of the type of dilemmas that face mental health professionals. We learn best from our patients, and these clinical situations better illustrate clinical wisdom than even the most erudite academic discussions. To protect the identities of the persons discussed, the features of those involved have been altered and many actual events have been combined to create composite case illustrations.

This volume is not a definitive discussion of the subject. Although we have a much greater understanding of traumatized patients and an enhanced armamentarium of treatment interventions, there is still much to be learned. We must continue to wrestle with important issues, recognizing that not all the extreme beliefs about childhood abuse may be factually accurate, but still acknowledging the tragedy and suffering of children who grow up in malevolent environments. We must hear the experiences of our patients and help to give them voice, but must better comprehend the vagaries of memory and understand that psychological reality is not necessarily the same as objective reality. We must acknowledge and value new treatments, but continue to rely on the traditional foundations of psychotherapy. As clinicians, we must combine our best knowledge, skill, and expertise to be of maximal help to relieve the distress of our patients.

James A. Chu, M.D.
Belmont, Massachusetts

PART ONE

THE NATURE AND EFFECTS OF CHILDHOOD ABUSE

CHAPTER 1

The Rediscovery of the Abuse of Children

PSYCHOLOGICAL TRAUMA is an affliction of the powerless. At the moment of trauma, the victim is rendered helpless by overwhelming force. When the force is that of nature, we speak of disasters. When the force is that of other human beings, we speak of atrocities. Traumatic events overwhelm the ordinary systems of care that give people a sense of control, connection, and meaning. . . . They confront human beings with the extremities of helplessness and terror, and evoke the responses of catastrophe.
—Judith Lewis Herman, *Trauma and Recovery* (1992, p. 33)

Traumatization is part of the human experience. Whether by acts of nature or by acts of man, catastrophic events can overwhelm human beings' ability to cope and result in a variety of post-traumatic responses. If the traumatization is severe or prolonged, or occurs early in life, post-traumatic stress disorder (PTSD) and dissociative disorders are likely to develop. The traumatic etiologies of these disorders are numerous and are generally thought to include war-time combat, physical or sexual assault, psychological terror, accidents and natural disasters, and other kinds of exposure to shocking or terrorizing events.

Exposure to traumatic events is common in our society. A sampling of 5,877 adults in the general U.S. population (part of the National Comorbidity Study [NCS]), estimated the lifetime exposure to severe traumatic events at approximately 61% in men and 51% in women (Kessler, Sonnega, Bromet, Hughes, & Nelson, 1995). Other recent studies have demonstrated similarly high levels of traumatic exposure (Breslau, Davis, Andreski, & Peterson, 1991; Resnick, Kilpatrick, Dansky, Saunders, & Best, 1993). However, it is unclear how this high prevalence of exposure to traumatic events translates into rates of post-traumatic and dissociative disorders. Not every shocking experience, and perhaps not even most traumatic events, results in serious psychopathology. The NCS determined a lifetime prevalence of PTSD at 7.8% (Kessler et al., 1995)—much higher than previous general population estimates of around 1% (Davidson, Hughes, Blazer, & George, 1991; Helzer, Robins, & McEvoy, 1987), probably due to differences in diagnostic criteria and assessment procedures. In the NCS, traumas in men that were most likely to result in PTSD included rape, combat exposure, childhood neglect, and childhood physical abuse; women were more likely than men to become symptomatic following rape, sexual molestation, physical attack, being threatened with a weapon, and childhood physical abuse. Of particular note was the finding that although men were more likely to be exposed to traumatic conditions than women (61% vs. 51%), women were twice as likely as men to develop PTSD (10% vs. 5%). This result might point to women's increased vulnerability to develop PTSD, or to the more severe sequelae of certain forms of traumatization since women were more than 13 times more likely than men to be the victims of rape or sexual molestation.

The nature and severity of the traumatic events may influence whether prolonged psychological effects will occur. Post-traumatic responses to brief or single overwhelming events in an otherwise intact person tend to be less severe and not long-lasting. Many such experiences spontaneously resolve, becoming muted with time and encapsulated deep in the psyche, reappearing only in nightmares and under conditions of severe stress. Persistent and disabling trauma-related responses are usually seen only in those who have been exposed to particularly severe or chronic traumatization. The most severe post-traumatic and dissociative disorders most commonly result from certain types of prolonged childhood abuse, chronic combat experiences, and long-term battering relationships. There are undoubtedly individual variations in response to stressful events, with some persons having a greater-than-normal capacity to cope with trauma and recover from such experiences. Trauma research has not yet sufficiently explored populations that have been exposed to trauma and do *not* develop post-traumatic or dissociative disorders. However, patients with severe and persistent post-traumatic and dissociative disorders often have histories of extreme trauma such as malignant childhood abuse. It is likely that experiences of this sort would be poorly tolerated by any individual, regardless of coping capacity or resilience.

Chronic childhood traumatization poses a particular problem in our society. Often unrecognized or unacknowledged, such experiences have profound effects on the psyche. Severe childhood abuse, if untreated, results in a variety of post-traumatic responses and alterations in personality development. Furthermore, because the innate capacity to use dissociative defenses is greatest in childhood (Bernstein & Putnam, 1986; Saunders & Giolas, 1991), traumatized and abused children are at most risk for developing severe dissociative disorders, including dissociative identity disorder. Given the prevalence of child maltreatment in our country, it is not surprising that the post-traumatic and dissociative disorders seen in many acute care settings are often due to severe and persistent childhood traumatization.

It is extraordinary that our current awareness of the extent and nature of child abuse in our society is relatively recent. In academic and training programs in the 1970s and early 1980s, the problem was understated. Future health professionals received little formal training concerning adults who were suffering from post-traumatic effects of childhood maltreatment. These deficits were particularly evident in the medical profession. Medical students were taught to look for signs of physical maltreatment and "failure to thrive"—those babies who simply didn't grow and develop normally as a result of severe neglect and malnutrition. However, there was no real awareness of the magnitude of the problem or the long-standing effects of early abuse and neglect. Even residency programs in psychiatry and graduate training in psychology—whether psychodynamically or empirically oriented—offered little information about how childhood abuse can affect adult mental functioning and no specific training in the recognition and treatment of adult survivors of childhood abuse. It has only been in the past 10 to 15 years that both public and professional attention has been drawn to this issue. Much of our current understanding of the prevalence and effects of childhood abuse, particularly sexual abuse, has derived from the efforts of the work of pioneering professionals in the 1970s and early 1980s, many of whom came from within the women's movement and were investigating sexual violence against women. Their studies led them to uncover the extent of such abuse against children. As a result, we are now beginning to understand the magnitude of childhood abuse and the enormous impact of trauma on the psyches and lives of abuse survivors.

A HIDDEN EPIDEMIC?

In the 1970s, governmental child protective services were established, requiring that human services professionals report all cases in which there is a strong suspicion of child maltreatment. Since then, there has been a phenomenal rise in the number of reported cases of suspected child abuse. A report from the Department of Health and Human Services (U.S. Department of Health and Human Services, 1990) chronicled a rise from 60,000 reported cases in 1974 to more than 2,400,000 cases in 1989. The nature of the suspected maltreatment included emotional abuse and neglect, as well as physical and sexual abuse. The rate of reported childhood maltreatment has continued to rise, with more than 2,800,000 cases reported in 1994 (U.S. Department of Health and Human Services, 1996a).

Does this dramatic increase imply more instances of abuse or simply more reporting? Three sequential studies mandated by congress monitored the prevalence of child abuse and neglect from 1979 to 1993 (U.S. Department of Health and Human Services, 1981, 1988, 1996b). The most recent of these studies, the Third National Incidence Study on Child Abuse and Neglect (NIS-3)(U.S. Department of Health and Human Services, 1996b), estimated that in 1993, 1,553,800 children were moderately or severely harmed as a result of abuse or neglect; this represents a prevalence rate of 2.3% of all children. These findings include 217,700 cases of sexual abuse, 381,700 cases of physical abuse, 204,500 cases of emotional abuse, and 879,000 cases of neglect. An estimated 1,500 children died as a result of their abuse in 1993. The numbers of abused and neglected children in 1993 were two-thirds higher than in 1986. Even taking into account the greater number of children in the population, a child had more than 1.5 times the risk of experiencing maltreatment in 1993 than in 1986. The NIS-3 concluded that although recognition of maltreatment by community professionals has improved, there have been substantial increases in the number of children who are abused and neglected. Just as alarming as the rates of child maltreatment, the NIS-3 found that child protective agencies investigated the cases of only 28% of children recognized as harmed in 1993, a substantial decrease from 44% investigated in 1986. The actual number of annual investigations remained approximately the same over this period, suggesting that child protective services have been stretched past capacity.

There has been much progress in the recognition of child maltreatment and the treatment of its effects. However, we are now seeing evidence of a new and related societal phenomenon: chaos and chronic exposure to danger and violence in some areas of our inner cities. Such urban war zones have led to the destruction of any sustaining social fabric in these communities, exposing millions of children to traumatic events. Many of these children have been chronically brutalized and terrorized and present extraordinary dilemmas for treatment and psychosocial interventions.

Maria, a 22-year-old African-American woman, was admitted to a psychiatric facility after being found dazed and intoxicated near an inner city emergency room. Initially she was disoriented and disorganized, going from states of some coherence to states in which she was either mute or terrified. Over several days, this lability subsided and she was able to report growing up in a dangerous housing project where crime and drug use were rampant; it was not unusual for her to hear gunshots after dark. In her relatively young life she had been physically and sexually abused by a brother and an uncle, had witnessed innumerable assaults on family and friends, had been gang raped at 14, and was involved with drugs and alcohol. The brother who molested her was in jail on drug offenses, but she lived with her grandmother, older sister, and an uncle who was under house arrest; this uncle continued to physically and sexually abuse her and to prostitute her to others. She refused to leave the home because she saw herself as the protector of her sister and grandmother, who could become targets of her uncle's violence. She refused all social interventions, fearful that telling would lead to retributions by her uncle. She did agree to see a therapist, but previous attempts at therapy had failed due to the patient's inability to extricate herself from ongoing abuse.

It is clear that these kinds of situations cannot be solved simply by improvements in clinical treatments. A solution will require the implementation of a broad social agenda that seeks to redress the misfortune of the impoverished, disadvantaged, and demoralized persons in our society. If we continue only to blame those who are caught in a spiral of adversity, helplessness, and passivity, we condemn them to an endless cycle of violence that will result in high costs in terms of both future financial resources and human suffering.

SEXUAL ABUSE: THE SECRET TRAUMA

Much progress has been made in establishing the prevalence and detrimental effects of child abuse, particularly sexual abuse and incest. Prior to the past two decades, incest was not only considered infrequent, but also not necessarily harmful. In the late 1970s and early 1980s, a number of important contributions were made by investigators who were concerned about the neglected issues that affected women and girls. The work of these professionals flew in the face of societal complacency and began exposing some of the realities of childhood abuse. While working with child protective agencies, clinicians such as psychiatrists Jean Goodwin and Suzanne Sgroi and doctor of nursing Anne Burgess began to investigate the effects of abuse on children and published authoritative texts on the treatment of sexually abused children (Burgess, Groth, Holmstrom, & Sgroi, 1978; Goodwin, 1982; Sgroi, 1982). Harvard psychiatrist Judith Herman began hearing story after story concerning incest in her adult patients diagnosed with borderline personality disorder. She found the incest stories convincing and began studying sexual violence. The result was the stunning book *Father–Daughter Incest* (1981), a scientifically credible work that documented the nature and undeniable harmful effects of sexual violation which she found to be more common than had been previously believed. Psychologist Christine Courtois began studying rape in a college setting in the 1970s. It became clear that many of the harmful effects of rape were derived not only from the current sexual assault, but from the backgrounds of childhood sexual abuse of many of the rape victims. Courtois chronicled her findings, first in a paper (1979) and later in a comprehensive volume, *Healing the Incest Wound* (1988), which was one of the first authoritative texts to describe treatment for adult survivors of familial sexual violation.

Research on the prevalence of childhood sexual abuse has yielded disturbing information. In 1986, sociologist Diana Russell's *The Secret Trauma: Incest in the Lives of Girls and Women* reported the results of a landmark survey on the prevalence of sexual abuse in women in the general population (1986). In this study of 930 women from a cross section of socioeconomic and ethnic backgrounds, more than one third reported some kind of unwanted sexual contact in childhood. About half of the reported sexual abuse was incestuous—sexual abuse perpetrated by a family member. These findings were considered surprisingly high when first reported, but have stood up well in subsequent studies. In her groundbreaking work, Russell discussed the effects of childhood sexual abuse, which ranged from benign to life destroying, depending on the circumstances of the abuse. However, Russell's work and other subsequent studies have made it clear that the sexual abuse of girls is widespread and that it occurs throughout all socioeconomic levels.

The prevalence of the sexual abuse of boys has been more recently studied, most notably by psychologists Diana Elliott and John Briere (1995) at the University of Southern California, and by psychiatrist David Finkelhor and colleagues at the University of New Hampshire (Finkelhor, Hotaling, Lewis, & Smith, 1990). Both studies found that one in six men in the general population reports having had some kind of sexual abuse in childhood. These and other studies lead to the unfortunate conclusion that childhood physical and sexual abuse is widespread in our society and is perpetrated on both girls and boys. Although both physical and sexual abuse occur among all children, girls appear to be somewhat more likely than boys to be sexually abused, and boys more likely than girls to be physically abused.

Most abuse-related research in recent years has dealt with physical and sexual abuse, or with just sexual abuse. Sexual abuse is relatively easier to define than physical abuse, and both are easier to quantify than emotional abuse or neglect. However, this focus on physical and sexual abuse should not detract from understanding that other kinds of abuse, including the witnessing of violence, emotional abuse, and serious neglect (all of which are more common than physical and sexual abuse), have deleterious effects on the psychological development of children. Some severely abused patients, after years of struggle, have eventually come to terms with having been physically harmed, but have had a much more difficult time with their emotional abuse. As one patient reported, "I can accept that I was hit and raped, but I can't get over having been hated."

How do we interpret the disturbing findings concerning the abuse of children? Will all or most of the children who have suffered abuse go on to develop serious lifelong psychiatric or psychological difficulties? The answer is almost certainly that many will not. Considerable evidence indicates that children can rebound from even severe stress. We know that most children are enormously resilient, and those who suffer mild or time-limited abuse may spontaneously heal if placed in a normally nurturing environment. A single instance of sexual abuse perpetrated by someone outside the family—such as an encounter with a stranger who exposes himself or a baby-sitter who fondles a youngster—may have a relatively minor impact on the child, particularly if the child has strong family support.

However, a certain subset of the population of abused children will go on to suffer serious consequences. Clinical experience and a growing body of research suggest that certain kinds of abuse are profoundly damaging. When abuse occurs within the family, the effects are likely to be far more long-standing. Particularly when the abuser is a parent or caretaker, there is a profound violation of trust, and the child has no refuge or support that might help to mitigate the effects of the trauma. In psychiatric patients being treated for abuse-related disorders, the vast majority report intrafamilial abuse. The abuse is often reported as occurring within the home, behind closed doors, and hidden by a veil of secrecy; it is precisely this most damaging kind of abuse that is unreported. Many patients tell stories of terrible abuses that occurred in families which appeared normal or even exemplary. One patient reported sexual abuse by her father and grandfather, both of whom were Baptist ministers in her small southern town. Another patient chronicled pervasive sexual molestation and chronic terrorization in a family voted "Family of the Year" two years in a row in her New England community.

The type and chronicity of the abuse also has profound effects on the child. A substantial number of traumatized children have been subjected to repeated assault, chronic terrorization, or neglect and will have potentially lifelong impairments and disability. The actual numbers of such children are not known, but if the evidence of clinical populations is any indication, chronic and damaging abuse is far from rare. Physical or sexual assault is an obvious gross violation of the child's bodily and psychological integrity, and repeated molestation will almost certainly lead to specific kinds of psychiatric disorders. Many of the psychiatric patients being treated for these disorders report multiple kinds of abuse, including not only physical and sexual abuse, but also pervasive experiences of profound neglect, emotional attacks, and terrorization. In the context of many kinds of chronic traumatization, the child undergoes profound changes in the way he or she views the world and himself or herself. The child views other people with mistrust and avoids them as potentially dangerous, and sees himself or herself as defective and unlovable. This combination of disconnection and isolation from others, combined with self-hate, becomes the legacy for the abused child. As he or she grows into adulthood, this legacy becomes the foundation for patterns of thinking and behavior that destroy the potential for future fulfillment and functioning.

THE TRADITION OF DENIAL

What has contributed to our collective blindness concerning the abuse of children? There are many important factors, the most important being denial. In a paper describing the "child sexual abuse accommodation syndrome," psychiatrist Roland Summit (1983) discussed the ways in which child abuse and the societal reactions to it combine to conceal the abuse, thus accommodating our need not to know:

Child victims of sexual abuse face secondary trauma in the crisis of discovery. Their attempts to reconcile their private experiences with the realities of the outer world are assaulted by the disbelief, blame and rejection they experience from adults. The normal coping behavior of the child contradicts the entrenched beliefs and expectations typically held by adults, stigmatizing the child with charges of lying, manipulating or imagining from patients, courts and clinicians. Such abandonment by the very adults most crucial to the child's protection and recovery drives the child deeper into self-blame, self-hate, alienation and revictimization. (p. 177)

The societal denial of the reality of childhood abuse and our collective need not to know should not be underestimated—there are powerful personal and professional reasons for not knowing. The abuse of children is an ugly reality. Moreover, particularly for professionals and those entrusted with safeguarding the lives and welfare of members of our society, acknowledgment of childhood abuse carries the moral imperative to do something about it, and it is easiest to deny the existence of any problem. Our collective denial, reinforced by the abusive family's culture of secrecy, permits the youngest and most vulnerable to continue to suffer.

Even among enlightened and sensitive professionals, the harsh facts concerning abuse are easily repressed. For example, in spring 1992, a national organization released the results of a large-scale study of rape in the United States (National Victim Center, Crime Victims Research and Treatment Center, 1992). The grim statistics demonstrated that one in eight women in the U.S. is likely to be the victim of forcible rape during her life. Even more striking were the findings that nearly 30% of rape victims were younger than 11 years old and that more than 60% of rape victims were under age 17. These statistics actually *underestimate* the prevalence of rape because although each victim was counted only once, some victims reported having been raped on multiple occasions (as is often the case in incestuous abuse). The results of the study were covered in the national press and appeared on network television. In the subsequent weeks, fewer and fewer professionals—including clinicians who were interested in issues of childhood abuse—had any recollection of the essential results of this study. Only 3 months later, an informal poll of an audience of more than 200 at a national conference on sexual abuse showed that not one person recalled hearing about the study or the results. Although this might be partially ascribed to the process of normal forgetting (in which even important events are progressively unavailable to conscious memory), the all-too-human need to deny these findings is likely to have played a major role in the lack of recall.

This kind of professional denial has historical precedence. In the late nineteenth and early twentieth centuries there was considerable interest in early traumatic experiences and their role in producing psychological dysfunction. The French physician Pierre Janet published studies in trauma and dissociation that are remarkably advanced in light of current findings (1907). In 1896, the father of psychoanalysis, Sigmund Freud, proposed his seduction theory, in which he attributed early sexual molestation as the cause of hysterical illnesses (1962). However, within a few years Freud appeared to have abandoned this theory. Instead, he developed the theory of infantile sexuality and postulated that the majority of reports of sexual abuse were caused primarily by childhood sexual wishes and fantasies rather than actual occurrences (Herman 1981, 1992; Masson, 1984). As noted psychoanalysts Elizabeth Zetzel and W. W. Meissner (1973) later wrote:

> The abandonment of the seduction hypothesis and the realization that the patient's reports of infantile seduction were not based on real memories but fantasies marked the beginning of psychoanalysis as such. The importance of reality as a determining factor in the patient's behavior faded into the background. . . . The focus of analytic interest turned to the mechanisms by which fantasies were created. (pp. 72–73)

Thus was the foundation laid for professionals to dismiss the realities of their patients' reports for generations. As recently as the mid 1980s, respected psychiatrists might have interpreted a patient's report of early sexual molestation by her father as "fantasies derived from Oedipal wishes" (meaning that as a child the patient had fantasized the incest because she wished for a kind of sexual involvement with the parent of the opposite sex). This view implied that adult women were often unable to distinguish between fantasy and reality, and blamed the patient for her own sense of victimization. Even in the mid 1980s, psychodynamic psychiatry was still dominated by classic psychoanalytic thinking, in which conflicts about sexual drives, instincts, and fantasies were considered more important than the possible reality of actual abuse. In fact, even when professionals believed that sexual abuse had actually occurred, the major concern was the intrapsychic conflicts produced by the fulfillment of so-called Oedipal wishes, and not the direct effects of the molestation.

Many theories have been advanced to explain why Freud abandoned his seduction theory. Herman (1992), whose work helped bring to light the realities of incestuous sexual abuse, argues that Freud's original ideas were not sustainable in the moralistic double standards of the Victorian era in the absence of a political environment that could support such theories. We may again be witnessing the backlash of denial in our society. Fueled by some instances of naïve or questionable therapeutic practices, many professionals and members of the public now seem to be willing to dismiss the damaging effects of abuse as predominantly false memory or self-pity, or as being a part of a culture of blaming others for personal inadequacies—all thought to be encouraged by unscrupulous or misguided therapists. Against this new wave of denial, some attitudes of concern for the rights of the disadvantaged must be preserved.

The extent of childhood abuse in our society is not simply a health issue. It is also a moral and political issue. Our denial and lack of awareness tacitly sanction the abuse of a substantial number of children. Studies and clinical work with psychiatric patients show that 20% or more of both inpatients and outpatients report a devastating combination of long-term physical and sexual abuse (Bryer, Nelson, Miller, & Krol, 1987; Chu & Dill, 1990; Saxe et al., 1993; Surrey, Michaels, Levin, & Swett, 1990), often in combination with neglect, emotional abuse, and witnessing violence. Extrapolating from these observations, millions of persons today are suffering or have suffered such experiences. This kind of abuse, captivity, and torture is not tolerated in any other group in Western society, with the exception of some chronically battered women. It is ironic that in the U.S. there are fewer strictures on becoming a driver than on becoming a parent. In order to drive a motor vehicle, one must obtain a license. Driver education programs are universal in our schools, yet little or no training is formally available or seen as necessary to rear children. We assume that the ability to parent is somehow innate or at least learned from being adequately cared for. In many instances, this assumption is correct, but in many other instances it is tragically wrong. As a society, we give all adults the right to have children without providing them the education to know how to do so, and we are complacent in allowing parents, many of whom are young and troubled, to struggle with the critical job of caring for children. The legacy of our complacency is a tide of human suffering and even death that has resulted in untold human, financial, and moral costs. We will require moral courage to be willing to openly look where we have previously refused to see.

THE THERAPEUTIC CHALLENGE

This volume is about the treatment of adults who have grown up bearing the scars of severe and chronic childhood abuse. These persons cannot simply go on with their lives: This kind of abuse cannot be forgotten, disregarded, or left behind, and it continues to have profound effects in almost every aspect of the victims' feeling and functioning. Severe and long-standing trauma introduces a profound destabilization in the day-to-day existence of many survivors. They feel unpredictably tortured by unwanted thoughts, feelings, and reminders of abuse. They are tormented by chronic anxiety, disturbed sleep, and irritability. They experience symptoms that alter their perceptions of their environment, disrupt their cognitive functioning, and interfere with a sense of continuity in their existence. They are subject to powerful impulses, many of which are destructive to themselves or others. They have explosive emotions that they cannot always control. They experience self-loathing and feel little kinship with other human beings. They long for a sense of human connection, but are profoundly alone, regarding other people with great mistrust and suspicion. They want to feel understood, but cannot begin to find the words to communicate with others about their most formative experiences. They wish for comfort and security, but find themselves caught up in a world of struggle, hostility, disappointment, and abandonment that recapitulates their early lives.

The therapists and other mental health professionals who treat these patients become a part of this world. Together with their patients, clinicians struggle to provide support, comfort, understanding, and change. Using treatment as a catalyst for change, clinicians attempt to provide the structure through which survivors of childhood trauma may begin to undo the devastation of their early lives and go on to grow and flourish. Given patience, understanding, skill, good judgment, determination, and luck, survivors of profound child abuse and their therapists may end up on solid ground, with a new-found stability and hope for future growth and fulfillment.

CHAPTER 2

Adult Symptomatology Related to Childhood Trauma

I N RECENT YEARS, much clinical inquiry, research, and controversy have focused on the identification of symptoms or problems related to childhood abuse, which has proved to be a difficult task. The nature and circumstances of past trauma differ considerably from person to person, and the nature of problems related to varieties of childhood abuse are similarly diverse. Clinical observations and studies since the 1970s have shown that childhood traumatization, particularly sexual abuse, is associated with a wide variety of psychiatric difficulties, including depression, anxiety, emotional lability, impaired self-esteem, social withdrawal, self-destructive behavior, alcohol and drug abuse, eating disorders, and various physiologic changes (Bryer, Nelson, Miller, & Krol, 1987; Finkelhor, 1984; Gelinas, 1983; Herman, Russell, & Trocki, 1986; Shapiro, 1987; Summit, 1983; Swanson & Biaggo, 1985). Although many of these difficulties are important, they are nonspecific—that is, they can result from a wide variety of different causes. These problems lack the specificity to childhood trauma that would help in finding cases of early abuse or designing treatment.

Recent research and clinical studies have shown that severe childhood trauma is more specifically associated with at least three major areas of psychological disturbance: dissociative symptoms including dissociative identity disorder (DID) as the most severe form (Bernstein & Putnam, 1986; Chu & Dill, 1990; Kirby, Chu, & Dill, 1993; Putnam, Guroff, Silberman, Barban, & Post, 1986; Ross, Anderson, Fleisher, & Norton, 1991; Saxe et al., 1993, posttraumatic stress disorder (PTSD) symptoms (Coons, Cole, Pellow, & Milstein, 1990; Donaldson & Gardner, 1985; Ulman & Brothers, 1988); and disruption of personality development and maturation such as that seen in borderline personality disorder (Goldman, D'Angelo, DeMaso, & Mezzacappa, 1992; Herman, Perry, & van der Kolk, 1989; Herman & Schatzhow,

1987; Ludolph et al., 1990; Ogata et al., 1990; Westen, Ludolph, Misle, Ruffins, & Block, 1990; Zanarini, Gunderson, & Marino, 1987). This triad of areas of psychological disturbance is a common clinical presentation that appears to be a direct result of severe childhood trauma. Dissociation appears to be an available psychological defense for children whose limited coping capacities are overwhelmed by extremely traumatic events (Braun, 1990; Putnam, 1985). Dissociation enables such events to be temporarily forgotten, or at least emotionally distanced. Post-traumatic symptoms are also logical consequences of childhood abuse. Adults with abuse backgrounds show many different kinds of intrusive reexperiencing of the abuse (Chu, 1991, van der Kolk & Kadish, 1987), as well as attempts to avoid recollecting the abuse and the chronic bodily overactivation of PTSD. Finally, symptoms of borderline personality disorder—including ongoing relational disturbances, difficulty tolerating intense affects, behavioral dyscontrol, and self-hate and emptiness—are logical consequences of the failures of attachment and the inadequate care and protection that are common in dysfunctional and abusive families.

Not all adults with histories of childhood abuse experience dissociative, post-traumatic, and severe personality disorder symptoms. However, clinical observations suggest that many individuals who have been severely and persistently abused and who have disabling psychiatric difficulties show evidence of this triad of symptoms. Moreover, many of these patients also commonly have secondary symptoms, most notably substance abuse (Kessler et al. 1995; Loftus, Polonsky, & Fullilove, 1994; National Victim Center, Crime Victims Research and Treatment Center 1992), and eating disorders (Hall et al., 1986; Welch & Fairburn, 1994). These kinds of difficulties may be considered secondary (but not necessarily less important) because they are not direct effects of early abuse, but rather are the ways in which traumatized persons try to cope with the effects of the abuse.

Symptoms related to somatization are also common in patients with histories of abuse. These may be primary symptoms that are direct results of the trauma, such as conversion disorders (e.g., hysterical blindness, paralysis), somatic reexperiencing (i.e., "body memories"), and stress-related symptoms (e.g., migraine headaches), or secondary effects such as somatization disorder and hypochondriasis. The study of somatiform disorders traditionally has focused primarily on patients in medical settings who have medical complaints unrelated to physical or biologic dysfunction. Hence, somatiform disorders in traumatized psychiatric patients are not well understood. However, rates for both somatization disorder (Loewenstein, 1990; Morrison, 1989; Pribor et al., 1993) and hypochondriasis (Barsky, 1996; Barsky et al., 1994; Pribor & Dinwiddie, 1992) have been found to be quite high in patients who experienced early abuse, and this area of study should be of great interest and clinical investigation in the future.

Severely traumatized patients commonly present with a bewildering range of psychiatric symptomatology and represent diagnostic and treatment challenges. It is understandably difficult to know how to approach patients who manifest such a complex array of symptoms. Perhaps it is because of this complexity of symptoms that these patients are seen as difficult to treat and that much time and effort on the part of both the patient and therapist are often wasted in misdirected therapeutic efforts. The discussion in this volume examines symptomatology that results from chronic and severe early traumatization and the treatment of complex childhood abuse survivors. These discussions are clinically oriented, set out a rational paradigm for treatment, and explore the complicated dilemmas encountered in the treatment of these patients.

DISSOCIATION AS A RESPONSE TO CHILDHOOD ABUSE

Histories of childhood abuse are extremely common among psychiatric patients. However, only recently have these high rates of abuse been acknowledged. In the early 1980s, clinicians who were treating traumatized patients began to understand the links between early abuse and adult psychiatric symptoms. Some of these clinicians began to realize that abuse experiences were much more common in psychiatric patients than had previously been acknowledged. To examine this issue more closely, a number of studies investigated psychiatric patients' current symptomatology and past life experiences. For example, Chu and Dill's 1988 study examined nearly 100 women subjects concerning psychiatric symptoms and childhood experiences (1990). The responses were analyzed for reports of childhood abuse and any correlations with adult symptomatology. Using a questionnaire originally developed in another study (Bryer et al., 1987), physical abuse was defined as being "hit really hard, burned, stabbed, or knocked down," and sexual abuse was defined as "pressured against your will into forced contact with the sexual parts of your body or his/her body." The results were striking. Two thirds of the group reported significant physical or sexual abuse in childhood. One half of the entire group reported physical abuse, and more than one third of the group reported sexual abuse. Moreover, most of the women who reported sexual abuse in childhood also reported physical abuse. The validity of these findings was underscored by almost identical results in similar studies of both inpatients (Saxe et al., 1993) and outpatients (Surrey, Michaels, Levin, & Swett, 1990).

Dissociative symptoms were prevalent in the patients in the Chu and Dill study. As measured by the Dissociative Experiences Scale (DES, see Appendix), developed by psychologist Eve Bernstein and psychiatrist Frank Putnam at the National Institute of Mental Health (NIMH; 1986), 24% of the entire subject group (women consecutively admitted to the hospital) showed levels of dissociation higher than Bernstein and Putnam had found in patients with a diagnosis of PTSD, and 6% showed levels similar to those of patients with DID. Similar levels of dissociation have been documented in other clinical populations of inpatients (Saxe et al., 1993). In a study of 484 patients around Winnipeg, Canada, psychiatrist Colin Ross and his colleagues (1991) found approximately 20% of patients had dissociative disorders and 5% had DID.

Higher levels of dissociative symptoms have been correlated with childhood abuse in a number of studies (Chu & Dill, 1990; Kirby et al., 1993; Saxe et al., 1993; Surrey et al., 1990). For example, the Chu and Dill study not only documented that reports of abuse and dissociation are common in psychiatric patients, but, as anticipated, that reports of childhood abuse are correlated with higher levels of dissociative symptoms. Both physical and sexual abuse were independently correlated with higher level of dissociative symptoms, and the combination of both kinds of abuse was related to even higher levels of dissociation. The relatively high level of dissociative symptomatology in a large percentage of psychiatric patients challenges the belief of most clinicians that trauma-related disorders are relatively rare in civilian populations.

THE NATURE OF CHILDHOOD ABUSE EXPERIENCES

Even in looking at research findings concerning dissociation and childhood abuse, it is unclear that childhood abuse per se produces psychological harm. Given the large numbers of children who are subject to abuse, only a subset of them seem to develop substantial psychological harm. Further research has strongly suggested that various parameters of abuse may result in more damaging effects (Briere & Conte, 1993; Herman & Schatzhow, 1987; Kirby et al., 1993). The parameters of traumatic experience that contribute to detrimental effects are generally considered to be severity, chronicity, early age of onset, and intrafamilial abuse.

As would be expected, more severe childhood abuse is associated with greater levels of symptomatology. Multiple kinds of abuse (e.g., physical plus sexual abuse) and more invasive sexual abuse (intercourse vs. sexual fondling) are associated with higher levels of dissociation (Chu & Dill, 1990; Kirby et al., 1993). Other factors such as violence, physical injury, multiple perpetrators, and fear of dying have been associated with amnesia for abuse (Briere & Conte, 1993; Herman & Schatzhow, 1987). Consistent with these findings, more severe abuse appears to be the norm among hospitalized patients being treated for post-traumatic stress disorders. For example, in one study, more than 93% of patients being treated for sexual abuse reported childhood experiences of attempted or completed intercourse (Kirby et al., 1993). This is not to suggest that less severe abuse is benign, but that severe abuse leads to more disability and a greater need for acute psychiatric care.

Chronic physical and sexual abuse beginning early in childhood is also common among patients being treated for post-traumatic sequelae. In one study, approximately 80% of such patients reported their physical and sexual abuse as very frequent, for example, "continuous," "every week," and "more times than I can count" (Kirby et al., 1993). Patients who had had chronic abuse had strikingly higher dissociative symptoms in adulthood. These patients also had disturbingly early ages of onset of their physical and sexual abuse. Nearly 60% reported that the abuse first occurred prior to age 5, and more than 70% reported that it occurred prior to age 11. Early age of onset was also correlated with high levels of adult symptomatology. Other studies have demonstrated that both early age of onset and chronic sexual abuse are associated with greater dissociative amnesia (Briere & Conte, 1993; Herman & Schatzhow, 1987). These findings challenge one of our most deeply held societal beliefs: that children grow up largely protected from extreme stress. It appears that a substantial number of young children are subjected to their own private hell.

Another erroneous belief is that children are most at risk of being damaged by abuse from persons outside the family. Stories concerning the molestation of children by day-care personnel, priests, and others in positions of authority are highlighted in the media. However, among psychiatric patients reporting abuse, major childhood abuse often occurs within the family, and intrafamilial abuse is much more likely than extrafamilial abuse to be damaging. Although the psychological damage inflicted by persons outside the home should not be minimized, such abuse may represent the tip of the iceberg of harmful abusive experiences. In Russell's study (1986) of women in the general population, approximately one half of all sexual abuse victims were molested within the family. In contrast, in other studies of psychiatric patients (Chu & Dill, 1990; Kirby et al., 1993), the rate of intrafamilial abuse in patients who reported abuse was much higher (77%). This difference in the rate of intrafamilial abuse between the general population and a psychiatric population strongly suggests that many of the psychiatric patients experienced psychological harm because their abuse was incestuous. In fact, when using dissociative symptoms as indications of psychological harm, Chu and Dill found that in psychiatric patients intrafamilial abuse was correlated with more adult dissociation, whereas extrafamilial abuse was not as clearly harmful (1990).

The damaging effects of intrafamilial abuse do not imply that abuse which occurs outside the home is benign. Severe extrafamilial abuse may have profound deleterious effects on a child's development. Even more alarming, the signs of abuse in a child may not be obvious. Often, evidence of serious childhood abuse is never suspected by caring families. In fact, in a prospective study of young children, psychiatrist Frank Putnam (personal communication, 1994) found a significant number of children who had suffered abuse but who were completely asymptomatic. Severe abuse is sometimes accompanied by post-traumatic experiences that make it difficult for children to report them. Furthermore, sexual abuse in particular is often accompanied by such a sense of shame that children may be reluctant to reveal what happened. Families have sometimes guiltily berated themselves for having missed ongoing abuse outside the home, when the only sign at the time was the child being quieter and preoccupied, or more labile and oppositional than usual; these are not unusual behaviors in children. However, even when abuse is not known to families, a warm, caring, and nurturing family environment is reparative. The innate resiliency of most children may lead to substantial spontaneous healing from brief traumatic experiences if given the necessary nurturing environment.

DONNA'S STORY

The presentation of patients with difficulties related to childhood abuse can be confusing and complex. Clinical examples best demonstrate how various complex psychological difficulties can present in clinical settings and how the clinician can understand them and provide adequate treatment. The following extended clinical vignette of a patient, Donna, illustrates the mixture of post-traumatic, dissociative, and characterologic features that can be perplexing to most clinicians.

Donna was first hospitalized when she was 26 years old. She was a college graduate who was working as a teacher's aide. She was unmarried and had few friends and little social interaction other than intermittent contact with a younger brother. She was admitted following a serious suicide attempt and remained hospitalized for more than 4 months because of unremitting, driven suicidality. Despite hospital staff attempts to keep her from harming herself, Donna ingested overdoses of saved-up medication, mutilated her arms and throat with a stolen metal fork, and attempted to strangle herself with a latex glove. Given repeated attempts to harm herself and her difficulties working productively with hospital staff, she was regarded with anxiety and frustration.

When calm, Donna was a pleasant-looking, somewhat overweight young woman who could be disarmingly direct, humorous, and engaging. However, she could also be angry and demanding. Donna felt demeaned by the necessary safety precautions and the restrictiveness of her treatment, which allowed her little privacy and limited personal freedom. She felt abused by the hospital staff and did not hesitate to tell them so. She repeatedly berated them for being cruel, insensitive, and incompetent. She repeatedly demanded more privileges and accused the staff of intentionally punishing and hurting her. Donna's treatment team tried to be reasonable, and on one occasion when she seemed to be a bit calmer and less overtly destructive, the team allowed her to go out on the grounds with a group of patients and a staff member. She proved unable to maintain the responsibility for this limited privilege; she ran off from the group, escaped from the grounds, bought razor blades, and cut her arms severely in the bathroom of a local bus depot. After being discovered, she was brought back to the hospital and the cycle of misery and mutual mistrust continued. After an extended hospitalization, Donna's self-destructiveness seemed to abate and she was eventually discharged to a halfway house for psychiatric rehabilitation. However, conflicts over her safety soon erupted and she was asked to leave for self-destructive behavior and violating rules about use of alcohol. She went to another halfway house and arranged to return to work.

Donna had difficulties at work; she had serious control struggles with her supervisors as well as problems with absenteeism. When she didn't feel well—which occurred 1 or 2 days every 2 weeks or so—she did not go to work, which created a serious reliability problem. And as she had predicted, Donna was a victim of prejudice when it became known that she had psychiatric problems. At times she was treated as though she didn't have any problems and was only trying to get out of working when she called in sick. At other times, she was labeled as unstable and incompetent even in situations that would have been stressful to anyone. Donna's behavior varied wildly. She was sometimes able to work competently, but at other times seemed so distraught, helpless, and childlike that she was unable to care for herself. This variability of behavior was confusing to those who were attempting to treat her. Some believed she was just regressing and was capable of pulling herself together and that she just wasn't trying; others felt that she had little or no control over herself.

Donna's treatment remained problematic. She was treated with every therapeutic modality in common use, but nothing led to sustained improvement. She received intensive individual psychotherapy. She was given medications, including powerful antidepressants and antipsychotics. She participated in group treatment. Nothing appeared to be effective. Not only was she despondent and suicidal, but she often became panicked and agitated. She complained of hearing voices inside her head that told her to kill herself, and of seeing frightening images of threatening figures at night. Often when alone, she would try to harm herself, cutting or scratching deep wounds on her forearms or other parts of her body. Periodically, new symptoms appeared, including episodes of seizure-like spasms during which she would seem to lose consciousness and convulse on the ground.

Donna remained suicidal. She would frequently present to her therapist looking withdrawn, depressed, and distressed. When asked what was troubling her, she would respond somewhat incoherently, "I don't feel like myself." Attempts to draw her out further were largely futile. She would sometimes mutter or become mute, looking around the room apparently frightened, mouthing inaudible words. This behavior would usually escalate into her becoming more upset and agitated, even to the extent of running from the room or trying to hurt herself.

Hospitalization was frequently required, and the hospitalizations continued to be chaotic. Donna would often be agitated and self-destructive, banging on walls and attempting escape from the ward whenever the door was opened. During some of these episodes she could only be contained by being placed in physical restraints, which caused her to cry for help and piteously sob. Staff members were frustrated by their inability to help Donna. Some continued to feel sympathetic to her. Others, particularly those who bore the brunt of her verbal (and occasional physical) attacks, were hostile to her and interpreted her behavior as manipulative and attention seeking.

Of particular note was Donna's response after being restrained. She would gradually quiet down, and then two or three hours later, would appear to wake up and, in a childlike way, ask the nurse observing her, "What happened?" This response would generally outrage some staff, who were often convinced that Donna was aware of what she was doing and should be more honest and cooperative.

For the first several years of her treatment, Donna continued to do poorly. Repeated crises occurred, many of which resulted in hospitalizations. Even during better periods of outpatient treatment, the unexpected often occurred. On some occasions, Donna would seem to be well grounded and able to discuss her current life situations with increasing insight and more of a sense of trust in her treatment team. At other times, Donna was less coherent and engaged. She was frequently suicidal, and sometimes her treatment was focused only on attempts to contain her self-destructive impulses and to have her agree to not kill herself, at least until the next appointment. Despite continued therapy and changes in medication, she was sometimes mute, seeming to respond to frightening internal experiences.

Emergency situations were frequent. On several occasions, medical treatment for drug overdoses was necessary. Sometimes Donna would call for help in a crisis. At other times, Donna would hurt herself without calling. Her forearms became the site of multiple self-inflicted lacerations and sometimes subsequent serious cellulitis. She claimed to experience no pain, only relief, when cutting herself and stubbornly resisted any suggestions that she stop this self-mutilation. On at least three occasions, Donna was at risk of death because of drug overdose or for serious medical problems, such as the possibility of amputation of an arm due to infection.

Donna's treatment finally changed during a hospitalization. A perceptive nurse approached the treating psychiatrist and told him about striking behavior when Donna was placed in restraints that made the nurse wonder whether Donna had a history of childhood abuse. Specifically, Donna would cower in a corner and put her hands over her head as if fending off attack and then react as if she were being beaten. This observation explained Donna's difficulties as perhaps being trauma related. For example, her sense of detachment was consistent with depersonalization and derealization (distortions of her perceptions in which the world around her and her body seemed unreal or detached). Her "waking up" after being in restraints or following a "seizure" could be true psychogenic amnesia. And her ability to abruptly switch from suicidal patient to competent teacher's aide could be interpreted as a kind of switching between self-states. Even more clearly, perhaps some of her hallucinations, intense psychological distress, and stereotypical behavior while being restrained could be understood as reexperiencing of past traumatic events.

Further inquiry revealed that Donna had only fragments of memories of events before age 12. She remembered a few specific incidents, but recalled almost nothing about such things as routine home life, the house where she grew up, friends, teachers, school, or other early childhood experiences. All she remembered clearly were her adolescent and adult years: details about high school and college, her struggle to leave home against her mother's wishes, her parents' divorce, and then the numbing depression and desperate wishes to kill herself. Donna had no memory of overt physical or sexual childhood abuse. She was able to describe a chaotic family with a father who was alcoholic and threatening at times. Her mother also appeared to be chronically overwhelmed and sometimes suicidal, often relying on Donna for comfort and support.

During this period of treatment, Donna continued to have terrible symptoms. She began to have nightmares, often waking her roommates with screams of terror. She began to have vivid memories of being both the victim and witnessing the abuse. She recalled details of how her parents were constantly battling, describing physical assaults between her parents, some of which appeared to be attempts to injure or kill each other. During a hospitalization, she began to have acute reexperiences of a series of physical assaults that had occurred when Donna was between the ages of 5 and 12. She believed that on multiple occasions when she was left alone with her father he became drunk and violent, repeatedly assaulting her.

Therapy became acutely painful for Donna as she felt tortured in her body and mind. The psychological toll was devastating as she spent several months coming to terms with her past. The breakthrough of traumatic memories overcame her brittle defenses—denial and dissociation. She could no longer block out past events; they invaded her being day and night. She could no longer function as a teacher's aide and had to take a leave of absence from her job. In retrospect, the exploration of Donna's childhood abuse was far too rapid and intense, resulting in serious impairment of her functioning. Even so, the years of struggle in treatment with the slow abatement of her mistrust of others, and her learning to control destructive impulses and feelings, made it possible for this regression to last only a few months.

The ultimate validation of understanding the role of trauma in Donna's life was that she actually got better. Several months after the first memory, she was asymptomatic for the first time in her life. She was not particularly depressed, not anxious, and modestly hopeful about her future. The seizures vanished and the nightmares abated. Even more remarkably, she no longer hated herself or was disliked by others. A new person—warm, compassionate, and funny—began to emerge from behind a mask of fear, defensiveness, and self-hate.

Donna eventually returned to work and tried to create a normal life, and more than ever she was successful. She was able to maintain an apartment and live by herself. She was increasingly able to make and keep friends, and she enlarged her network of friends and acquaintances. At age 35 she had a boyfriend for over a year. However, her life was not trouble free. There were periods in which she was devastated by additional unexpected recollections. Far from being the end of treatment, the recovery of her past was the beginning of the rebuilding of her life and her reengaging with the world. She faced the need to examine her fundamental assumptions about the world and herself, and to face the fears and hopelessness that still interfered with her ability to function. Nonetheless, she was able to proceed with the journey from feelings of self-hatred to self-worth, from helplessness to self-empowerment, from despondency to hope. Donna emerged from the nightmare of her struggles with dignity and a depth of character that only adversity can forge.

CHAPTER 3

The Repetition Compulsion Revisited: Reliving Dissociated Trauma*

FORMALLY DEFINED, dissociation is the disruption of the normal integration of experience. Dissociation is a common experience under stressful conditions. This feeling of fragmentation has become a part of our common lexicon, and we speak of "falling apart," "not being myself," or even "having a nervous breakdown." This sense of fracturing results in psychic distress and a paralysis of functioning in which access to thoughts, normal abilities, and judgment becomes limited. Under moderate stress, dissociation is usually transient and reversible, as the stressful events are progressively integrated into the rest of normal experience. Truly extreme, overwhelming, and prolonged stress, however, can have long-lasting pathological effects. Persons undergoing this kind of traumatization feel shattered in a fundamental way.

The concepts of dissociation and dissociation in response to trauma were well described by the French physician and theorist Pierre Janet (1907) in the early part of this century, but were largely supplanted by Freud's psychoanalytic concepts of repression and the unconscious (1955b). Both psychoanalytic and dissociative concepts involve the psychological separation of experience, but in different ways. The classic psychoanalytic concept, based on Freud's topographic theory (1953), assumes that persons have a single or unitary psychological state that is experienced as conscious, un-

*Portions of this chapter are adapted from the article "The repetition compulsion revisited: Reliving dissociated trauma" (Chu, 1991b).

conscious, and preconscious (i.e., unconscious, but almost conscious) in familiar model of *horizontal splitting*:

Conscious
Preconcious
Unconscious

In contrast, the model of dissociation suggests that experience can be split in more complex ways. For example, rather than having a unitary experience, the dissociative model suggests that over time, one's experience can vary over a number of different experiential states, which is called *vertical splitting*:

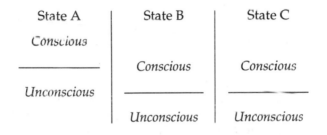

State A	State B	State C
Conscious		
	Conscious	*Conscious*
Unconscious		
	Unconscious	*Unconscious*

Each state may differ in terms of what is conscious and unconscious. Furthermore, when one is in a particular state, one may have access to certain kinds of mental information specific to that state and less access to information associated with other states. The study of "state-dependent learning" supports such a model of the human psyche. Research findings suggest that emotions, learning, memory, and recall are highly state dependent, and that when in one emotional and physiologic state, it is more difficult to access memories and experience of a different state (Eich & Metcalfe, 1989).

Psychiatrist Bennett Braun (1988) described the various components of experiential states. In his BASK model of dissociation, he identified four parameters of normal experience: behavior, affect (emotion), somatic sensation, and knowledge. A fifth parameter might well be added: identity. Thus, each experiential state has its own unique set of behaviors, feelings, sensations, cognitive awareness, and identity attached to it. These states may vary considerably. For example, the parameters connected with someone listening to a lecture (listening and taking notes, a low level of emotional activity, body at rest, alert mental processes, an identity as a student) are quite different from the parameters of the same person performing athletic activity (running and jumping, emotions and senses attuned, the body in motion, an identity as physical being). In Braun's model of dissociation, all these parameters can be split off from each other in a variety of ways. For example, when overwhelmed, persons often can describe events that have occurred (cognitive awareness), but have little access to feelings (affect).

State changes are not associated with only pathological conditions. Over time, even during the course of a day, most persons experience many different experiential states. Optimally, each state is functionally correlated with specific activities or the particular external environment. The individual has considerable control over the nature of his or her experiential states, can adapt to changing situations, and has a continuous sense of the same identity over many different states. From the perspective of state theory, in pathological dissociation, the individual loses control of state changes, has a diminished ability to adapt to the environment, and lacks a continuous sense of identity. Thus, a rape victim with post-traumatic stress disorder (PTSD) is suddenly triggered into a flashback of the rape during a violent scene on television, and the patient with a severe dissociative disorder has many different states that are not always appropriate to the external environment.

A leading researcher in the field of dissociation, National Institute of Mental Health psychiatrist Frank W. Putnam remarked that all of psychiatry can be seen in the context of state theory, and that therapeutic interventions are geared to help persons change from a more dysphoric state to a less dysphoric state (personal communication, 1989). For patients with more biologically based disorders such as true affective disorders or psychosis, the intervention is often medication that helps them achieve mood stability or a more organized state. In working with patients with post-traumatic and dissociative disorders, psychological interventions are designed to help patients move into a more desirable experiential state—to become grounded from flashbacks or to achieve control over involuntary switches in personality states.

Dissociative experiences range from normal to pathological. Routine adult dissociative experiences include certain kinds of splitting of awareness—for example, what many of us do while driving a familiar route to work. We remember little about the drive, having been internally preoccupied with personal concerns. Yet a split-off part of our awareness must be paying attention to the road, because most people do not suffer accidents in this situation. A relatively high level of dissociative experiences are normally seen in young children. Young children commonly use dissociative mechanisms and show evidence of dissociative experiences. Consider a five year-old on Saturday morning in front of the television: Part of the child's experience is split off and transported into cartoon land in a particularly intense way so that the child is often oblivious to events occurring in the room. The phenomenon of imaginary companionship—a dissociative experience—in young children is also considered normal. The child attempts to deal with unwanted impulses and feelings by splitting them off and disowning them as belonging to another imagined being. This kind of dissociation in children is accepted as a normal part of the developmental process. If seen in adulthood, imaginary companionship would be considered pathological as a kind of dissociative identity disorder. Psychologist Rosalyn Schultz (personal communication, 1988) did a survey of patients with dissociative identity disorder (DID) compared to those without DID. She asked persons in each group if they recalled having imaginary companions as children. Curiously, the patients with DID recalled *fewer* imaginary companions. Upon careful consideration, this finding makes sense. After all, in order to report having had an imaginary companion, one would not only have to separate out and disavow a part of the self, but to *reintegrate* that part. Patients with DID may have been subject to a level of chronic traumatization that never allowed them to reintegrate parts of themselves.

The innate capacity to dissociate is greatest in childhood and normally decreases with age, although it briefly increased in adolescence (Bernstein & Putnam, 1986; Saunders & Giolas, 1991). It is only in the presence of ongoing traumatization that high levels of dissociative capacity are maintained into adulthood (Braun & Sachs, 1985; Kluft, 1984b). "Normal" adults, that is, those who have not been exposed to extreme and chronic childhood trauma, do have some capacity to use dissociation (e.g., adult-onset PTSD in which knowledge of events is often separated from feelings and meanings associated with the trauma), but do not develop florid dissociative disorders even in response to very overwhelming experiences. For example, the hostages released after years of captivity and torture in the Middle East showed some trauma-related symptoms but no evidence of extreme dissociative symptoms.

The concept of dissociation has proved to be extremely valuable in understanding the effect of traumatic events on the psyche. In response to severely traumatic events, dissociative symptoms serve an important defensive function. When a person is overwhelmed, the experience is fragmented and separated into compartmentalized components. Different parts of the experience can be dissociated, i.e., disconnected. In the face of severe stress, it is common for persons to feel numb (separating feelings from awareness of current events), with a sense of detachment from their surroundings (derealization) or from their own bodies (depersonalization). In the face of extreme stress, dissociative amnesia can occur, in which the person actually forgets, dissociating cognitive awareness of events, or can feel as though the events are occurring to someone else; these latter responses are more common in traumatized children than in adults. Many other kinds of defensive dissociative experiences are less well named. For example, the ability to withdraw from reality and to remain internally preoccupied for long periods (up to several hours) is common in persons who were extensively traumatized in childhood. The ability to ignore pain is also frequently observed. In more severe dissociative disorders, dissociated internal thoughts may be perceived as thought insertion (foreign thoughts that feel ⌈placed in the mind) or even as auditory hallucinations. Finally, in response to the most severe childhood traumatization, we see the dissociative ability to function as a series of different self-states or personalities as the person attempts to adapt as well as possible to intolerable events and irreconcilable ⌊feelings.

DISSOCIATION AND THE *DSM-IV*

Dissociative symptoms are inherent elements of certain psychiatric disorders. The dissociative disorders all have dissociative symptoms as their central characteristics. As defined by the current American Psychiatric Association's *Diagnostic and Statistical Manual of Mental Disorders (DSM-IV)* (American Psychiatric Association, 1994), the dissociative disorders include dissociative amnesia, fugue states, depersonalization disorder, dissociative identity disorder, and dissociative disorder, not otherwise specified. Dissociative amnesia—the inability to recall specific events or periods of time *not* attributable to organic etiologies such as intoxication or neurologic injury— is occasionally seen in adult-onset traumatic events and is usually confined to the trauma itself. Pervasive dissociative amnesia, including major gaps in memory and ongoing periods of lost time, is more consistent with adults who have histories of severe childhood trauma and is usually seen together with other dissociative symptoms as part of a more severe dissociative disorder. Similarly, dissociative fugue (assuming another identity and sometimes traveling to another locale) and depersonalization are rarely seen alone and are usually one of a variety of dissociative symptoms in a severe dissociative disorder. DID involves a sense of internal fragmentation of the sense of self that ranges from dual personalities (infrequent), to persons with 3 to 20 personalities (most common), to persons who are "poly-fragmented," or appear to be shattered into dozens or even hundreds of personality states (less frequent). Dissociative identity disorder, not otherwise specified (DDNOS) is a catch-all category for dissociative disorders that do not fall into other groups. However, included in the DDNOS category is a commonly seen group of patients who do not have the extreme identity separation of DID but who have a range of dissociative experiences and who experience themselves as fragmented in their sense of self. Patients with this kind of DDNOS recognize that they do not actually change their identity, but feel so different at times that they see themselves as a series of different "me's." In general, the severity of dissociative symptoms appears to be consistent with the severity of early traumatization. That is, less severe abuse results in few dissociative symptoms (e.g., a tendency toward depersonalized states), and more severe abuse results in more complex dissociative disorders such as DID.

PTSD also includes dissociative symptoms. PTSD has been classically seen as a biphasic disorder with persons alternately experiencing phases of intrusion and numbing. The intrusive phase is associated with recurrent and distressing recollections in thoughts or dreams, as well as reliving the events in flashbacks. The numbing phase is associated with efforts to avoid thoughts or feelings associated with the trauma, emotional constriction, and social withdrawal. This biphasic pattern is the result of dissociation: Traumatic events are distanced and dissociated from usual conscious awareness in the numbing phase, only to return in the intrusive phase. In addition, patients with PTSD have long-standing heightened autonomic activation that results in chronic anxiety, disturbed sleep, hypervigilence, startle responses, and irritability. It is this last set of symptoms that has caused PTSD to be classified with anxiety disorders rather than with dissociative disorders, although there remains considerable controversy over this classification. Both the dissociative disorders and PTSD involve some kind of environmental or psychological stress as a central cause or etiology because dissociation seems to play a major role in the psyche's efforts to deal with the stress.

THE RETURN OF DISSOCIATED EXPERIENCES

The reexperiencing of previously dissociated traumatic events presents in a variety of complex ways. The central principle is that dissociated experiences often do not remain dormant. Freud's concept of the repetition compulsion is enormously helpful in understanding how dissociated events are later reexperienced. In his paper "Beyond the Pleasure Principle," Freud (1955a) described how repressed (and dissociated) trauma and instinctual conflicts can become superimposed on current reality:

> The patient cannot remember the whole of what is repressed in him, and what he cannot remember may be precisely the essential part of it. . . . He is obliged to *repeat* the repressed material as a contemporary experience instead of *remembering* it as something in the past. (p. 18)

Freud posited that these repressed (in its more common meaning versus the more technical psychoanalytic meaning) experiences are likely to recur and to be reexperienced. He theorized that this compulsion to repeat served a need to rework and achieve mastery over the experience, and perhaps had an underlying biologic basis as well. The most perceptive tenet of Freud's theory is that previously dissociated events are actually *reexperienced as current reality* rather than remembered as occurring in the past. Although

Freud was discussing the trauma produced by intense intrapsychic conflict, clinical experience has shown that actual traumatic events that have been dissociated are often repeated and reexperienced. Past events, feelings, behaviors, or even somatic sensations are superimposed on current experience in the form of intrusive thoughts, feelings, sensations, dreams, or full flashbacks. As in Freud's description of the repetition compulsion, persons are obliged to repeat these experiences rather than simply remember them. These repetitions range from the need to repetitively talk about ordinary traumatic experience (e.g., a minor car accident), to full-blown PTSD symptoms, including recurring dreams and nightmares, intrusive thoughts, and vivid recollections of the event.

The most striking examples of the emergence of dissociated experiences are the flashbacks seen in patients with PTSD. These patients are thrust back into the traumatic events both in their dreams and while awake. Any therapist who has experienced a patient's full-blown flashback has felt the powerful pull into the actual experience of the events along with the patient. The reliving of the trauma is indeed experienced as a real and contemporary event. That is, the patient does not talk about feeling as if he or she remembers the experience; rather, he or she feels the experience in the present. For example, the Vietnam veteran with combat-related PTSD, walking down the street of his hometown, may be triggered into a reliving of his combat experiences by the sound of a car backfiring. This sound, which is similar to the sound of gunfire, may thrust the veteran into reliving a firefight with the Vietcong. He may actually have vivid sensory experiences—visualizing, hearing, and even smelling the combat scenario. He may feel as young as he was at the time of the battle and may experience the intense fear, horror, helplessness, and even bodily sensations of those past events. The power of such an experience is phenomenal and points to the extraordinary ability of the psyche to distance and dissociate experiences, as well as to bring them back into consciousness with full force.

Full and vivid reexperiences of traumatic events are often seen as sequelae of a single or a limited number of traumatic events experienced in adulthood. Although most adults who suffer from this type of PTSD are able to report what happened to them, the overwhelming feelings associated with the events and the meaning of the experiences are dissociated from day-to-day consciousness. When the awareness, affect, and meaning of the trauma are reexperienced all together, they may be relived in very powerful ways. Therapists who work with PTSD patients are familiar with the pull into old experiences such that patients lose awareness of their current reality and surroundings. Therapists are also familiar with the difficult task of attempting to help patients remain in current reality while they are consumed by the past. Even this may have some untoward results because the patients may then superimpose their experience onto the current situation, as in the following example:

Beth, a pleasant, shy woman in her late 20s, entered treatment about 3 months after being brutally raped by multiple men in a park near her home. Her therapist was a young man who had recently finished his residency and was pursuing training in psychoanalysis. Understanding that Beth's current panic attacks, nightmares, and depression were probably related to the recent rape, the therapist encouraged her to tell him about it. After some resistance to discussing the circumstances of the rape, Beth began to have a vivid flashback of the actual events right in the therapist's office. She began screaming and fell to the floor, fighting off attackers as if she were currently being molested. The therapist, who lost his usual composure when his patient began screaming, was forced to abandon his own chair in an attempt to restrain her from banging into the office furniture and injuring herself. At first, he was unable to make any contact with Beth, who continued to scream and struggle with her eyes tightly shut. She seemed to be in dire physical and emotional pain. Eventually, the therapist was able to engage her attention enough to let her know that he was there. With great effort, Beth was able to describe to him the rapists and the events she was experiencing, and he reminded her that she was in his office and that there was no one else present. To this she demanded, "Then why are *you* hurting me?"

Despite the pitfalls of being confused with the perpetrators of abuse, it is exactly this contact between the PTSD patient and another person that begins a therapeutic and potentially reparative process. Traumatic events are often experienced with an intense sense of *aloneness*. It is only with the support and sense of connection with another person that the events and all the attendant feelings can be tolerated, retained, and integrated into memory as past experience, rather than remaining a dissociated psychological time bomb that is waiting to explode into consciousness. The sense of interpersonal connection is crucial because reliving trauma without appropriate interpersonal support will cause the patient to be overwhelmed again and retraumatized by the experience. Reliving traumatic events in the context of a supportive interpersonal relationship makes true abreaction and catharsis possible and begins the reparative process.

Adult-onset PTSD commonly occurs in the aftermath of such events as combat, assaults, rape, accidents, and natural disasters. However, the prototypical model of adult-onset PTSD can be quite misleading. The person who is disconnected from emotional experience of the trauma is prone to report the experience in a rather constricted or matter-of-fact manner. Such persons often deny the importance of these traumatic events in an understandable attempt to keep the overwhelmingly dysphoric feelings from consciousness. Such a presentation commonly leads mental health professionals to collude with the denial and to ignore the importance of trauma in producing emotional disturbance and psychiatric illness. Patients may present with a wide variety of distressing symptoms such as depression or anxiety, or with dysfunctional behaviors such as addictions or self-destructive behaviors, but may deny the importance of known traumatic events. Interestingly, if questioned about whether it feels as though the events happened to them, they often report that they know about the events, but feel as though they happened to somebody else. Clinicians ignore this kind of history at their patients' peril. Too much time and effort are sometimes expended on fruitless treatment programs to control symptoms, including endless trials of medications or psychotherapy directed to issues unrelated to the trauma, as in the following example:

> Susan, a woman in her early 40s, was admitted to the hospital for suicidal depression. She had been treated for several years for what appeared to be classic major depression. She was tearful and angry as she talked about the hopelessness of her life. She was convinced that there was no hope of ever feeling better and she looked at death as a source of potential relief. Under the care of her attending psychiatrist, Susan went through a sophisticated biologic work-up and underwent a series of medication trials that failed to improve the depression. Finally, she was given a course of electroconvulsive treatments that seemed to result in modest improvement. She bought a bouquet of flowers for the staff and was discharged from the hospital, only to make a near-lethal suicide attempt on the afternoon of the day of discharge. The hospital staff and her attending psychiatrist were frustrated about her lack of improvement and angry that she withheld her suicidal plans from them. One staff member even commented that the bouquet looked funereal, and was furious about how the patient had "set us up." However, after regaining some professional composure, the psychiatrist and staff agreed to Susan's readmission for further evaluation and treatment. Susan's current difficulties and past history were reexamined. The treatment team had been well aware throughout the course of treatment that the patient had undergone a horrible traumatic incident some years previously. After giving her infant child a prescribed antibiotic medication for an ear infection, the child had gone into anaphylactic shock and died in her arms. Because Susan was able to report the events, and even denied any persistent feelings about the death, it had been assumed that it was no longer a major issue. As Susan once again began to talk about the tragic death of her child, it became clear that there were major unresolved issues of grief, loss, anger, and guilt. As she relived and shared some of the old feelings with her therapist and the staff, she began to appear less depressed. She appeared warmer and more engaged with others and was eventually discharged uneventfully. One year later, Susan again became severely depressed and required hospitalization. At the time she complained of chest pains that her attending psychiatrist thought were side effects of her new antidepressant medication. However, an observant staff member noted that she was admitted on Mother's Day, and her pain was then more correctly understood as heartache.

Bodily sensations or somatic symptoms that have to do with past traumatic events can also be dissociated from usual awareness. It is common, for example, for rape victims to have bodily sensations consistent with the actual kind of sexual assault, including abdominal, genital, or rectal pain, nausea, choking, and shortness of breath. Other somatic manifestations of trauma are more difficult to explain. Bruises, redness, chafing, or even boils that are consistent with the events that they are reexperiencing have been observed to appear on a person's body. These marks then disappear as the person becomes reoriented to his or her current surroundings. There is no accepted medical explanation of these stigmata. Clearly, so-called somatic memory is more complicated than is currently understood and can have powerful effects on bodily appearance and functioning. A medical evaluation of any persisting somatic difficulties is always warranted to rule out true physical etiologies, but post-traumatic causes should also be considered. Medical interventions are generally fruitless for somatic symptoms related to trauma and may only further harm the patient. Of course, the presence of other post-traumatic difficulties makes a diagnosis of PTSD-related somatic symptoms more likely. The following example illustrates a case of adult-onset PTSD with prominent physical symptoms:

Harry, a 37-year-old man, was seen in psychiatric consultation after a full medical evaluation failed to disclose any cause for his excruciating abdominal pain and intractable nausea and vomiting. He couldn't keep down food or fluids and was in danger of becoming dehydrated. After a period of medical and psychiatric hospitalization, he was slightly improved and was discharged on a regimen of powerful painkillers and tranquilizers. Harry's treatment over the next 2 years was chaotic. He underwent bouts of severe depression and was briefly readmitted to the hospital on two occasions when he became suicidal. In therapy, he continued to have abdominal pains and would frequently double over when discussing painful feelings. Even narcotic pain medication was ineffective in relieving the severe abdominal cramping. In therapy sessions, Harry was somewhat self-preoccupied, but very likable. He enjoyed telling stories about his past romantic encounters and all the scrapes he had gotten himself into. Over time, he also explored a rather painful childhood and more recent losses and disappointments. Harry gradually improved, experienced less depression, and was able to reengage with old friends in a better, more mutually supportive manner. However, he was unable to return to work because of his disabling abdominal pain, nausea, and vomiting. Finally, in the third year of treatment, Harry came to a therapy session looking somber. He told his therapist that he had something to talk about that he had never discussed with anyone else. Hesitantly, he began to relate an episode that had occurred in his early 20s. As a way of fleeing a difficult home environment, he had joined a paramilitary organization and had been part of a brief, disastrous mercenary guerrilla operation in Latin America. He described the combat experience in painful detail while feeling intense abdominal pain. He had, at one point, shot a comrade in the head after the comrade had been mortally wounded in the abdomen but was not dead. It was at this point in telling his story that he experienced the full horror, pain, nausea, and disgust of his combat experiences. These revelations were a turning point. After some additional months of treatment Harry was free of physical symptoms for the first time in years and was able to function without the use of medications. He received a job offer from an old employer, returned to work, and was able to finish his course of therapy.

In both the clinical examples of Susan and Harry, cognitive awareness of the trauma was present, as were the dissociated feelings and bodily symptoms. It is important to understand that the link between knowledge and feelings could not be made easily in either case because of the enormous psychological benefit of not knowing. This seeming inability to put together simple events and feelings is a defensive function that protects the psyche from truly overwhelming circumstances and events. There is extraordinary psychological pain involved in finally understanding the whole of the traumatic experiences, and considerable strength and courage are needed to face the devastating reality of those events.

DISSOCIATION IN RESPONSES TO CHILDHOOD-ONSET ABUSE

When children, particularly young children, are faced with abusive experiences, they employ a host of dissociative defenses (Bernstein & Putnam, 1986; Braun, 1990; Putnam, 1985). Moreover, children's dependency makes them more likely than adults to be the victims of chronic traumatization. Psychiatrist Lenore Terr, who has made pioneering advances in the study of the effects of psychic trauma in children, specifically points to *chronic* traumatization as a cause of extensive dissociation in children (1991). The research of Kirby, Chu, and Dill (1993) suggests that factors such as early age of onset, severity, and chronicity are all implicated in the development of severe dissociative symptoms. Unfortunately, these factors are common in the histories of many adult patients who report childhood abuse. In fact, among many patients hospitalized for dissociative and post-traumatic problems, early, severe and persistent childhood abuse seem to be more the rule than the exception.

There are particular differences in post-traumatic and dissociative symptomatology between persons who have been first traumatized as adults and those who were traumatized as children. Because children have a greater innate dissociative capacity, as well as less capacity to tolerate stress, severely abused children develop more dissociative symptoms, including more dissociative amnesia. In fact, several studies have demonstrated that extensive childhood abuse prior to adolescence frequently results in either partial or complete amnesia for the abusive events (Briere & Conte, 1993; Herman & Schatzhow, 1987; Loftus, Polonsky, & Fullilove, 1994; Meyer-Williams, 1994; Terr, 1988). Although this degree of amnesia may seem extreme, it is common for patients with severe traumatic histories to have extensive loss of memory for childhood events. Typical reports include statements such as, "I don't remember anything before the age of 12," or "I remember some fragments about school, but I couldn't tell you much about my childhood." Of note is the amnesia for virtually *all* events, not just the abusive events, suggesting that overwhelming trauma may lead children to process their experiences in a way that holds them separate from ordinary conscious awareness. In the absence of organic reasons for such amnesia, these kinds of statements are highly significant and suggest that there may be reasons why a person might not remember substantial portions of their lives. (Please see Chapter 5 for more details about memory.)

Even patients who can recall that they were abused often do not acknowledge the impact of the abuse, or do not connect the abuse with current difficulties. Again, the psychological gain is in not knowing because the reality of the abuse and the implications of the abuse are too overwhelming to be appreciated as a whole. Not acknowledging abuse does not free persons from reexperiencing aspects of the abuse. Instead, such persons are frequently tormented by intensely dysphoric feelings such as helplessness, depression, anger, and isolation that derive from the unacknowledged or forgotten abuse. Moreover, because such patients are unable to report the core reasons for their distress, neither they nor clinicians are able to make sense of their painful lives. Because most survivors of childhood abuse carry an internal sense of defectiveness, they assume (as do some of their treaters) that they are simply inherently crazy or bad. It is chilling to realize that it is often easier for many persons to accept that they are inherently defective than to acknowledge the enormity and the ongoing impact of their childhood abuse.

Not knowing the source of their distress, many abused persons attribute their feelings and behaviors to circumstances around them. They are often extremely reactive to relatively minor current events (e.g., the announcement of a therapist's vacation) that trigger intense waves of depression and helplessness or bouts of rage associated with unacknowledged or poorly remembered childhood abuse. To make matters worse, in many situations these persons may be aware that their own reactions are excessive, intensifying the belief that they are somehow defective. This dilemma is a constant source of difficulty in therapeutic settings, where frustrated and perplexed therapists have essentially colluded with traumatized patients in the belief that they are abnormal. The seemingly irrational reactions of the traumatized person, the denial of the source of the reactions, and the mutually held view of the person as defective all contribute to a painful and dismal downward spiral in many therapeutic relationships.

A more subtle difficulty for persons with early childhood abuse has to do with communication. Prior to adolescence, and especially in early childhood, the primary modality of experiencing the world is not verbal and linguistic as it is in adults, but is largely sensorimotor. Traumatic events that occur early in childhood are encoded in the psyche in a modality that is primarily nonverbal. Additionally, recent neurologic studies of the effects of abuse on brain function suggest that trauma results in overactivation of right brain (nonverbal) activity as compared with left brain (verbal) activity (Schiffer, Teicher, & Papanicolaou, 1995). Thus, when traumatic events are relived in current reality, they retain a strikingly nonverbal quality. In the clinical arena it is common to encounter patients who are otherwise highly intelligent, verbal, and articulate, but who literally seem to have no words to describe their traumatic childhood experiences. Furthermore, many persons who were abused as children were told not to tell and were threatened with harm to themselves or their families. Even though such threats may have been made years ago, they remain vivid and real to adult patients. For all these reasons, early childhood abuse remains both literally and figuratively unspeakable.

The inability to find words to describe feelings and events concerning early abuse has additional implications. Adult mental functioning depends on verbal ability to organize and contain powerful emotional processes. For example, the verbal thought, "I am afraid because I feel as though everyone will humiliate me like my father did" is much more manageable than nameless dread. Thus, the difficulties that traumatized patients have in being able to verbalize their experiences make them more vulnerable to being repeatedly overwhelmed. This inability to verbalize experience also results in patients being unable to communicate with and receive support from others. It is common for patients to be flooded by powerful but wordless feelings and memories, but to feel intensely alone even in the presence of a therapist or other supportive persons. Finally, intense nonverbal experiences often leave little alternative to traumatized patients other than acting out. Because the underlying basis of this kind of acting out cannot be communicated and may involve avoidance, flight, or even self-destructive acts, such behavior is often poorly understood and characterized as deliberate misbehavior. However, true acting out is not just another undesirable and difficult patient behavior, but an opportunity for the patient and therapist to begin to search for words to describe the patient's chaotic and inarticulate internal world.

ISSUES CONCERNING CLINICAL PRACTICE

Despite current understandings of the role of trauma in psychiatric illness and the prevalence of dissociative symptoms, mental health professionals are not routinely trained to detect either covert trauma or dissociation. Specific questions about dissociative symptoms are generally not included as part of a formal mental status examination. Routine examinations may reveal much about mental processes, but do not investigate abnormal experiential state changes, gaps in memory, or distortions in perceptions that result from traumatic experiences. The questions needed to elicit evidence of dissociative symptoms are simple, for example, "Do you have problems with your memory or gaps in your memory?" "Do you ever have the feeling that you are detached from your body or your surroundings are foggy or unreal?" "Do you ever feel that you function so differently at times, almost as if you were another person?" The Dissociative Experiences Scale (Bernstein & Putnam, 1986; see Appendix) offers a number of questions that are useful for clinicians who are not accustomed to asking about different types of dissociative symptoms.

Asking about childhood abuse poses a considerable challenge to even experienced clinicians. Perhaps the best clinical practice is a combination of being open and flexible in trying to understand patients' difficulties, paying attention to the basic tasks of taking a past personal history, and making ongoing assessments of patients' mental status. There is considerable controversy concerning direct inquiries about childhood abuse. Critics of this practice caution that such questioning may produce false reports of abuse. This concern must be balanced against the clinical reality that childhood abuse is associated with so much shame and denial that patients often do not volunteer such information. The failure to inquire may result in not knowing or ignoring critical clinical information. Clinicians can find ways to ask questions that are relatively neutral (e.g., about difficult or painful past experiences) that do not lead the patient to answer in any particular way. Similarly, clinicians must also find ways to ask about dissociative and post-traumatic symptoms because these also may not be volunteered or clinically apparent. Clinicians who are astute in their observations and practice, and who strive to understand their patients in light of both current symptoms and past histories, may be the best hope for helping traumatized patients achieve a sense of coherence about their pasts and fulfillment in their troubled lives.

CHAPTER 4

Childhood Trauma and Borderline Personality Disorder*

FOLLOWING THE rediscovery of the prevalence and effects of childhood abuse in the 1970s and early 1980s, many clinicians began to employ techniques previously used only for persons with adult-onset posttraumatic stress disorder (PTSD; e.g., combat-related PTSD). As described later in this chapter, many of these treatments that focused on aggressive abreaction of trauma resulted in poor clinical outcomes such as profound regression, more symptomatology, and increased morbidity. Clinicians studying and treating such patients were compelled to reassess their understanding of traumatized patients and to acknowledge the profound effects of early abuse on the development of personality structures. These clinicians began to accept that many patients with childhood abuse had significant personality disorders—mostly borderline personality disorder or borderline traits—that vastly complicated the treatment process. However, many therapists were reluctant to apply the borderline classification to traumatized patients due to the negative and pejorative connotations that had come to be associated with the borderline diagnosis.

There have been two distinct views of borderline personality disorder in psychiatry. On one hand, theoretical observations and scientific inquiry have contributed to valued understandings concerning borderline patients. Early concepts of borderline personality disorder placed it between psychosis and neurosis (Knight, 1958) and emphasized the psychotic core that lay beneath a thin layer of normal neurotic functioning (Hoch & Cattel, 1959). Subsequent investigators (e.g., Grinker, Werble, & Drye, 1968; Gunderson & Singer, 1975; Kernberg, 1967) described this diagnosis more in

---

*John G. Gunderson, M.D., contributed to this chapter, and portions of this chapter are adapted from the article "Treatment implications of past trauma in borderline personality disorder" (Gunderson & Chu, 1993).

specific models of intrapsychic functioning and patterns of behavior in relation to the external world. Based on these observations, the *DSM-III* (American Psychiatric Association, 1980), and more recently the *DSM-IV* (American Psychiatric Association, 1994), defined borderline personality disorder in terms of a series of criteria that are necessary to make the diagnosis.

The other view of the borderline personality disorder has to do with the negative associations and connotations connected with this diagnosis. As psychiatrist Paul Russell succinctly wrote (unpublished manuscript), "diagnosis borderline; prognosis pain." In his sympathetic description of the vicissitudes of borderline patients and their treatment, Russell repeatedly emphasized how their difficulties with interpersonal connections compelled them to repeat and reenact painful conflicts in the therapeutic relationship. Notwithstanding such discussions, the borderline diagnosis has been associated in the minds of many mental health professionals with difficult patients, mostly women, who are angry, affectively labile, intrusive, anxiety-provoking, unlikable, and ungratifying. As psychologist John Briere (personal communication), has noted, the term *borderline* has become so pejorative that professionals use it to describe not only difficult patients, but also colleagues they dislike. To counteract this prejudice, noted psychiatrist George Vaillant (1992), in a paper titled, "The beginning of wisdom is never to call a patient borderline," advocates the use of other diagnoses that may be applicable but are less emotionally laden.

Elucidating the role of childhood trauma in the development of borderline personality disorder has done much in terms of both understanding the development of borderline symptomatology and in helping clinicians be more sympathetic to the dilemmas of many traumatized patients. Before clinicians understood how a traumatic environment affects personality development, classic psychoanalytic theories emphasized the failures of the developing child to build certain kinds of mature intrapsychic structures and implied a kind of subtle defectiveness. For example, psychiatrist Otto Kernberg (1967, 1968, 1970) emphasized the lower-level defenses of borderline patients and their vulnerability to transient psychosis. He hypothesized that there was a failure of normal psychological development early in life, particularly around the necessary integration of conflictual feelings about primary caretakers. Psychoanalyst Margaret Mahler's (1971, 1972) and psychiatrist James Masterson's (1972) contributions pointed specifically to the rapprochement subphase of the separation-individuation process around the age of 18 months as a time of difficulty. They hypothesized that disruptions of attachment can occur in the mother–child relationship if a proper balance of holding and letting go does not occur.

In recent years, more attention has been given to actual occurrence of traumatic childhood experiences in borderline patients. Several studies

(Herman, Perry, & van der Kolk, 1989; Herman & van der Kolk, 1987; Ludolph et al., 1990; Ogata et al., 1990; Westen, Ludolph, Misle, Ruffins, & Block, 1990; Zanarini, Gunderson, & Marino, 1987) have demonstrated high rates of traumatic childhood experiences in adolescent and adult borderline patients, generally in the range of 60%–75%. These traumatic experiences include physical and sexual abuse and witnessing violence. This growing body of evidence suggests that childhood abuse is often a critical factor in the development of borderline psychopathology. This kind of understanding shifts the conceptual paradigm of borderline personality disorder. Rather than simply focusing on traditional concepts concerning impairments of intrapsychic structure, one must also consider the developmental adaptations of young children subjected to cataclysmic events. In this context, the intrapsychic structures and behaviors of borderline patients can be understood in a model that emphasizes adaptation rather than pathology (Saunders & Arnold, 1993).

In clinical settings many borderline patients report extensive histories of childhood emotional, physical and sexual abuse, profound neglect, and the witnessing of violence. However, it is not the trauma per se that results in borderline personality disorder; after all, a significant minority of borderline patients do not have evidence of obvious childhood trauma. Rather, it is the gross disruptions of normal familial attachments and the massive failure of adequate care and protection of the child that result in distortions of normal characterologic development. Experiences of intrafamilial abuse and neglect are extreme manifestations of the failure of normal parental attachment and nurturance. Often these disruptions of attachment and nurturance have been neither subtle nor limited to the rapprochement subphase, but have existed throughout multiple phases of childhood development.

In her book *Trauma and Recovery*, psychiatrist Judith Herman (1992) makes a persuasive argument that the term *chronic post-traumatic syndrome* should be used to describe the characterologic adaptation to abuse in place of the negative diagnostic label *borderline personality disorder*. Although this idea has considerable merit, it blurs the distinction between symptoms of Axis I and Axis II disorders. In the *DSM* classification, Axis I disorders are seen as syndromes that are superimposed on an existing Axis II personality substrate. In other words, Axis I disorders are seen as symptoms, and Axis II disorders are seen as long-standing personality characteristics. As one chronically traumatized patient stated succinctly, "It's not 'problems' or 'beliefs' or 'patterns of thinking' that I can simply reason through. It's *me*, it's who I am." Although an understanding of the role of trauma in the development of borderline personality disorder may help both patients and clinicians struggle through difficulties, it does not diminish the intensely painful and often slow process of changing the sense of self, the adaptations made to the world, and the meanings attached to formative experiences.

REFRAMING THE DIAGNOSIS OF BORDERLINE PERSONALITY DISORDER

The *DSM-IV* (American Psychiatric Association, 1994) provides the following criteria for borderline personality disorder:

> A pervasive pattern of instability of mood, interpersonal relationships, and self-image . . . as indicated by at least five of the following:
>
> (1) frantic efforts to avoid real or imagined abandonment . . .
> (2) a pattern of unstable and intense interpersonal relationships characterized by alternating between extremes of overidealization and devaluation
> (3) identity disturbance: markedly and persistently unstable self-image or sense of self
> (4) impulsiveness in at least two areas that are potentially self-damaging . . .
> (5) recurrent suicidal threats, gestures, or behavior, or self-mutilating behavior
> (6) affective instability due to marked reactivity of mood . . .
> (7) chronic emptiness or boredom
> (8) inappropriate, intense anger or difficulty controlling anger . . .
> (9) transient, stress-related paranoid ideation or severe dissociative symptoms
> (p. 654)

In light of evidence of a history of significant trauma in many borderline patients, borderline symptomatology has become more understandable. The intensity of the borderline patient's relationships and the wild oscillations between idealization and devaluation may well be better understood as recapitulations and reenactments of early abusive relationships. The set of assumptions concerning interpersonal relationships for persons who have experienced abuse is based on their experiences with caretakers' narcissistic preoccupation, control, manipulation, and exploitation. It is hence not surprising to find that traumatized patients continue to engage others (including therapists) in repetitions of the most powerful interpersonal dynamics they have experienced. They reenact the roles of both abuser and victim because in their families one had to be either one or the other. For the therapist who becomes part of this world and who is subject to the interpersonal struggles of the reenactments, the experience can indeed be intense and unpleasant. Yet the patient's dilemmas can be viewed as deficits in learning and deprivation concerning interpersonal experiences rather than as malicious or deliberate. And although abuse-related interpersonal dynamics and dysfunctional behaviors must be challenged, therapists can have more empathy and patience with the necessary and inevitable struggles.

Borderline patients' behavioral dyscontrol, impulsivity, affective lability, and poor affect tolerance can similarly be traced to early abuse. After all, how do children normally develop behavioral control and affect tolerance? Good parents routinely buffer and shield children from situations that produce overly intense affect and out-of-control impulses. If the child is over-whelmed, parents or caretakers serve to mitigate and ameliorate the situation and to soothe the child. Parents assist children throughout their developmental years with the gradual process of learning affect tolerance and behavior control, often intuitively utilizing the principle of optimal frustration, in which the child is progressively exposed to challenging situations in an incremental and step-wise manner, but never allowing the child to become truly overwhelmed. For example, most mothers can distinguish the fussy crying of an infant or a young child (which may not require intervention, allowing the child to learn to cope with low to moderate distress) from the cries that signal marked distress or terror (which require immediate intervention). In abusive family environments, these principles are pervasively ignored or violated, and it is often the case that one or more of the caretakers routinely subjects the child to situations in which the child is overwhelmed by unbearable affects and intense impulses. It is hence not surprising that many of the adult borderline patients who come from such backgrounds have difficulties with these basic psychological and behavioral tasks.

Borderline patients' fear of abandonment and intense anger may be understood as deriving from actual abandonment, maltreatment, and deprivation. The continuing expectation of being victimized and the recapitulation of abusive and failed relationships leads to a growing reservoir of bitter disappointment, frustration, self-hate, and rage. The result is episodic expressions of intense and poorly controlled anger that break through a barrier of fragile and brittle control. Given borderline patients' inability to utilize supportive relationships, angry outbursts and impulsive and self-destructive patterns of releasing tension—such as suicide gestures and repetitive self-injury—may be the only outlet for the intolerable experience of explosive rage.

Most of the major theories regarding the development of a sense of self, including psychoanalytic, object relations, and self-psychology theories, point to the importance of a positive, supportive, and validating relational context during critical developmental years. More recent ideas, particularly concerning the psychology of women, point not only to the importance of the early relational environment, but to the necessity of ongoing relationships that validate one's sense of self, self-worth, and cultural role (Jordan, Kaplan, Miller, Stiver, & Surrey, 1991). For the adult who has been subject to chronic childhood abuse, the family culture has fostered only confusion about identity, emptiness, and negative views of the self. There is overwhelming consensus that one of the damaging effects of early abuse is the development of self-hate (Carmen, Rieker, & Mills, 1984; Gelinas, 1983; Herman, Russell, & Trocki, 1986; Herman, 1981; Shapiro, 1987; Shengold, 1979, 1989; Summit, 1983). Chronic early victimization frequently creates a set of assumptions in which children view abuse and exploitation as inevitable and even normative (Carmen & Rieker, 1989; Shengold, 1989). Because young children remain relatively undifferentiated from parental figures on whom they remain physically and emotionally dependent, they cannot see themselves as being victimized and cannot express rage against their abusers. Rather, they view themselves as justly deserving of the abuse and hence bad and defective (Shengold, 1979; Summit, 1983). Psychiatrist Leonard Shengold (1989) descriptively called this "soul murder":

> If the child must turn to the very parent who inflicts the abuse and who is felt as bad for relief of the distress that the parent has caused, then the child must break with what has been experienced, and out of a desperate need for rescue, must register the parent, *delusionally*, as good. Only the mental image of a good parent who will rescue can help the child deal with the terrifying intensity of fear and rage that is the effect of the tormenting experiences. . . . It is this inhibition of the ego's power to remember and test reality that makes soul murder so effective as a continuing force. The absolute need for good mothering makes the child believe in the promise that her parents . . . will be good and rescue her, and to believe that she herself must be bad. (pp. 26–28)

Paradoxically, this sense of responsibility for the abuse gives many abused children the illusion of control: they feel as though they somehow caused the abuse and if they could only be "good" that the abuse would stop (Summit, 1983).

In a paradigm that takes into account the actual occurrence of major trauma in the early background of borderline patients, one must move away from the prevailing view of a subtle kind of degeneracy, that is, that borderline patients inherently have abnormal or excessive reactions to current untoward life events. Rather, one must see many patients with borderline personality disorder as having adapted to overwhelming life events by developing certain patterns of relating and specific defenses, and by viewing themselves and reacting to others on the basis of long-standing and unresolved abusive experiences. These patterns of adaptation can be seen as currently dysfunctional but eminently understandable in view of past life experiences. This kind of attitudinal shift may be crucial in ameliorating the pejorative associations common to the borderline diagnosis and in providing effective treatment.

TREATMENT IMPLICATIONS FOR TRAUMATIZED PATIENTS

In the mid to late 1980s there was considerable debate about traumatized patients, especially those with dissociative disorders, as to whether these patients actually had dissociative disorders or were "just" borderline. Some clinicians viewed trauma-related treatment as ineffective and over-gratifying and argued that the primary treatment should be containment of behaviors through strict limit setting and maintenance of clear boundaries. Although this contention was reductionistic and simplistic, many patients who have dissociative and post-traumatic disorders also have borderline personality disorder, and part of their treatment involves containment, good boundaries, and clear limits. After all, the severe and persistent intrafamilial abuse fosters not only the development of post-traumatic conditions, but also the failure of adequate caretaking and relational support that lead to borderline psychopathology. In clinical settings, a majority of patients with severe PTSD and dissociative disorders related to childhood abuse have borderline personality disorder or similar difficulties in personality functioning. This observation that severely traumatized patients present with post-traumatic and dissociative symptomatology *and* characterologic difficulties is supported by research which suggests that a high percentage of patients with the most severe dissociative difficulties—those with dissociative identity disorder—also have borderline personality disorder (Horovitz & Braun, 1984).

Understanding the traumatic antecedents in many patients with the combination of dissociative and post-traumatic symptomatology and borderline personality disorder raises important clinical issues. Much of the literature on the treatment of PTSD focuses primarily on the treatment of adult war veterans and others who have been traumatized as adults. Effective treatment paradigms for this population place a priority on abreaction (Foa, Steketee, & Rothbaum, 1989; Keane, Fairbank, Caddell, & Zimering, 1989). The positive value of abreaction is thought to involve the reexperiencing of the traumatic event in a context of high social support so that the experience is tolerated, attitudinally reframed, and integrated into conscious experience. For example, in the treatment of adults who have been through wartime experiences or similar events, abreaction is sometimes brought about by *exposure* or *flooding* techniques whereby the patient is deliberately exposed to stimuli designed to trigger reexperiences of the traumatic events (e.g., Vietnam veterans being shown clips from the movie *Platoon*) in a supportive and controlled environment. Such therapeutic strategies have been shown to be effective in alleviating acute symptomatology.

There are no similar studies of the use of abreactive techniques in survivors of childhood trauma. Based on clinical experience, however, it is widely believed that the eventual reexperiencing and working through of childhood trauma has a beneficial therapeutic effect. Persons who have been able to successfully abreact abusive childhood events often experience dramatic changes in their lives, reporting that they are able to proceed with their lives unencumbered by their pasts. This process involves changes such as a reduction in dissociative symptomatology, fewer and less troubling intrusions of the abusive experiences, a new sense of identity as being psychologically healthy and functionally competent, an improved ability to relate to others.

The clear value of abreaction of childhood trauma in some patients led to an erroneous belief system that continues to be remarkably ubiquitous among many patients and their therapists. In this belief system, it is felt that in any clinical situation in which a history of childhood abuse is discovered, all efforts should be made to immediately explore and abreact those abusive experiences. Moreover, many clinicians appear to feel that if current difficulties seem related to past abuse, the treatment of choice is to abreact the etiologic abuse. Unfortunately, in the treatment of many patients, such a belief system is conceptually flawed and inappropriate and can have untoward effects such as increasing acute symptomatology and difficulties with functioning and coping, as illustrated in the following clinical example:

> A 22-year-old woman was admitted to an inpatient psychiatric facility after an overdose of her antianxiety medication. She had a long history of severe depression, panic, suicidal impulses, poor relationships, and a low level of functioning. She had recently begun treatment with a new outpatient therapist. In the context of therapy, the patient began to reveal evidence of severe early childhood sexual abuse. The patient began telling more information about the abuse and became increasingly fearful, isolated, and suicidal. She was referred for hospitalization in order to work through the abuse issues. Following her admission, the patient was noted to have flashbacks of presumed childhood sexual abuse. She and her therapist were insistent on the need to get the bad feelings out in order to heal from the abuse. The patient was encouraged by her therapist to explore these issues in therapy and she related horrific details of repeated victimization that she reported she was just remembering. On the ward, her behavior became more and more out of control, particularly at night, necessitating intensive suicide precautions and even the intermittent use of restraints for head banging. After 6 weeks of hospitalization she was unable to be discharged and was put on a leave of absence at her job.

The psychological driving force behind these premature attempts at abreaction appears to be the repetition compulsion—the intense psychological need to recapitulate and reexperience repressed material, even at the expense of the pleasure principle (Freud, 1955a). The presumed psychological gains of this process are potential mastery of the experiences and release of intense affects related to the repressed experiences. Unfortunately, many patients are once again overwhelmed and retraumatized by these experiences, and little or no working through or resolution takes place.

The key element that appears to be missing in these attempts at abreactive therapy in patients with trauma-related syndromes and borderline psychopathology is the ability to utilize social supports. The various models of successful use of abreaction assume that patients are able to utilize a high level of social and interpersonal support. Unfortunately, the ability to relate to and feel supported by others is a primary area of disability in many patients with histories of severe childhood abuse. It is essential to understand that these relational difficulties also occur within the therapeutic relationship, often in a particularly intense fashion. The therapist is viewed with great suspicion, and many severely abused patients are unable to take the emotional risk to have a normal level of trust in the relationship. Characteristically, when faced with any major stressor (internal or external), severely abused patients flee into isolation as the perceived safest alternative and/or they resort to ingrained and familiar but dysfunctional solutions such as impulsive and self-destructive behaviors. Because therapy involves intimacy, vulnerability, and the potential for arousing painful and overwhelming feelings, the therapist and the therapeutic process are experienced as major stressors and may precipitate negative therapeutic reactions.

A general principle of treatment with traumatized borderline patients is that early phases of psychotherapy need to address their vulnerability to stress prior to active work with traumatic memories. Premature attempts at abreaction result in increased symptomatology and decreased ability to function because the patient feels alone and overwhelmed in reexperiencing the intense dysphoria of the traumatic events. It is now acknowledged that an initial period of establishing safety and building ego strength is essential prior to the recovery and working through of childhood trauma, as described in Part II of this book (see also Chu, 1992c; Herman, 1992; Lebowitz, Harvey, & Herman, 1993). Developing and establishing a stable therapeutic alliance is an essential task of this early work. However, the development of a supportive and moderately trusting relationship is a major undertaking. This sometimes lengthy process has few shortcuts, and the therapist who either ignores this task or is convinced that it is not necessary for a particular patient risks a poor clinical outcome. Stated in another way, the ability of the patient to develop a moderately stable sense of trust in others is the rate-limiting task of the therapeutic work with many traumatized patients; the therapy can proceed only as quickly as this difficult task is accomplished.

One of the more important ways of encouraging an attachment and developing a sense of alliance is therapists' validation of the essential elements of patients' abuse. Whereas an earlier generation of psychoanalytically oriented therapists may have been concerned about the symbolic distortions of such retrospective accounts of abuse, it is now clear that such accounts, when viewed critically, are often fundamentally realistic (Herman & Schatzhow, 1987; Westen et al., 1990). A skeptical response may appear hostile and may be damaging to the fragile therapeutic alliance. Therapists who focus only on the intrapsychic conflicts produced by past abuse, or on possible distortions of initial accounts of abuse, may be guilty of empathic failure. Such stances tend to devalue patients' perceptions of their experiences, resulting in increasing patients' sense of shame and fearfulness within the therapy or even precipitating flight. This is not to suggest that therapists should encourage patients to believe in the literal truth of *all* recollections (including those that may be poorly or hazily remembered) or to conjecture about what might have happened. Similarly, therapists should not conclude that all borderline patients, or all patients with certain behaviors or traits, have been subject to gross abuse. Rather, when appropriate, therapists can ally with their patients' sense of having been victimized, which can help these patients begin to understand their own feelings and behaviors.

Acknowledging the reality of past victimization is also helpful when coping with issues concerning therapeutic responsibility. Most patients with histories of abuse are burdened by undue feelings of responsibility for their having been violated or abandoned. The coping strategies and defenses characteristic of traumatized patients make them particularly likely to take flight or to become defensively angry in response to interventions that emphasize their being responsible for creating their own problems. It is necessary to help patients distinguish clearly between the need to take responsibility for caring for themselves in the present and wrongly assuming the responsibility and blame for having been abused in the past.

An approach that emphasizes the importance of empathizing with patients' abuse experiences and their adaptation to such experiences may conflict with traditional therapeutic approaches. Interpretations concerning the centrality of anger in the patient's life or exposing the manipulativeness of patients' actions are often counterproductive early in the therapy. These types of interventions may ask patients to "own" their angry feelings and behavior prior to validating the reasons why they are angry or behave in dysfunctional ways. Such approaches may be especially likely to evoke negative therapeutic reactions in traumatized patients with borderline characteristics (Adler, 1985; Brandchaft & Stolorow, 1987; Kolb & Gunderson, 1990). Indeed, early confrontations and interpretations have been shown to be a major reason why borderline patients drop out of psychotherapy (Gunderson, et al., 1989). Interpretations that identify a patient's angry motives and feelings usually need to be accompanied by empathy and validation of past trauma. For example, the therapist could convey that the patient's anger about past abuse is understandable, but that angry feelings must be identified and expressed in a manageable fashion.

Reports of successfully treated patients have documented the importance of support and the significance of patients' developing a positive dependency on the therapist (Waldinger & Gunderson, 1987; Wallerstein, 1986). Early interventions are most successful when behaviors (including those that may be dysfunctional, such as self-destructive behavior or flight) are understood and interpreted as being normative, sometimes even admirable, adaptations to childhood experiences, but misplaced and dysfunctional in the present context. More generally, whereas virtually all patients must make a personal commitment to their own self-care before they can work as allies in treatment, those with histories of severe abuse require added support during the early phases of treatment, gentleness about interpretations directed at their traumas, and patience about expecting them to engage in stable therapeutic alliances or to do transference-based work.

Validation of trauma and other supportive interventions are the first step in the treatment of traumatized patients. Empathy and understanding alone can result in patients becoming mired in a chronically victimized and helpless position. As the therapy continues, ongoing efforts to maintain a sense of engagement must be supplemented by interpretations and confrontation, for example, around dysfunctional behaviors and dissociated affects such as hate and aggression. However, an empathic sense of the traumatic antecedents of patients' feelings and behaviors will make such interventions more acceptable. Establishing empathic resonance prior to an interpretation or confrontation is essential (Chu, 1992a). As Mann (1973) noted, the

> gentle, caring concern of the therapist for the patient may well be the most important element in a proper, effective confrontation. . . . It communicates to the patient his privilege to choose the direction that he would like to move in rather than communicating a directive to which the patient feels impelled to yield. (p. 44)

CHAPTER 5

The Nature of Traumatic Memories of Childhood Abuse*

DISSOCIATIVE AMNESIA is at the core of the controversy concerning traumatic memory of childhood abuse. The idea that overwhelming experiences can be forgotten and then later recalled has its origins in major schools of thought concerning intrapsychic experience. Early in this century, French physician Pierre Janet (1907) described psychogenic amnesia and theorized that traumatic events could be dissociated from conscious awareness, only to be remembered at some later point in time. Sigmund Freud's psychoanalytic theory included the belief that events that were traumatic or resulted in intense intrapsychic conflict could be repressed and become unconscious, and could later be repeated and reexperienced (1955a, 1955b, 1962). Freud described repression as an active process, itself unconscious, that holds unacceptable or overwhelming thoughts and impulses outside conscious awareness. These theoretical constructs laid the groundwork for modern investigators who were interested in the effects of traumatic events on memory.

In the clinical arena, psychogenic amnesia has been observed for overwhelming and traumatic experience. For example, psychiatrist Bessel van der Kolk and his colleagues reported a clinical anecdote of a woman who was repeatedly arrested for pulling fire alarms and shouting for people to get out of buildings that she believed were on fire (van der Kolk & Kadish, 1987). The authors believed that she was completely amnestic for having survived the infamous Coconut Grove nightclub fire, where hundreds had perished more than 30 years previously. In the course of treatment, she re-

---

*Julia A. Matthews, Ph.D., M.D., Lisa M. Frey, Psy.D., and Barbara Ganzel contributed to this chapter, and portions of this chapter are adapted from the article "The nature of traumatic memories of childhood abuse" (Chu, Matthews, Frey, & Ganzel, 1996).

covered the memory of being in the burning building that was filled with smoke and toxic gases. Numerous anecdotal accounts of amnesia for traumatic childhood events have been documented. For example, a recent media story reported the experience of Ross Cheit, an associate professor of political science at Brown University (National Public Radio Morning Edition, February 1996). In 1992, Professor Cheit learned that his nephew was joining a boy's chorus. He became quite depressed and could think of no reason for his depression. However, he soon had the abrupt recovery of memories of childhood sexual molestation by an administrator of a boy's chorus in a summer camp. Professor Cheit set out to corroborate his memory. He found other men who had been molested at the same camp as boys, as well as two former employees of the camp who had witnessed some episodes of sexual molestation. He subsequently located and telephoned the perpetrator, who admitted to the acts. He filed civil suit against the organizers of the boys' chorus; the case was settled in 1994. Professor Cheit was not in psychotherapy at the time of his recovered memory.

Also striking are the many adult patients who report extensive amnesia for childhood events. To some patients, much of their childhood is foggy. Others can recount the events of their past, but feel as though it happened to someone else. Many patients describe a kind of "Swiss cheese" memory with gaps in their recall of their early experiences, or even complete amnesia for any events during some months or years. In clinical settings, this level of psychogenic amnesia may be highly significant, and many patients with this kind of amnesia eventually report recovered memories of extensive childhood abuse.

Many clinicians and investigators accept recovered memories of childhood abuse as essentially valid reports of repressed or dissociated early experiences. Indeed, for some patients, clinical work with recovered memories has led to resolution of psychiatric symptomatology and to an enhanced understanding of the traumatic etiologies of their difficulties. Recently, however, a number of investigators have questioned the validity of recovered memory and have argued that such memories can be false and that many clinicians may be colluding in the creation of pseudomemories. In particular, a heated debate has emerged in recent years regarding therapists' role in the retrieval of dissociated memories of childhood abuse. Several recent authoritative reviews have been written on this controversy of traumatic amnesia (see Appelbaum, Uyehara, & Elin, 1997; Brown, 1995; Brown, Scheflin, & Hammond, 1997; Meyer-Williams & Banyard, 1997; Scheflin & Brown, 1996). The goal in this chapter is to provide an integrated view of trauma and memory by reviewing recent findings concerning the psychobiology of traumatic memory, progress in cognitive memory research, issues concerning memory distortion, prevalence studies of traumatic amnesia, and clinical practice concerning traumatic memory.

THE PSYCHOBIOLOGY OF TRAUMATIC MEMORY

The psychobiology of learning and memory suggests that traumatic memory is different from ordinary memory. Many investigators propose that the symptoms of post-traumatic stress disorder (PTSD) result from the multifaceted neurohormonal changes that occur in response to acute and chronic stress (Charney, Deutch, Krystal, Southwick, & Davis, 1993; Krystal et al., 1989; van der Kolk, 1994; van der Kolk & Saporta, 1991; van der Kolk & van der Hart, 1991). These changes may powerfully affect the ways in which memory is encoded, stored, and retrieved. (It should be noted that although many physiologic changes have been observed in PTSD patients, many of the stress-responsive neurohormonal changes—especially in the brain—have been observed only in animal models, and the applications of these models to humans with PTSD remains speculative.) At least three stress-responsive neurohormonal systems have emerged as critical in the development of PTSD:

1. Catecholamines, including adrenaline, noradrenaline, and dopamine, that modulate bodily activation and arousal particularly in stressful emergency situations
2. Hormones of the hypothalamic-pituitary-adrenal (HPA) axis, including corticotrophin-releasing factor (CRF), adrenal corticotrophic hormone (ACTH), and glucocorticoids, that have an essential role in maintaining physiological and psychological homeostasis; and
3. Substances produced by the body in response to stress.

Persistent increases in catecholamine activity, alterations in hormonal functions in the HPA axis, and opioid responses have all been documented in patients with PTSD (Charney et al., 1993; McFall, Murburg, Roszell, & Veith, 1989; Pitman, van der Kolk, Orr, & Greenberg, 1990; Southwick et al., 1993; van der Kolk, 1994; Yehuda, Giller, Southwick, Lowy, & Mason, 1991).

Patients with PTSD exhibit multiple symptoms of heightened arousal, including exaggerated startle response, increased response to stress-related stimuli, panic attacks, and hypervigilance (American Psychiatric Association, 1994; Charney et al., 1993; van der Kolk, 1994). Many investigators have suggested that the physiological arousal found in PTSD is caused by chronic elevations in both central and peripheral catecholemine function (see Charney et al., 1993; Southwick et al., 1993; van der Kolk, 1994). In the model of inescapable shock, for example, laboratory animals that are unable to avoid aversive stimuli show dramatic increases in catecholamine activity and persistent elevations of catecholamines that are slow to subside. Even brief reexposure to the aversive stimuli results in a similar increase in catecholamine activity with a delayed decline (van der Kolk, 1987).

In extensive animal studies, neurophysiologist James MacGaugh (1989, 1992) and others have shown substantial effects of neuromodulators such as catecholamines on retention of newly learned material. Exposure to catecholamines immediately post-learning affects learning in a dose- and time-dependent fashion. For example, low to moderate levels of epinephrine enhance retention of newly learned material. However, higher doses interfere with learning. Thus, an attenuated catecholamine response to a traumatic event might enhance memory, whereas unusually high levels of catecholamines (such as seen in persistent stress) might block memory formation.

A recent study examined the hypothesis of catecholamine enhancement of memory retention (Cahill, Prins, Weber, & McGaugh, 1994). Participants in the study were shown slides of a neutral story and a more emotional story about a boy in a life-threatening situation. One group of participants was given propranolol, a drug that blocks the activity of the β-adrenergic system and hence inhibits the release of catecholamines. The control group received a placebo. The group receiving the drug showed no difference for memories of the neutral story, but had significantly decreased recall for the details of the more emotional story compared to the control group. This study in humans begins to demonstrate the effects of catecholamines of the β-adrenergic system in making traumatic memories more indelible than ordinary memories.

Hormonal activity in the HPA axis is highly responsive to acute stress, producing an immediate increase in CRF, ACTH, and glucocorticoids (Sapolsky, Krey, & McEwen, 1986). Glucocorticoid receptors are particularly abundant in the hippocampus, a brain structure thought to be central in memory function. There is evidence for glucocorticoid toxicity to the hippocampus, resulting in actual neuronal cell death. Hippocampal cell death occurs with aging and is accelerated by stress. Hippocampal neuronal degeneration has been demonstrated in monkeys after either prolonged stress or prolonged administration of glucocorticoids (Sapolsky, 1986; Sapolsky, Uno, Rebert, & Finch, 1990), suggesting a possible mechanism for some of the changes in memory function seen in PTSD. Reduced hippocampal volume (as measured by magnetic resonance imaging) and memory deficits have been demonstrated in veterans with combat-related PTSD (Bremner et al., 1995) and in patients with PTSD associated with childhood physical and sexual abuse (Bremner et al., 1997). These findings suggest that some memory difficulties found in PTSD may not be reversible and that treatment interventions should be on coping with and compensating for these deficits.

Uncontrollable stress results in stress-induced analgesia in both animals and humans, and is attributed to the release of endogenous opioids (Hemingway & Reigle, 1987; McGaugh, Introini, & Castellano, 1993; Willer, Dehen, & Cambier, 1981). Endogenous opioids are known to have in-

hibitory action in the amygdala (McGaugh, 1989, 1992), a brain area believed to be central in the emotional evaluation of information (Davis, 1992).
MacGaugh's studies in animals showed that low doses of opioids sup-
presses learning and diminishes the enhancement effects of epinephrine
(McGaugh et al., 1993).

A considerable body of research points to state dependence in learning,
memory, and recall (Eich & Metcalfe, 1989; Tobias, Kihlstrom, & Schacter,
1992; van der Kolk, 1994). Findings from research in state-dependent learning suggest that when in one emotional and physiologic state, it is more difficult to access memories and experience of a different state. Because the
traumatic experience induces a marked physiological arousal and altered
neurohormonal state, it is likely that both the encoding and recall of memory are specific to this state. This may contribute to the phenomena of amnesia and dissociated memory in PTSD, because when one is not
physiologically aroused, it may be more difficult to access the traumatic
state. Conversely, when presented with triggers reminiscent of the trauma,
access to the traumatic state may be facilitated, leading to flashbacks and
other reexperiencing phenomena (Rainey et al., 1987; Southwick et al., 1993;
van der Kolk & van der Hart, 1991).

Finally, based on clinical observation, some investigators (Crabtree, 1992;
Kolb, 1987; van der Kolk & Ducey, 1989; van der Kolk & van der Hart, 1991)
have suggested that traumatic memories are stored segregated from ordinary narrative memory and are less subject to ongoing modification in response to new experiences. In contrast to narrative memories that are
integrative and malleable, and thus fitted into the individual's personal cognitive schemas, traumatic memories are inflexible, nonnarrative, and disconnected from ordinary experience. This lack of integration may be the
basis for dissociated remembering through behavioral reenactment, somatic
sensation, or intrusive images that are disconnected from conscious verbal
memory of events. Because the memories are unassimilated, they retain
their original force; they are "unremembered and therefore unforgettable"
(van der Kolk & Ducey, 1989). Ordinary narrative memory is dynamic and
both changes and degrades over time. In contrast, traumatic memory may
be less changeable and has been described as "indelible" (Le Doux, 1992).

THE CONTRIBUTIONS OF MEMORY RESEARCH

Research concerning the types of memory and the malleability of memory
has been useful in elucidating the particular nature of traumatic memory.
Much of the experimental research and the more recent debate about traumatic memory has concerned concepts of unconscious memory. It should be
noted, however, in comparing experimental findings to theories about

trauma, that the term *unconscious* has been used to describe both nonconscious memory processes demonstrated by laboratory investigations and the psychodynamic unconscious as described by Freud. Both uses of the term imply nonconscious mental processes, outside conscious awareness, that may exert influence on behavior, thought, or experience. The psychoanalytic use of the term has additional implications (i.e., memory that is suppressed by the active process of repression).

Multiple Memory Systems: Explicit and Implicit Memory

Since the late nineteenth century, the study of memory has produced descriptions of several forms of memory, suggesting that memory is not a unitary entity, but more likely a multidimensional function consisting of various domains and representations of recollections (Polster, Nadel, & Schacter, 1991). In the modern era of memory research, neuropsychological studies on patients with amnesia have repeatedly shown that these patients could acquire various skills (e.g., on cognitive and perceptual tasks) despite having no memory of the episodes during which the skills were learned (Cohen & Squire, 1980; Daum, Channon, & Canavar, 1989; Jacoby, Lindsay, & Toth, 1992; Jacoby & Witherspoon, 1982; Sartori, Masterson, & Job, 1987; Warrington & Weiskrantz, 1982). Subsequent research demonstrated similar nonconscious learning and memory in normal subjects (Graf, Mandler, & Haden, 1982; Jacoby et al., 1992; Jacoby & Witherspoon, 1982; Tulving, Schacter, & Stark, 1982).

Two separate and distinct memory systems have been described by many investigators (Kihlstrom & Hoyt, 1990; Tulving, 1972, 1983). Harvard research psychologist Daniel Schacter coined the currently accepted descriptive distinctions of two primary memory systems: explicit and implicit (Graf & Schacter, 1985; Schacter, 1985, 1987, 1990, 1992). Explicit memory consists of the recollection of prior experiences with intentional or conscious recall, and is generally considered to include verbal and visual memory (i.e., recollections in the form of words or mental images). Implicit memory refers to changes in performance or behavior based on prior experiences of which one has no conscious recall, including conditioned responses. Implicit memory may be the active process in affective and somatic memory (i.e., recall or reexperience of emotions and bodily sensations) (Crabtree, 1992; Erdelyi, 1990).

Research on priming, a type of implicit memory, has shed further light on the nature of conscious and nonconscious mental processes. Priming refers to facilitation of a simple cognitive task (e.g., object recognition, word completion) as a result of a prior encounter with the cue and independent of conscious recollection of that encounter (Schacter, 1992). For example, college student subjects who are shown word lists are more likely to recognize those words in other lists even after several weeks when they have no conscious recollection of the original words. Even more remarkably, persons with organic amnesia (e.g., stroke patients who are unable to prospectively retain information) do similarly well on such tasks, indicating that implicit memory is a nonconscious process that operates separately from conscious recall. The findings strongly suggest that memory and memory processing are highly complex, with multiple memory systems involved in the acquisition, retention, and recall of information. This theory of separate and independently functioning memory systems supports the clinical observation in PTSD patients that certain kinds of emotions and somatic sensations may be experienced without conscious awareness of their traumatic origins (Braun, 1988; Chu, 1991b).

THE MALLEABILITY OF MEMORY

Recent studies of memory have shown that memories can be remarkably inaccurate, in contrast to earlier ideas that precise details of a traumatic scene are permanently etched in memory in a potentially retrievable manner (Brown & Kulick, 1977). Despite the difficulties of simulating traumatic experiences in the laboratory, investigators have studied the nature of memory in stressful experiences. Experimental procedures have included testing college students under demanding conditions (Eriksen, 1952, 1953; Tudor & Holmes, 1973) and exposing subjects to shocking photographic material (Christianson & Loftus, 1987; Kramer, Buckhout, Fox, Widman, & Tusche, 1991). Subjects in these studies are often remarkably inaccurate in recounting details of their experience (e.g., who made statements to whom, where they were at the time, what time of day it was), although experiences that were central to the individual seem to be accurately retained (Christianson & Loftus, 1987, 1991; Holmes, 1990; Kramer et al., 1991). A number of investigators have suggested that an individual's recall of central detail is a direct function of the intensity of the affect associated with the experience: The more emotional the experience, the better selected central details are remembered (Christianson & Loftus, 1991; Holmes, 1990).

The role of suggestion in the malleability of memory has also been well established in laboratory studies (Loftus, 1979; Loftus, Korf, & Schooler, 1989; Schooler, Gerhard, & Loftus, 1986; Schumaker, 1991). In some protocols, such as those designed by research psychologists Elizabeth Loftus and James Schooler, participants are shown pictures, slides, or videotape of an event and are then asked to recall the event. When participants are given even subtle cues or suggestions regarding the event, they often make errors concerning peripheral details of the event. For example, in one experiment

(Schooler et al., 1986), participants were shown slides of an automobile accident. For one set of participants, the slides contained a yield sign. For another set of participants, the slides did not contain a yield sign, but its existence was suggested in a questionnaire about the slides. When asked, many subjects in both groups reported seeing the sign and could provide a verbal description of the sign. These studies demonstrate that memory is not a static phenomenon, but can be influenced by a variety of factors, including the retrieval context.

Actual traumatic events can be misremembered. Studies of memory of the space shuttle *Challenger* explosion showed that many subjects had incorrect recollections of the events (Neisser & Harsch, 1992; Warren & Swartwood, 1992). Moreover, a participant's certainty that he or she had accurate recall was *not* related to actual accuracy. Loftus (1993) described other situations in which serious life-and-death situations such as war and accidents were misremembered. However, the central features of the events (e.g., the fact of the *Challenger* explosion, wartime events, and accidents), were accurately retained.

Despite evidence that memory content can be influenced by suggestion, emotional arousal, and personal meaning, the bulk of memory research supports the accuracy of remembered events that are known to have occurred. However, there is also evidence that persons can have memory for events that did *not* occur. One well-known personal pseudomemory was described by the Swiss psychologist Jean Piaget (1962), the well-known theorist of cognitive development in childhood. During his childhood, Piaget had clear visual memory of someone trying to kidnap him from his pram when he was 2. The memory also involved his nanny chasing away the potential kidnapper and then going home and telling the family. When Piaget was 15, the nanny returned to the Piaget family and confessed that the incident had never occurred. Her motive had been to enhance her position in the household, but she subsequently had suffered guilt about the fabrication and about the watch she had received as a reward.

In a *Fresh Air* radio interview with Terry Gross (November 1989), Chef Julia Child reported on another pseudomemory. She described being repeatedly approached by fans who insisted they saw her throw a chicken on the floor and saw her drink wine from a bottle. Child denied ever having done these things, although admitted to once having flipped a potato pancake onto the stove. On NBC's *Saturday Night Live*, Julia Child was lampooned in a sketch in which she became intoxicated and created mayhem in her kitchen. It is possible that viewers may have confused the parody with the actual cooking show. However, this anecdote suggests that memory content may comprise a combination of actual events, displaced events, and fantasy.

An experiment by Loftus and her colleagues (1993) further demonstrated that vivid visual memories can be created simply by being told of events by another person. In the experimental protocol, one family member attempted to instill a memory of an episode of being lost at the age of 5 in another family member. All family members agreed that the episode had never occurred. In one example, a story was told to Chris, age 14, by his older brother:

> It was 1981 or 1982. I remember that Chris was 5. We had gone shopping at the University City shopping mall in Spokane. After some panic, we found Chris being led down the mall by a tall, oldish man (I think he was wearing a flannel shirt). Chris was crying and holding the man's hand. The man explained that he had found Chris walking around crying his eyes out just a few moments before and was trying to help him find his parents. (p. 532)

Over the following days, Chris began to have fragmentary memories of this event. By the end of 2 weeks, he had a vivid memory of being lost:

> I was with you guys for a second and I think I went over to look at the toy store, the Kay-bee toy and uh, we got lost and I was looking around and I thought, "Uh-oh. I'm in trouble now." You know. And then I . . . I thought I was never going to see my family again. I was really scared you know. And then this old man, I think he was wearing a blue flannel, came up to me . . . he was kind of old. He was kind of bald on top . . . he had like a ring of gray hair . . . and he had glasses. (p. 532)

Even after being told about the experiment, Chris still had trouble believing that the incident had not occurred.

Is there a population of persons who are susceptible to creating pseudomemories? Psychologist Ira Hyman and colleagues have attempted to implant false memories of childhood events in college students. Participants were asked to describe both real events (from information supplied by parents) and false events. In one study (Hyman, Troy, & Billings, 1995), over several interviews, approximately 6% of participants developed vivid pseudomemories of false events, as in the following description.

First Interview

> INTERVIEWER: The next one is attending a wedding. At age 6 you attended a wedding reception and while you were running around with some other kids you bumped into a table and turned over a punch bowl on a parent of the bride.
> SUBJECT: I have no clue. I have never heard that one before. Age 6?
> INTERVIEWER: Uh-huh.
> SUBJECT: No clue.
> INTERVIEWER: Can you think of any details?
> SUBJECT: Six years old, we would have been in Spokane, um, not at all.

Second Interview

> INTERVIEWER: The next one was when you were 6 years old and you were attending a wedding.
> SUBJECT: The wedding was my best friend in Spokane, T_____ . Her brother, older brother, was getting married, and it was over here in P_____ , Washington, because that's where her family was from and it was in the summer or spring because it was really hot outside and it was right on the water. It was an outdoor wedding and I think we were running around and knocked over like the punch bowl or something and um made a big mess and of course got yelled at for it. But uh.
> INTERVIEWER: Do you remember anything else?
> SUBJECT: No.
> INTERVIEWER: Okay. (p. 191)

In a similar subsequent experiment, researchers found that vivid pseudomemories increased from 9% to 25% if participants were asked to imagine the false events in detail (Hyman & Pentland, 1996). These studies support the contention that pseudomemories can be induced, particularly with repeated suggestion, rehearsal, and the use of imagery. It should be noted, however, that only a minority of participants responded to cues to remember false events, suggesting that certain individuals may have more vulnerability than others to creating pseudomemories.

The creation of pseudomemories in children has been studied by psychologists Stephen Ceci and Mary Lyn Huffman (1997). In their studies, preschool children were interviewed on multiple occasions and were given suggestions about fictitious events. For example, in one protocol (Ceci, Huffman, Smith, & Loftus, 1994), children were asked to "think real hard before answering" about a variety of different events, including a presumably false experience of "get[ting] your hand caught in a mousetrap and go[ing] to the hospital to get it off." Over the course of 10 interviews, a majority of 3- and 4-year-old children remembered these false events as true, as did a lesser number of 5- and 6-year-olds. Neither parents nor the researchers were able to convince some of the children that the events had not occurred. Videotapes of some of the interviews of children were shown to experts in the field of children's forensic testimony. These experts were unable to distinguish between true and false accounts. These studies support the intuitive notion that younger children have difficulty distinguishing between reality and fantasy, and are vulnerable to suggestion. This type of research further complicates the issue of validity of memory, not only in children who report abuse, but in adults as well. Even if adults report having always remembered past events, it is possible that the original events could have been misremembered.

The now well-known case of Paul Ingram added evidence to the notion of the creation of pseudomemory. As described by social psychologist

Richard Ofshe (1992) as well as Loftus (1993), Ingram, the chair of his county Republican party committee, was accused of sexually abusing his daughter and other children and participating in satanic cult activities, including ritual sexual abuse and murder. At first, he denied everything. However, after interrogation and pressure from advisors, Ingram began to have vivid memories of his involvement in the alleged abuse. Ofshe, an expert witness, attempted to test Ingram's suggestibility. He told Ingram that he had been accused of forcing his son and daughter to have sex together, an event that his children had agreed had *not* occurred. Ingram initially had no memory of this event, but after being urged to think about the scene, he began to vividly recall it and eventually confessed to the alleged activities. This apparent pseudomemory does not necessarily invalidate Ingram's other recollections. In fact, another psychologist involved with the case reported that Ingram was convicted of six counts of child molestation after "care was taken to eliminate those allegations that could have been contaminated by the investigator's questioning or by contact with the daughters and Mr. Ingram" (Peterson, 1994). However, this case raises issues concerning the effect on memory of questioning, suggestion, and interrogation in both legal and clinical settings.

The contributions of memory research raise many thorny questions, some of which challenge traditional psychodynamic concepts. For example, cognitive psychology research does not empirically substantiate the existence of the psychoanalytic theory of repression, an active ego-defensive process. Memory research does not provide an explanation of how traumatic memories that were once conscious become nonconscious other than through normal forgetting, selective inattention, or avoidance. However, it is problematic to extrapolate experimental findings to clinical situations. As a number of investigators have noted, experimental conditions are often quite different from actual clinical situations (so-called *ecological factors*) (Erdelyi, 1985; Holmes, 1974, 1990; Schacter, 1990). Experimental investigations of traumatic memory are limited by the ethical constraints of exposing subjects to truly overwhelming or very prolonged traumatic events. Thus, results from experimental psychology may provide limited understanding of the actual impact of traumatic events. Nonetheless, a clear understanding of the mechanisms of memory is critical in evaluating clinical reports of traumatic memory and clinical situations.

STUDIES OF TRAUMATIC AMNESIA

Memory loss as a component of stressful events is a part of our cultural heritage (e.g., movies or books about a person who has been through some kind of trauma and has lost his or her sense of identity and memory of the event).

However, there has been little study of actual traumatic amnesia. In the past two or three years, the debate concerning recovered memory has stimulated numerous studies and publications on this subject. There is now a burgeoning literature concerning the prevalence and nature of traumatic amnesia.

CLINICAL STUDIES OF TRAUMATIC AMNESIA FOR CHILDHOOD ABUSE

Until recently, the only published study concerning the nature of amnesia for childhood abuse and validity of recovered memories was reported by psychiatrist Judith Herman and colleague Emily Schatzhow (1987). Their study involved 53 women who had sought treatment in time-limited incest survivors' groups. A majority of these women reported that they had experienced some kind of amnesia for their sexual abuse at some time in the past. Twenty-six percent reported that they had severe amnesia (e.g., no memory for the abuse), 36% reported moderate amnesia (e.g., remembered only some of the events), and the remaining 38% always remembered the abuse. More amnesia was correlated with early age of onset of the abuse, chronic abuse, and severity of abuse such as violent or sadistic abuse. Perhaps even more notable was that the overwhelming majority of these women were able to find some corroborating evidence of the abuse. Seventy-four percent were able to find convincing evidence that the incest had occurred, for example, family members who confirmed it, or diaries and other evidence of a deceased brother who had been the abuse perpetrator. Another 9% found family members who indicated that they thought the abuse had likely occurred, but who could not confirm it. Eleven percent made no attempt to corroborate their abuse, and 6% could find no validating evidence despite efforts to do so. Critics of this study note that some of the subjects were young at the time of their traumatization and that their inability to remember may have been normal infantile amnesia, and that clear, independent corroboration of abuse was not obtained (Ofshe & Singer, 1994; Pope & Hudson, 1995).

Similar rates of amnesia have been found in other studies. In one study (Gold, Hughes, & Hohnecker, 1994), patients who reported sexual abuse upon initial intake at an outpatient mental health center were asked detailed questions about their ability to recall the abuse. Thirty percent had periods of no memory of the abuse, 40% had some partial memory (i.e., suspicion of abuse but no clear memory, memory of some aspects, memory of some but not all episodes), and 30% reported complete and continuous memory. Another study investigated the experiences of 60 patients in psychotherapy who recalled being sexually abused (Cameron, 1994). Of the participants in this study, 42% had a period of complete amnesia for the abuse, 23% reported partial amnesia, and 35% believed they had no amnesia.

Psychologists John Briere and John Conte (1993) asked therapists to administer a questionnaire to their patients who reported sexual abuse memories. The questionnaire consisted of a variety of scales about current symptomatology and past life experiences. Of the 450 participants who reported childhood sexual abuse, 53.9% reported having had some amnesia for the abuse between the time of occurrence and age 18. Greater levels of amnesia were correlated with greater current levels of psychiatric symptoms, early age of onset, and severity (e.g., multiple perpetrators, physical injury, fear of death if they revealed the abuse). The researchers also asked about factors that were likely to produce greater psychological conflict, such as enjoyment of the abuse, acceptance of bribes, and feelings of guilt or shame. These factors were not correlated with amnesia, suggesting that it may be the noxiousness of the experience itself, not intrapsychic conflict, that produces amnesia. Critiques of this study note methodological problems, including a skewed subject sample and various interpretations of the term *remembering* (Loftus, 1993; Ofshe & Singer, 1994; Pope & Hudson, 1995). For example, Loftus (1993) noted that the question concerning forgetting could be interpreted as volitional suppression of the memory (e.g., "There were times when I could not remember because I could not remember without feeling terrible").

In their article on traumatic memory, attorney Alan Scheflin and psychologist Daniel Brown (1996) cited two Dutch studies on repressed memory or dissociative amnesia. Psychiatric patients with histories of sexual abuse reported high levels of chronic and severe abuse with symptoms including dissociation, hallucinations, self-injury, and suicidality (Ensink, 1992). This study directly addressed the difference between avoiding thinking about the abuse and inattention and true amnesia. A substantial number of the participants (28%) reported periods in which they "hardly gave any thought" to their abuse histories, and a similar number (29%) "had intervals in which they had completely forgotten it." In another recent study of severely sexually abused women (Albach, Moorman, & Bermond, 1996), 35% reported amnesia for sexual abuse at some period in their lives. Of note is that amnesia was determined by the question, "Did you really forget it or did you just not think about it?" Only those who reported actual forgetting were deemed to have experienced amnesia. A much larger number (85%) reported avoiding thinking about the abuse. Psychotherapy was reported as not being the cause of memory recovery in most of the study participants with traumatic amnesia.

A study by Loftus, Polonsky, and Fullilove (1994) reported more conservative estimates of amnesia for sexual abuse in a clinical population. A substantial proportion (54%) of 105 women in outpatient treatment for substance abuse reported childhood sexual abuse. Most (81%) reported remembering part or all of the abuse, and 19% reported that they forgot the abuse for a period of time. In this study, amnesia was not correlated with either severity of abuse or intrafamilial abuse. Critiques of this study noted the absence of independent corroboration and the methodological problems of defining the nature of the forgetfulness (Pope & Hudson, 1995).

PREVALENCE OF AMNESIA FOR CHILDHOOD ABUSE IN NONCLINICAL POPULATIONS

Studies of persons in nonclinical populations—who presumably have fewer distressing symptoms than patients in clinical populations—have nonetheless shown high rates of amnesia for childhood abuse. Psychologists Linda Meyer-Williams and Victoria Banyard studied women (Meyer-Williams, 1994) and men (Meyer-Williams & Banyard, 1997) who had been treated for sexual abuse 17 years earlier in a city hospital, and asked them to participate in a study about hospital services. Thirty-eight percent (38%) of the women and 55% of the men did not recall the abuse or chose not to report it. (These findings are strikingly similar to an unpublished study—Widom (1996) cited in Meyer-Williams & Banyard (1997)—which reported that 32% of women and 58% of men did not report court-substantiated childhood sexual abuse when interviewed 20 years later.) Many of the women in Meyer-Williams's studies who did not report the abuse did disclose other intimate details about their lives, including subsequent sexual victimization. There is hence a strong implication that many were actually amnestic for the experiences. There was a correlation between amnesia and age at time of abuse, which would be expected because verbal recall of events experienced prior to age 3 is limited. However, this factor alone could not explain the degree of amnesia in the subject population. Few of the women had been under 3 years of age, and there was actually greater amnesia in the group that was aged 4 to 6 at the time of abuse versus the under-3 group. More amnesia was associated with cases in which perpetrators were family members. Amnesia was not correlated with any particular kind or severity of abuse, for example, fondling versus penetration. Critical reviews of this study warn against interpreting the data as representing amnesia because the subjects were not asked directly whether they remembered the abuse (Ofshe & Singer, 1994; Pope & Hudson, 1995). Thus, the absence of responses about early abuse could be based on avoidance or normal forgetting.

Another nonclinical population was studied by psychologists Shirley Feldman-Summers and Kenneth Pope (1994). Their survey of 330 randomly chosen psychologists showed 24% reporting a history of physical abuse and 22% reporting a history of sexual abuse. Of the participants with histories of abuse, 40% reported a period when they had no memory for the abuse, and 47% reported that they had obtained some kind of corroboration of the abuse experiences. Fifty-six percent identified psychotherapy as a factor in recalling the abuse.

Many of these studies have the disadvantage of being based on self-report. Studies that are clearly retrospective in nature and rely on a clinical population seeking treatment for sexual abuse may also have limitations concerning the applicability of the findings. Meyer-Williams's (Meyer-Williams, 1994; Meyer-Williams & Banyard, 1997) and Widom's (1996) studies are perhaps the most persuasive because they involved nonclinical populations and prospectively followed traumatized groups. However, all these studies and clinical observations, taken as a whole, support the idea that traumatic experiences may lead to profound alterations of mental processes, including amnesia. As noted by Scheflin and Brown (1996), who reviewed 25 studies on traumatic amnesia:

> Partial or full amnesia was found across studies regardless of whether the sample was clinical, non-clinical, random or non-random, or whether the study was retrospective or prospective. Every known study has found amnesia for childhood sexual abuse in at least a portion of the sampled individuals. (pp. 178–179)

Some relevant and coherent evidence comes from psychiatrist Lenore Terr's (1979, 1983, 1985, 1988, 1991) pioneering work with children subjected to psychic trauma. Although Terr's work has been faulted for not being entirely based on empirical data, her observations of hundreds of children over decades has clear face validity. In an overview of the effects of trauma on children, she noted that distinct differences are seen in children who have experienced limited, circumscribed trauma (type I) versus those who have been subjected to chronic traumatization (type II) (Terr, 1991). Terr's description of memory in children who have experienced limited trauma suggests that traumatic memory has a quality that is different from normal memory:

> Verbal recollections of single shocks in an otherwise trauma-free childhood are delivered in an amazingly clear and detailed fashion. . . . A few details from a traumatic event of childhood may be factually wrong because the child initially misperceived or mistimed the sequence of what happened. But children with type I disorders seem to remember the event and to give impressively clear, detailed accounts of their experiences. This remarkable retrieval of full, precise, verbal memories of almost all single-blow traumas makes one conclude that these memories stay alive in a very special way. . . . (p. 14)

In contrast, Terr (1991) also observed that chronically traumatized children often experience extensive amnesia:

> Children who experience type II traumas often forget. They may forget whole segments of childhood—from birth to age 9, for instance. Where one sees the

difference between these "forgetful" children and ordinary youngsters is in the multiply traumatized child's relative indifference to pain, lack of empathy, failure to define or acknowledge feelings, and absolute avoidance of psychological intimacy. Repeatedly brutalized, benumbed children employ massive denial. . . . (p. 16)

Terr's observations demonstrate the existence of various kinds of memory in response to traumatic events in childhood. In one study of preschool children who had been subjected to known traumatic events (Terr, 1988), verbal recall of the events depended on the child's age when traumatized and on the chronicity of the trauma. Children under 28 to 36 months tended to have less verbal (explicit) memory of their experiences, a finding that is consistent with the development of verbal abilities around this period (Miller, 1979; Terr, 1985; Meyer-Williams & Banyard, 1997). However, even some of these very young children appeared to have implicit memory of the traumatic events, engaging in behavioral reenactments (e.g., trauma-related play, fears, dreams) of the events despite having no conscious recall. Terr (1988) also noted that of 13 children over the age of 28 months at the time of being traumatized, 7 had experienced single, brief events and generally had good verbal recall. The other 6 children, who had been subjected to more chronic traumatization, generally had impaired verbal memory of the events, but engaged in behavioral reenactments.

Important implications from Terr's work begin to explain that both a heightened clarity of memory (hypermnesia) and impairment of memory (amnesia) can result from traumatization. She postulated hypermnesia for traumatic events in situations that involve limited trauma, and she observed amnesia as a result of chronic traumatization. She also offered evidence that there may be nonconscious memory of traumatic events even when there is no conscious recall. However, it should be emphasized that the accuracy of memory, particularly recovered memory, following chronic traumatization, is not well established. Given that chronically traumatized children use massive denial and dissociative defenses, these children may not encode traumatic memories with the hypermnestic clarity that is characteristic of single-event traumas. Thus, chronically traumatized patients are most likely to suffer amnesia for their abuse, and, given the level of denial and dissociative defenses they use, the accuracy of recovered memory in these patients may be most vulnerable to distortions and errors.

CORROBORATION OF RECOVERED MEMORY OF CHILDHOOD ABUSE

Additional studies have dealt with the validity of memory of childhood abuse. Psychiatrist Richard Kluft (1995) reviewed records of 34 dissociative identity disorder patients in his practice for evidence of confirmation or dis-

confirmation of recovered memory. A majority (19) had obtained clear confirmation of childhood abuse. Three recovered memories that were later discon-
firmed. Of the 19 patients who obtained confirmation, 10 (53%) confirmed
events they had always remembered and 13 (68%) confirmed events first remembered in therapy (recovered memory). Both valid memories and
pseudomemories occurred in 2 patients. Many valid recovered memories
(85%) were accessed by hypnosis, challenging the widely held belief that the
use of hypnosis strongly contributes to the creation of pseudomemories.

Other recent data also support the validity of some recovered memory of
childhood abuse (Chu, Frey, Ganzel, & Matthews). In this study of 90 inpatients in a trauma program, there was a substantial rate of episodes of self-
reported complete amnesia for childhood physical (20%) and sexual abuse
(24%). The mean dissociative symptoms for all participants reporting abuse
was elevated and consistent with PTSD. More amnesia was correlated with
earlier age of onset of abuse. Most of the participants who reported a period
of complete amnesia for their abuse had attempted to obtain corroboration
of the events—14 of 20 for physical abuse and 19 of 25 for sexual abuse. The
overwhelming majority of those who attempted to corroborate their
abuse—13 of 14 for physical abuse and 17 of 19 for sexual abuse—found
clear validation for their recovered memories. Of particular note are the descriptions of a subset of severely and chronically abused participants with
high rates of amnesia. For the most part, these participants lost memory for
whole periods, recollecting neither traumatic events nor neutral or positive
experiences. These descriptions are strikingly similar to Terr's observation
of pervasive amnesia for chronically traumatized children and suggest that
the underlying mechanism for this kind of amnesia may not be repression
of overwhelming experiences or selective inattention to noxious events. Instead, the massive failure to integrate entire periods of childhood strongly
suggests that intensely traumatic experiences may result in a different way
of processing and storing information, supporting the notion that traumatic
memory is different from ordinary memory. This model is consistent with
the concept of dissociation, in which various mental contents exist in different states held separately from each other, adding evidence to the notion
that traumatic amnesia may result from dissociative phenomena rather than
the active psychoanalytic mechanism of repression.

IMPLICATIONS FOR CLINICAL PRACTICE

From both experimental investigations and clinical research, there appears
to be substantial evidence to support the existence of complex memory
processes that are affected by traumatic conditions. Limited trauma can result in memory enhancement, and overwhelming or repetitive trauma can

result in pervasive amnesia for the experiences. There is also evidence that correlates amnesia for traumatic events with early age of onset, chronicity, severity, and family members as perpetrators. Thus, children who experience abuse at young ages, who suffer multiple kinds of abuse, whose abuse continues over years, and who are abused by family members are most likely to develop serious dissociative symptoms, perhaps including dissociative amnesia. Unfortunately, at least in some clinical populations, this kind of abuse is more the rule than the exception.

It appears that horribly abused children do forget. However, when individuals begin to recover memories of past traumatic events, it remains unclear to what extent these memories reflect the actual events. Recall of single events of childhood trauma have been observed to have an unusual clarity. We cannot assume that there is similar clarity for recovered memories of chronic traumatization. In fact, the defenses used to cope with chronic traumatization—denial, depersonalization, and derealization—may make encoding of memory substantially less accurate. However, the essential features of recovered memories of severe childhood abuse cannot be dismissed out-of-hand. Although chronic traumatization may negatively affect the accuracy of memory, clinical observations and some research do support some of the validity of recovered memories of childhood abuse.

Therapists must understand the findings of memory research that memory content can be highly influenced by the mechanisms of memory retrieval, and caution must be exercised in inquiring about histories of childhood abuse. There is little evidence that direct questioning about abuse per se results in false memories of abuse. However, research concerning the use of suggestion and certain kinds of interrogation has shown that memory content can be affected by interactions with others and that pseudomemory can be induced. Hence, therapists must be careful not to inquire about possible abuse in a way that even subtly suggests a particular kind of response.

Therapists who treat survivors of abuse must not impose any particular idiosyncratic model of understanding or treatment on patients and must be open to understanding patients' difficulties in a variety of ways. Fantasies about abuse, suspicions or partly formed ideas about abuse, and dreams about abuse are not the same as actual abuse. Especially when memories are fragmentary, therapists must support the psychological validity of the memories but avoid coming to premature conclusions when there is insufficient evidence to support the actual occurrence of abuse. Similarly, when recovered memory begins to replace amnesia, therapists must remain open to the possibility of real abuse, but must also encourage patients to reconstruct their personal history in a way that is thoughtful, rational, and consistent with what is known about the past and current symptomatology. Therapists must also scrupulously avoid regressive clinical practices. Current reality, past realities, fantasies, dreams, and fears become inextricably entangled under conditions of profound regression, and may make it difficult or even impossible to establish a coherent personal history.

Understanding the role of childhood trauma and abuse in the development of psychiatric illness has helped many patients to deal with the horrors of past abuse and to reclaim a sense of normal human worth. However, work with traumatic memory has the potential not only for enormous benefits, but for serious detrimental effects as well. In order to be most helpful, therapists must combine an understanding of trauma, knowledge concerning memory processes, cautious inquiry, validation and support, and sound psychotherapeutic practices. Work of this kind may be maximally helpful to patients who suffer from sequelae of childhood abuse and who struggle to remember and make sense of their painful and chaotic lives.

PART TWO

TREATMENT PRINCIPLES FOR COMPLEX TRAUMA-RELATED DISORDERS

CHAPTER 6

Riding the Therapeutic Roller Coaster: Stage-Oriented Treatment for Survivors of Childhood Abuse*

C LEAR RECOGNITION of the profound effects of early abusive experiences and the complexity of adult syndromes related to such experiences underscores the need for a sophisticated understanding of the treatment process for childhood abuse survivors. Because of patients' many and varied presenting psychiatric symptoms, clinicians need to conceptualize a hierarchy of treatment approaches designed to address specific symptomatology. There is an evolving standard of care for complex traumatized patients, with a number of clinician-investigators advocating a variety of stage- or phase-oriented approaches (Chu, 1992c; Herman, 1992; Lebowitz, Harvey, & Herman, 1993). All these treatment models are based on the clinical experience that many survivors of severe childhood abuse require an initial (sometimes lengthy) period of developing fundamental skills in maintaining supportive relationships, developing self-care strategies, coping with symptomatology, improving functioning, and establishing a basic positive self-identity. This early phase of building a solid foundation of ego functioning is essential prior to embarking on any extensive exploration of childhood trauma or abreactive work.

Persons with severely traumatic backgrounds show a wide variety of attitudes in approaching therapy for their trauma-related difficulties. At one extreme, some persons assiduously avoid dealing with any recollections, feelings, or reminders of their childhood traumatic experiences. They at-

*Portions of this chapter are adapted from the article "The therapeutic roller coaster: Dilemmas in the treatment of childhood abuse survivors" (Chu, 1992c).

tempt to maintain rigid control over themselves and are vigilant about sup-
pressing thoughts and feelings that might trigger a reexperience of the
trauma. These persons, who include many male survivors of abuse, often do
not even present for treatment because they are generally intolerant of the
intense affects, dependency, and vulnerability of intimacy that tend to arise
in therapy. For the most part, they maintain themselves in a precarious balance, clinging to personal and vocational functioning to some degree, but
paying a psychological price in their stoic, chronically benumbed state. Another liability of this kind of rigid adaptation is the possibility of the breakthrough of unwanted thoughts and feelings that have been suppressed from
consciousness. If such breakthroughs occur, the result may be psychiatric
decompensation, including disorganization, self-destructive or aggressive
acting out, flight, or substance abuse.

It is generally accepted among clinicians who work with traumatized patients that the eventual abreaction and integration of childhood abuse experiences diminishes acute post-traumatic and dissociative symptomatology
and allows patients to develop a new perspective about themselves and the
world. However, a common clinical dilemma is observed in patients who
aggressively seek to uncover and explore their traumatic backgrounds long
before they are equipped to do so. Such patients (and their therapists) are in
a whirlwind of nearly constant crisis as they cycle through intense periods
of intrusive thoughts, feelings, dreams, and flashbacks, punctuated by brief
periods of numbing. Not only do such patients experience the internal compulsion to repeat the trauma, but they frequently naïvely believe they need
to "lance the abscess" of their abuse by explosively discharging unbearable
thoughts and feelings. Unfortunately, such a strategy is doomed to failure
because patients routinely feel overwhelmed by these thoughts and feelings.
These patients often overestimate their capacity for tolerating and containing
the torrent of intense experience that comes from premature attempts at
abreaction. Nonetheless, many of these patients dysfunctionally persist in
such efforts, as if just one more crisis will actually help them achieve some
sense of resolution in their tortured lives. Some of these patients a have a
kind of addiction to crisis. Although they experience crisis as intensely unpleasant, they feel most alive when battling their internal demons. Moreover,
because many of these patients have known crisis all their lives, the concept
of a deliberate, paced, and steady therapy is foreign to them. In therapies
that are out-of-control, it is common for therapists and patients to feel as
though they are riding a roller coaster with little sense of control or direction,
and to have a constant feeling of impending crisis and potential danger.

The pervasive myth that aggressive abreactive work will lead to rapid
improvement in most patients has its origin in treatment models developed
for combat-related post-traumatic stress disorder (PTSD) (Foa, Steketee, &
Rothbaum, 1989; Keane, Fairbank, Caddell, & Zimering, 1989). These mod-

els emphasize flooding patients with stimuli that trigger reexperiences of the traumatic events that are then abreacted in the context of high interpersonal support. The applicability of these techniques early in the treatment of patients with severe childhood traumatization and complex post-traumatic and dissociative symptoms is limited. As noted in Chapter 4, chronic early abuse has profound detrimental effects on the development of trust and the ability to use interpersonal support. When faced with the overwhelming thoughts and feelings related to abreaction, patients again flee into dysfunctional isolation and destructive behavior. Thus, the well-intended attempt at mastery of the traumatic experience results only in a retraumatization of the patient through a repetition of the trauma without therapeutic benefit. Would continued flooding of the patient with traumatic material eventually result in some benefit? Clinical evidence points to only continued negative effects of such a course of treatment. Some long-term therapies have made heroic attempts to push through repeated abreactions, sometimes in the context of prolonged inpatient hospitalizations. Most of these attempts have resulted in only profound regression, increased symptomatology, and potential for increased morbidity and mortality.

Therapists must avoid using strategies that repeatedly overwhelm patients without leading to significant resolution of the trauma. They must provide education (and limits, when necessary) about the need to do solid ego-supportive psychotherapy before proceeding with abreactive work. It may be tempting to pursue the traumatic etiology of a symptom, for example, if the patient is in crisis due to flashbacks, feelings, or somatic sensations having to do with a traumatic event, or is suicidal because of an abuse-related memory. Therapists must educate patients that pursuing this kind of strategy is akin to opening a Pandora's box. In fact, a major crisis, especially one that necessitates hospitalization, is usually a sign that the therapy needs to slow down and focus on basic therapeutic relational and coping skills. This kind of therapy may not appear as dramatic as aggressive abreactive work, but it has the best chance of helping patients achieve stability and the capacity for eventual exploration and working through of their early abuse.

Clinical experience with severely traumatized patients with complex post-traumatic and dissociative symptoms has shown that the best prognosis is for persons who attempt to gain control of their lives, challenge themselves to overcome obstacles, and persist in their efforts to attain a "normal" life (Chu, 1992c). In the face of an underlying reservoir of powerful feelings of despair related to their early abuse, these persons struggle to achieve healthy functioning in the world and in their interpersonal relationships. The initial achievements of these efforts may feel fragile and superficial. However, persistent efforts at functioning result in a sound foundation that consists of a positive sense of self-identity and self-worth, a sense of control over internal feelings and impulses, an ability to interact with the external environment, a daily structure that provides stability in daily living, and a true network of social supports. These accomplishments then may provide solid ground on which the patient may stand when exploring his or her early abuse. Establishing this solid ground is often an arduous and lengthy process, requiring hard work from patients, guidance from skilled clinicians, and the patience and persistence of both patients and clinicians.

The following treatment model divides the treatment course into early, middle, and late stages. The early stage consists of building the fundamentals of good ego functioning, including basic relational coping skills and a positive self-identity. The middle stage involves exploring and abreacting traumatic experiences. Finally, the late stage consists of stabilization of gains and increased personal growth particularly in relation to the external world. This division of the course of treatment is somewhat arbitrary because patients generally move back and forth between stages rather than progressing linearly. However, this delineation is useful in specifying the components and hierarchy of treatment. This discussion focuses extensively on the early stage of treatment because the dilemmas encountered here are the most formidable for patients and clinicians. The middle or abreactive stage of treatment is summarized in this chapter. For more lengthy descriptions of this process, there are fine texts that detail the abreactive and integrative process with traumatized patients (Courtois, 1988; Davies & Frawley, 1994; Herman, 1992) and those with dissociative disorders (Kluft & Fine, 1993; Putnam, 1989; Ross, 1989). The late stage receives the least emphasis because it is more familiar to experienced psychotherapists as the work with individuals who are largely functional but who have psychological impairments that affect the quality of their lives. Three areas that are part of the focus of early treatment—self-care, symptom control, and relational issues—are briefly described in this chapter; the scope and importance of these areas exceed the limitations of setting out the overall treatment model. A fuller exploration of these critical areas is found in the four subsequent chapters of this volume.

EARLY-STAGE TREATMENT

Abreaction and resolution of early traumatic experiences are limited by the ability of many childhood abuse survivors to relive the intense affects and experiences of the traumatic events, and their disability in utilizing supportive relationships, specifically including the therapeutic relationship. Abreactive work must be deferred pending the development of basic relating and coping skills. Certain areas of focus can be identified as crucial in the early stages of treatment. These are discussed here as part of the mnemonic

SAFER: self-care and symptom control, acknowledgment, functioning, expression, and relationships.

SELF-CARE

Survivors of childhood abuse are prone to become involved in a wide variety of self-destructive and dysfunctional behaviors (Briere & Runtz, 1988; de Yong, 1982; Himber, 1994; Shapiro, 1987; van der Kolk, Perry, & Herman, 1991). Chronic reexperiencing of the affects related to early abuse—including intense dysphoria, panic, helplessness, and hopelessness, as well as a chronic sense of aloneness and disconnectedness—often lead to suicidal impulses and behavior. Nonlethal self-mutilation is common (Himber, 1994; Shapiro, 1987), and, paradoxically, is often used as a soothing and coping mechanism. Patients with histories of extensive childhood abuse often describe their nonlethal cutting or burning as tension relieving rather than painful; this may have an underlying biologic explanation in the release of endogenous opioids (van der Kolk, 1987). Abuse survivors often exhibit other self-destructive and dysfunctional behaviors such as substance abuse (Kessler et al., 1995; Loftus, Polonsky, & Fullilove, 1994; National Victim Center, Crime Victims Research and Treatment Center 1992), eating disorders (Hall, Tice, Beresford, Wooley, & Hall, 1986; Welch & Fairburn, 1994), and addiction to risk-taking behaviors (van der Kolk, 1987). Revictimization is also remarkably common (Briere & Runtz, 1987; Chu, 1992b; Chu & Dill, 1990; Dutton, Burghardt, Perrin, Chrestman, & Halle, 1994; Follette, Polusny, Bechtle, & Naugle, 1996; Russell, 1986), including repetitions of emotional, physical and sexual abuse, even within the "safety" of the therapeutic relationship (Kluft, 1990).

Patients' propensities toward inadequate self-care through both self-destructive behavior and vulnerability to revictimization must be controlled prior to the beginning of any exploratory therapy. Failure to do so increases the likelihood of serious self-harm when traumatic material is broached. Analogous to the situation of abused children, abuse survivors must create an environment of personal safety prior to dismantling protective (albeit now dysfunctional) defenses.

Abuse survivors tend to be ambivalent about self-care. Perhaps one of the most damaging legacies of chronic childhood abuse is the compulsion to continue the patterns of abuse long after the original perpetrators are no longer actively abusive. In addition, a sense of inner worthlessness may make self-care seem internally consistent or unimportant. And perhaps most significant, alternative coping mechanisms that involve reliance on others may seem risky to abuse survivors who have backgrounds of abandonment and betrayal. Nonetheless, therapists need to insist that the therapy of patients with extensive childhood abuse focus on self-care. In the early stage of treatment, this often takes the form of therapists asking for agreement on a therapeutic agenda; for example, "I know that hurting yourself has been a long-standing coping mechanism for you, and that you may not feel that self-care is important. However, if we are to get anywhere in this therapy, you will have to make a commitment to work very hard to take care of yourself, even when you may not want to." It should be noted that in the early stage of therapy many patients lack the strength to fully achieve self-care. In many situations, lapses occur and patients retreat to self-destructive behavior. However, such lapses are only tolerable when patients are able to demonstrate a commitment to the principles of self-care over time. It is essential to the treatment that patients ally with their therapists around preventing self-harm, oppose their own self-destructive impulses, and understand the mechanisms of their vulnerability to revictimization. They must also begin to learn how to soothe themselves using alternative and less self-destructive ways of coping with stress.

SYMPTOM CONTROL

Many of the symptoms associated with severe PTSD and dissociative disorders need to be modulated and controlled in order to bring some stability into the patient's life. As long as symptoms such as abrupt state changes (including personality switching), amnesia, and reexperiencing of the trauma occur frequently, the patient is likely to remain in crisis. Some of the techniques for controlling these symptoms are more specific to the treatment of dissociative identity disorder (DID; see Chapter 11) but others, such as control of reexperiencing and modulating state changes, respond to more general interventions. Limiting the intrusion of traumatic thoughts and feelings during the initial phase of treatment is a major dilemma often encountered in the therapy of childhood abuse survivors. Although the therapist may understand that abreaction should be done only when the patient is optimally prepared, reexperiencing phenomena can and often do occur prematurely and at inopportune times.

The control of intrusive symptomatology can be gradually achieved, but only if the patient allies with the therapist in attempting to control the rate and nature of reexperiencing past abuse. Education about whether and how this can be done is the most important intervention concerning pacing of the therapy. This is a difficult proposition because this kind of symptomatology is inherently experienced as out of the patient's control. Efforts at control are at odds with the patient's own internal experience that control is impossible to achieve. Early in the treatment process, achieving adequate control may be difficult, and beginning steps to do so may be only minimally successful. However, the ultimate goal of the therapy has to do with achieving control over these experiences, and unless there is a concerted effort, this goal will not be accomplished. *Not* to strive for control is acceptance of the notion that reexperiencing phenomena are beyond patients' control and essentially dooms therapeutic efforts.

If patients are working in alliance with therapists and other treaters, many behavioral interventions can be effective. Most of these fall into the category of "grounding" techniques that reinforce the current reality when patients are beginning to be overwhelmed by trauma-related symptoms. Grounding techniques, if learned and practiced regularly, are effective in increasing voluntary control over post-traumatic and trauma-related symptoms. A well-lit environment can be helpful in grounding patients, particularly in the evening or at night; often, patients feel compelled to sit in half-darkened rooms, which increases their propensity to lose their bearings in current reality. Contact with other persons (particularly eye contact) is also enormously effective and conveys two critical therapeutic messages: Control of dissociative processes is possible, and other people can be helpful and safe. Finally, use of familiar and soothing objects can be helpful in reorienting patients who are having difficulty with reexperiencing phenomena or other dissociative symptoms.

ACKNOWLEDGMENT

Although intensive exploration of past traumatic experiences may be inadvisable in the early stage of treatment, acknowledgment of the central role of the early trauma is crucial. Childhood abuse is perhaps the most important determinant in the lives of trauma survivors, not only in terms of posttraumatic symptomatology, but also in terms of ability to cope with normal life experiences, especially interpersonal relationships. To ignore the role of abusive experiences is to tacitly collude in patients' denial of the impact of the abuse, as well as in their erroneous beliefs of personal defectiveness. The simple acknowledgment of the possible role of early traumatic experiences begins the process of helping survivors to understand many of their current difficulties as normally adaptive responses to overwhelming events.

Therapists must reiterate that although patients must shoulder the responsibility of the recovery process, they are not responsible for the abuse itself. Therapists often need to repeat variations of the normalizing message "You are not crazy or bad. You have had to adapt to very traumatic events, which has led you to feel and act in certain ways. You could not have stopped the abuse, and you are not responsible for having been hurt." Not surprisingly, this message is often poorly received. Patients who are abuse survivors are often ambivalent about acknowledging the role of trauma in their lives. Although they may be able to understand intellectually the relationship between their early abuse and their current difficulties, on an emotional level they tend to resist acknowledging any such linkage. This level of emotional denial is a continuing defense against the reality of the trauma in an effort to distance these overwhelming experiences, and against the powerful need to maintain a bond with idealized caretakers—even when the caretakers were perpetrators of abuse. The abusive experiences have formed the core of meaning in their lives ("I was hurt because I was so bad") and patients understandably resist seeing how much their lives have continued to center on flawed assumptions about themselves and others. It is striking that many trauma survivors continue to minimize obviously abusive experiences and their effects, and instead insist that they deserve the difficulties they have had in their lives. Virtually all victims of childhood abuse assume inappropriate responsibility for their own abuse. Even bright and perceptive patients who can acknowledge that no other children could deserve what they experienced maintain that they were to blame in their personal family situations. In the face of backgrounds of truly abusive experiences, such denial appears to be further evidence of the extent and unbearable nature of the abuse.

FUNCTIONING

In therapy, patients who suffered early abuse often become acutely symptomatic when they are overwhelmed by the reexperiencing of their trauma. Without persistent efforts on the part of both patients and their therapists to maintain some semblance of normal functioning, the reexperiences of trauma can rapidly intrude into every aspect of patients' lives. A syndrome of constant flashbacks, repeatedly occurring crises, desperate efforts to obtain comfort and reassurance, and dysphoric dependence on therapists is seen frequently in treatments that are out-of-control.

Maintaining functioning is far from a trivial matter. Without some kind of anchor in current reality, patients can become consumed by the emotional reality of their past abuse. That is, the feelings of victimization, hopelessness, powerlessness, and aloneness can overwhelm current realities. Patients may become intensely suicidal based on such feelings and are not able to perceive that their actual current lives are not abusive and well worth living. Too often, patients begin to unravel while beginning therapeutic work concerning past abuse. Such patients quickly become unable to function at all, and within a few months become bereft of any identity other than as victimized. This kind of result is not only a poor therapeutic outcome, but is a major problem that carries considerable risk in terms of increased symptomatology, permanent loss of functioning, and even suicide or aggression toward others.

Maintaining an appropriate level of functioning is often difficult but is essential. Therapists, even those who have been trained to be nondirective, need to respond with a clear *no* to the often-asked patient question "Do you think it might be worthwhile for me to take a few weeks off from my usual activities in order to get to the root of my difficulties?" Even if efforts to function seem to patients to be superficial or just going through the motions, they are important in balancing the internal pull toward becoming totally immersed in past events.

Therapists must emphasize the importance of maintaining both functioning and supportive relationships during the therapeutic process. Without this emphasis on functioning outside the therapy, problems such as regression and overly intense transferences are prone to flourish. Paid employment, a volunteer job, regular activities in the home, school, or training programs are preferable because they not only provide a positive sense of self, but compel patients to function in the current reality. If patients are unable to meet the challenges of vocational or educational settings, treatment programs such as therapeutic groups, day programs, or Alcoholics Anonymous/Narcotics Anonymous related activities are important as areas of functioning. Functional activity not only provides an all-important daily structure, but also enables patients to form a social network. And, patients' activities that are not therapy-related can provide a balance for the heavy emotional weight of patients' treatment. A sense of mastery in functioning helps to reinforce patients' sense of internal control of their own lives.

EXPRESSION

The intense affects associated with post-traumatic symptomatology must be expressed in a nondestructive and therapeutic manner. Although full exploration of the traumatic events may not be advisable in the early stage of treatment, patients do experience some of the overwhelming negative affects associated with the trauma, including such intolerable feelings as intense depression and hopelessness, panic and terror, and rage. Particularly because one of the goals of early therapy is to help patients avoid use of ingrained and destructive coping mechanisms, the therapy must help patients find healthier means of expression.

"Unspeakable" feelings need to find expression in words. However, in the early stages of treatment, verbalization of intense feelings may be difficult. This process may be facilitated through therapeutic nonverbal expression, and expressive therapies may have a special role in permitting and encouraging appropriate expression. After all, expressive therapies are specifically designed to help patients translate nonverbal feelings into words. It is common for abuse survivors who are unable to speak about their feelings to be able to find relief through art, music, or physical activity such as dance, exercise, or sports. Even writing is sometimes nonverbal: some patients describe sitting with pen and paper and allowing words to flow out on paper without conscious awareness of the content. In the early stage of therapy, such efforts should be directed primarily at therapeutic expression (e.g., venting tension) rather than exploration of traumatic events; they can be a powerful force in helping patients to find words for their previously unspeakable feelings.

Formal expressive therapy is best left to qualified expressive therapists. However, even verbal psychotherapists can help patients find nonverbal channels for explosive feelings. Therapists can support patients in pursuing expressive activities, or can simply encourage a program of regular physical activity. The latter modality can be an effective outlet for a variety of dysphoric affects. Intense panic and rage are visceral experiences that are normally felt in the body rather than the mind, and they are not easily verbally expressed even among those who have not been traumatized.

Training in relaxation techniques or use of hypnosis is often useful to combat both dysphoric feelings and the bodily overactivation that occurs in post-traumatic conditions. However, early in treatment, it is important that any such efforts be directed at containing feelings, especially anxiety, and not at exploring traumatic events.

RELATIONSHIPS

Perhaps the most important task of early-stage treatment is beginning to establish patterns of interpersonal relatedness that are mutual and collaborative. Survivors of childhood trauma bring the abuse-related interpersonal assumptions of their childhood environments into all their adult relationships, including the therapeutic relationship. Childhood abuse often transforms the therapeutic relationship into an emotional battlefield in which the patient and therapist take on abuse-related roles—most often victim or abuser, but sometimes rescuer or indifferent bystander (Davies & Frawley, 1994). The recapitulation and reenactment of early abusive relationships makes collaborative work on resolving past traumatic experiences impossible until mutuality is established.

In the early stage of therapy the patient and therapist must repeatedly renegotiate the therapeutic alliance. As the patient is repeatedly unconsciously compelled to precipitate abusive reenactments that disrupt the treatment relationship, the therapist must interpret the process and help the patient develop a sense of collaboration and mutuality. This process of disconnection and reconnection must occur on seemingly endless occasions with many variations before even a minimal sense of trust is formed. The following clinical example illustrates this process:

> Ruth, a 24-year-old woman with a history of severe childhood abuse complained angrily to her therapist that she was being treated unfairly concerning limits the therapist had set about emergency telephone calls. She claimed the therapist was being uncaring: "I thought you were the first person I ever met that I could trust, and now you do this. I can't believe you did this to me. You don't care about me and just want to get rid of me. You're just like everyone else—in fact you're worse because you *pretend* that you care." The therapist, although initially taken aback by the vehemence of the verbal barrage, recognized that both he and the patient felt abused and that mutuality needed to be reestablished. After a number of fruitless interchanges, he finally was able to say, "I'm sorry you feel so hurt. It was not my intent to abandon you. In fact, I was just trying to work out this relationship so that I could continue to help you over the long haul I would be interested in your ideas about how we might solve the problem of phone calls because it's important that we find ways to work together." Ruth became calmer and replied, "You're really interested in *my* ideas? I didn't know you cared about how I felt. In my family you could scream all you wanted and nobody heard or cared." In this way, mutuality was reestablished. However, the vicissitudes of the interpersonal process soon continued as the patient said, "But I still can't believe how you talked to me as though I was just a bother to you."

This is the "therapeutic dance," a seemingly endless cycle of disconnection and reconnection that occurs repeatedly, sometimes in the course of a single therapy session, and certainly over the weeks, months, and sometimes years in the early stage of therapy. This process makes this stage of therapy long and arduous. However, this process provides a new model of relatedness that is in sharp contrast to the abusive style of relatedness that the patient has experienced and expects. The therapy helps to introduce mutuality and collaboration in relationships, rather than control, aggression, abandonment, and betrayal that formed the core experiences of the patient's early life. Establishing and providing this alternative interpersonal process is the corrective emotional experience. Allowing patients to experience mutuality and collaboration provides them with a model to obtain support, resolve conflict, and feel a powerful sense of connection with others. The corrective emotional experience is *not* about taking care of patients. Therapists who expect patients to respond positively to a strategy of caretaking or reassurance will be ill equipped to weather the vicissitudes of the therapeutic process with abuse survivors. Although some caretaking is inevitable and respect is essential, these patients cannot be loved into health.

Despite therapists' efforts to be helpful and benign, they will not always be regarded as such. Therapists must recognize that no matter how kind, tolerant, or skilled they may be, they will find themselves as the objects of what psychiatrist David Spiegel (1986) calls "traumatic transferences," being regarded as abusers and being the object of patients' anger, suspicion, and even sadism. They must also be prepared to feel themselves being pulled into the position of feeling enmeshed, helpless, and violated, which are repetitions and reenactments of the experience of the abused child. Many, if not all, of these experiences are part of working with patients who have had horrific experiences. Therapists must be prepared to work with such situations and to deal with their own countertransferential feelings. Using the framework of the therapeutic dance to understand the cycles of the therapeutic relationship will assist therapists in helping advance the process and in formulating strategies to move the relationship toward a more psychologically healthy and stable collaborative position.

MIDDLE-STAGE TREATMENT

Psychiatrist Judith Herman (1992) speaks of abreaction as the reconstruction of a comprehensive verbal narrative of traumatic events, where "the therapist plays the role of witness and ally, in whose presence the survivor can speak the unspeakable" (p. 175). When traumatized patients have mastered the tasks of early therapy, they may then cautiously proceed to the exploration and abreactive work of the middle stage of treatment. Patients vary considerably in their ability to move beyond early-stage treatment. Some patients enter therapy with excellent coping skills and may quickly move toward middle-stage treatment. However, many others require months or years of preliminary work. Several caveats should be noted. It is uncertain what proportion of survivors of chronic and severe abuse will be able to abreact and successfully work through early traumatic experiences. Clinical evidence suggests that although many are able to do so, others may be able to achieve resolution and integration of traumatic backgrounds only to a minimal or partial extent. For such patients, stabilization and symptom management remain the long-term (and sometimes life-long) goals of treatment.

Significant regression is commonly observed in the face of abreaction of traumatic experiences. That is, under the stress of reexperiencing early abuse, patients may return to former patterns of isolation and dysfunctional or self-destructive behavior. If and when these patterns reemerge, clinical attention should return to early-stage issues until these issues are once again mastered. In fact, it is precisely because of the inevitable regressive pull of abreactive work that early-stage issues *must* be mastered. Patients need to establish powerful relational bonds and be prepared to withstand extremely dysphoric affects without resorting to dysfunctional behavior in order to tolerate abreactive work.

Abreactive work should always be undertaken from a position of strength rather than vulnerability. Without adequate preparation and support, patients are prone to reexperience traumatic events once again in isolation and to be repeatedly overwhelmed by them. Patients in acute decompensation often go through a long series of out-of-control abreactions, with therapists making sometimes heroic efforts to help contain these explosive events. Although abuse survivors may be able to vent affect and release internal tension through uncontrolled abreactions, these experiences have resulted in little lasting therapeutic value.

Abreactive work should not involve crisis. Achieving full understanding and integrating past traumatic experience may be painful, but should not result in patients feeling so overwhelmed that a crisis is precipitated. For the most part, effective abreactive work takes place in an outpatient office setting. Many patients enter therapy expecting to resolve traumatic issues through a cataclysmic catharsis. Although there may be breakthroughs of understanding and instances of intense emotional release, working through trauma is a progressive process that is accomplished over time. As early abreactive work is successfully completed, patients draw strength from new understandings about their lives and feel progressively freed from conflict, memories, and self-hate. This new strength is then an asset that allows them to go on to achieve resolution of other conflictual areas, or even to return and rework areas already broached. Working through each major issue or important event may entail a prolonged process lasting days, weeks, or months. Moreover, the process must often be repeated until all major issues or events are resolved.

Although patterns of abreaction differ according to the individual characteristics of patients, there are several common phases: (a) increased symptomatology, particularly more intrusive reexperiencing, resulting in (b) intense internal conflict, followed by (c) acceptance and mourning, which is transformed into (d) mobilization and empowerment.

An increase in the reexperiencing of traumatic events is a common early feature of the abreactive process. Again, it should be emphasized that this reexperiencing should occur without a major breakdown of functioning. The patient should have the ability to maintain grounding in current reality throughout the abreactive process. Acute reexperiencing may take many forms. Major traumatic events may be reexperienced with symptoms such as nightmares and disturbed sleep, increased anxiety, dissociative experiences, and generalized hyperactivity and autonomic hyperarousal. Other kinds of reexperiences may be more subtle. For example, the past experience of being subjected to pervasive hatred and denigration may be reexperienced as intense shame, self-hate, helplessness, aloneness, and despair.

The initial reexperiencing symptoms are often accompanied by the patient's efforts to deny any link to traumatic events or patients' use of dysfunctional defenses (e.g., isolation). The denial and defenses begin to break down as patients become able to utilize the support of the therapist and others in their lives. With the help of this kind of support and new-found coping skills, patients begin to tolerate the reality of past events and begin to attempt to reframe these events. Being able to remain connected with others is crucial in this process. These connections enable the patient to utilize the adult perspectives of others, perspectives that often cannot be gained by the patient alone. The events that were originally experienced (and are being re-experienced in the present) from the perspective of a helpless abused child can be seen from a more adult viewpoint.

New perspectives about past abuse produce intense internal conflict. For example, patients are often unable to let go of long-held feelings of self-blame at the same time that they begin to understand that they were not responsible for their abuse. Patients may retain a sense of identification with the perpetrators of abuse or may still feel intensely protective of them, even though they realize that they were victimized by them. Abuse survivors may also experience intense shame about not having been good or strong enough to stop the abuse, or having given in to the abuse, even though they understand that they were helpless in the abusive situation. Resolving such conflicts involves the patient's new, stronger, and healthier aspects understanding and developing compassion for the old and dysfunctional aspects. That is, patients must understand that some intrinsic aspects of themselves—including unpleasant feelings, thoughts, behaviors, and identities—were molded in painful ways by extreme events, and that these parts of themselves need to be accepted and nurtured rather than hated and rejected. Acceptance and integration of past feelings and behaviors, as opposed to rejection and disavowal, lead to the resolution of these internal conflicts.

Persons with unresolved abusive experiences frequently underestimate and minimize the extent of their own victimization as a way of protecting themselves from the full impact of the abuse. Despite the intense dysphoria that often accompanies fragmentary memories of the abuse, survivors are often stunned by the full realization of the extent and meaning of past abuse. One severely traumatized patient was finally able to give some eloquence to her experience after years of treatment:

I have been struggling for years to "get it." I've realized for some years now that I'm smart, but I still couldn't understand it. I went all around in circles rather than just realizing what had really happened. I now know why I couldn't understand it. To accept what happened takes away the whole meaning of my childhood. I had to believe I was hurt and hated because I was so bad, and so all these years I hurt and hated myself. And I was so alone with my self-hate—no wonder I tried to kill myself. It's so unbelievable that they could have done that to me if I didn't deserve it. It makes everything seem so pointless—nobody really benefited. It didn't have to be that way—but I guess I have to accept that it was that way.

As patients begin to accept the reality of their past abuse, they are often overcome by the extent of their former helplessness and by the abandonment and betrayal of important people in their lives. This part of the abreactive process often leaves patients emotionally drained, analogous to survivors of a natural disaster who are just beginning to take in the extent of the devastation that surrounds them.

Full realization of the extent of their abuse, and the subsequent toll it has taken on their lives, allows patients to begin to mourn the losses that have resulted from the abuse. This slow and painful process may involve patients examining each significant aspect of their pasts and reframing their understanding of the events and their meaning. Patients begin to accept that they were truly not to blame for their victimization and to understand how the early abusive experiences pervasively influenced the course of their lives.

Supported by these insights, patients begin the process of surrendering the role of victim and replacing it with a sense of self as a survivor of abuse. Over time, the abreactive process enables abuse survivors to mobilize their strengths and to gain control over their lives. Another patient remarked:

> I once read a story about a man who had been a political prisoner. For years he was kept in a cell that was 5 feet wide and 9 feet long, separated from anyone else. His routine was the same each day—he got up at 6 each morning, ate twice a day, and was allowed to bathe once a week. The rest of the time he spent walking up and down the 9 feet of his cell, back and forth, back and forth. As an old man, after almost 30 years, he was released and went to live with relatives. For the rest of his life, he got up at 6 each day, ate twice a day, bathed once a week, and spent his time walking back and forth in his bedroom—up 9 feet, and back 9 feet. I realize that's what I've done most of my life—living in captivity although I'm no longer a captive. I now know I don't have to stay in my cell. My life has been ruled by fear, but I finally feel as though I can escape and be free.

Pervasive distress becomes more focused as nameless feelings become understood and can be verbalized in words. For example, rather than experiencing wordless automatic terror and numbness in close proximity to all men, sexual abuse survivors may be able to recognize that there were specific men responsible for the abuse and to verbalize "These men are not the men that hurt me and are not looking for ways to destroy me." They may then be able to focus their fear, anger, and outrage on the perpetrators instead of displacing these feelings in a generalized fashion.

Abreaction of past trauma frees traumatized patients from fear of their own dissociated memories. Their nightmarish childhood realities lose the power to overwhelm and control them; huge and malevolent abusers are seen as somehow smaller and less powerful, and even horrific events become part of the past rather than repetitively intruding into the present. A remarkable transformation slowly occurs, as the sense of self is enhanced by an understanding that the patient has been able to tolerate and overcome his or her past abuse. Having understood and overcome extraordinary past circumstances, abuse survivors can find a new sense of competence, including a sense that they can protect themselves from future victimization. Having been able to acknowledge their own victimization and to come to terms with the realities of human failings such as selfishness, aggression, and malevolence, abuse survivors often begin to take on a depth of character in terms of self-understanding and true empathy towards others. After her long and continuing struggles to overcome the effects of abuse, one patient reported:

> You asked me earlier if I would like to trade places with someone else—someone that I admire. A few years ago I would have said "Yes!" in a minute, but now I don't think so. This is my life, and even though I wish sometimes it wasn't, it has made me who I am and I don't want to be someone else. I've had to look at myself and examine myself and learn how to accept myself, which has been incredibly painful. I know a lot more about myself and about others than most people, probably as a result of what I have been through. I like myself, and I really think that I'm okay. I've been told that adversity breeds character, and I suppose it's true, but I can't help thinking that I would have settled for a little less adversity and a little less character.

This discussion is not intended to be a comprehensive description of the intricacies of abreactive work. The most serious challenges of work with patients with complex post-traumatic and dissociative disorders has to do with the preparation for abreactive work. If adequate stabilization, containment, and ego-supportive preparation are done, abreaction should flow naturalistically from such work. One further caution and clarification should be noted: Therapeutic work with traumatized patients is not about abreaction as a goal. Abreaction is the means through which survivors of trauma begin to build a credible, personal narrative that helps them understand how they have become who they are, why they feel what they feel, and how they can go on with their lives.

LATE-STAGE TREATMENT

Abreaction and resolution of past abusive experiences enable trauma survivors to proceed with their lives relatively unencumbered by their pasts. Late-stage therapy involves consolidation of gains and increasing skills in creating healthy interactions with the external world. Resolution of all-encompassing and overwhelming past events reduces survivor's narcissistic preoccupation with their symptoms and difficulties. Moreover, an empowered sense of self leads patients to have increased confidence in their abilities to participate successfully in interpersonal relationships and other activities in ways that previously eluded them. In persons with a fragmented sense of identity, a profound sense of a new, integrated self arising from new psychic structures often emerges, which facilitates the ability to engage with the external world. Work with patients in the late stage of trauma-related treatment is similar to work with patients who enter therapy with good ego strength but who are experiencing serious impediments in their functioning. Another legacy carried by childhood abuse survivors is the need to expend much time and effort to undo what was done to them before they can really begin to grow in relation to the world.

It should be noted that it is common for patients in the late stage of therapy to find areas of yet unresolved trauma or trauma-related issues as they proceed with their lives and encounter new situations. This process should be construed only as a need to complete further abreactive work, not as a failure of therapy. In fact, previous successful experiences with abreactive therapy facilitate and often shorten any additional similar treatment.

A final quote from another patient illustrates the new perspective of those who have been able to rebuild their shattered lives:

> When I look back, it's incredible I ever made it this far. How many times did I feel I couldn't get any further? How many times did I try to kill myself? I think if I knew in the beginning what it would take to get to this point I never would have tried. There were so many years spent just getting through, and then so many years *undoing* what was done to me—so many years just getting to the point that I could have a chance just like anyone else. In a way, it's so unfair that I have had that job of undoing. I've had to struggle and struggle to do what seems so easy for everyone else. But I guess I've known that no one else could do it for me, although God knows I've needed a lot of help. Life isn't easy for me now a lot of the time, but I don't expect it to be. I feel lucky and very thankful for having the chance to do all the things I've done and to have a real future. It's scary to admit this, but I'm looking forward to the rest of my life.

CHAPTER 7

The Paradox of Self-Care*

THE CONCEPT OF self-care for adult survivors of childhood abuse is an inherent paradox. Learning self-care is an essential early step in the treatment of traumatized patients, but most persons who have been victims of early abuse have debased senses of self—as worthless and defective—and have no concept of the need to care for the self. Not only do traumatized patients often fail to care for their emotional well-being, but they fail to assume basic care for their physical health. Adults who have been chronically abused, particularly those who have been physically or sexually abused, have little sense of ownership of their own bodies. Patients often describe a kind of discomfort about their bodies: "I know that somehow this body belongs to me, but it doesn't feel like my body." When they look in the mirror they sometimes feel as though they are seeing someone else. Most of the feelings that traumatized patients have about their own bodies are negative—echoes of what they were told and how they were treated: "ugly," "fat," "disgusting," "cheap." Dissociative identity disorder (DID) patients have the most extreme distortions of the way they see their bodies; with a bit of mental legerdemain, patients see reflections in the mirror or photographs of themselves as having the imagined physical appearance and bodies of their alter personalities.

One of the destructive paradigms in abusive families is that the victimized child's mind and body are available for exploitation and adult impulses such as anger or sexual tension are vented on the child. It is not surprising that children who have been exploited in this way use themselves, particularly their bodies, to relieve tension or to act out impulses

---

*Portions of this chapter are adapted from "The Therapeutic Roller Coaster: Dilemmas in the Treatment of Childhood Abuse Survivors" (Chu, 1992c). The section "Silent Cries: Self-Harming in Abuse Survivors" draws on the clinical research and practice of Judith Himber, Psy.D., and portions were incorporated, as noted, from her article, "Blood Rituals: Self-Cutting in Female Psychiatric Patients" (Himber, 1994).

often resulting in self-harm. This tendency to use the self as a vehicle for tension release is heightened by the relational disturbances that result from the abusive early environment. When distressed, most humans seek connection with others in order to feel understood and to alleviate the distress. This avenue of assistance is unavailable to many abuse survivors since their cries for help have been met with either further abuse or indifference at best, and they have learned to avoid human connection.

The need for comfort and soothing is evident in all our relationships and is especially prominent with young children. Even the most independent toddler or young child is instinctively drawn to a protective adult in times of stress or fright. A normally nurturing parent establishes physical contact and comfort by picking up and holding an infant or toddler or by making connection through eye contact or words with an older child when the child has acquired the ability to use verbal communication. This behavior of seeking support from another human being is innate and is in marked contrast to the reactions of many patients with backgrounds of childhood abuse. In times of stress or difficulty, these patients flee from any kind of contact with others into a dysfunctional isolation, relying only on their own resources. One can only assume that the early experiences of many of the patients were sufficiently aversive that they virtually extinguished the innate response to seek contact with others when in distress.

COMORBID SUBSTANCE ABUSE, EATING DISORDERS, AND SOMATIZATION

Being unable to effectively use others for support, many abuse survivors seek relief in a variety of dysfunctional behaviors that do not rely on anyone else. Some patients attempt to numb themselves by drug or alcohol abuse, including excessive reliance on prescription medications. Others change the focus of their distress by engaging in eating disorder behavior or becoming excessively preoccupied with real or imagined somatic problems. Not surprisingly, histories of childhood abuse are common in patients with substance abuse (Kessler et al., 1995, Loftus, Polonsky, & Fullilove, 1994; National Victim Center, Crime Victims Research and Treatment Center, 1992), eating disorders (Hall, Tice, Beresford, Wooley, & Hall, 1986; Welch & Fairburn, 1994), hypochondriasis (Barsky, Wool, Barnett, & Cleary, 1994; Pribor & Dinwiddie, 1992), and somatization (Loewenstein, 1990; Morrison, 1989; Pribor, Yutzy, Dean, & Wetzel, 1993). Sometimes these problems have relatively minor impact, for example, in patients who occasionally abuse alcohol or drugs, struggle to be able to eat properly, or try to avoid becoming preoccupied with somatic concerns. In other instances, these problems are major impediments to effective treatment. To the extent that these problems are a prominent and consuming focus in patients' daily lives, they must be addressed as a first priority in treatment. Little, if any, work on learning the skills needed to address trauma-related difficulties can be done with patients who are recurrently intoxicated, endangering their lives through starving, binging or purging, or focusing their activities almost entirely on somatic concerns.

Primary problems such as out-of-control substance abuse, eating disorders, and somatization should be treated utilizing the standard basic principles established for the treatment of those disorders. Because these difficulties offer a kind of relief for patients, there is often considerable resistance to addressing them as problems. Patients sometimes regard them as secondary difficulties that will remit if only work is done on trauma-related issues. Patients may minimize their difficulties: "I only lose control of my drinking (or drugging, or eating) when I have flashbacks, and I need to work on my trauma," or, in DID patients, "I don't have a drinking problem—I don't even like to take aspirin; it's my alters that drink." This last statement is probably familiar to those who work in the addictions field as a form of common denial.

Modulating out-of-control behaviors should be undertaken prior to embarking on trauma-related treatment, and clinicians must be clear in their advice and expectations. Referral to inpatient or outpatient substance abuse treatment programs, Alcoholics Anonymous, Narcotics Anonymous, eating disorders programs, or other resources, or establishing effective protocols for somatization may be an important part of addressing self-care. Somatization may offer particular treatment difficulties because most work in this area has been focused on patients in medical and surgical settings. It may be useful to establish a program of regular and predictable medical appointments with a primary care physician who can both provide support and exercise appropriate limits concerning access to excessive and harmful medical care (Barsky, 1996). In addition, an educationally oriented cognitive–behavioral treatment, particularly in a group format, has been found helpful in alleviating some patients' somatic concerns (Barsky, 1996; Salkovskis, 1989).

SILENT CRIES: SELF-HARMING IN ABUSE SURVIVORS

Self-cutting is common among psychiatric patients, particularly adolescents (DiClemente, Ponton, & Hartley, 1991), eating disorder patients (Favazza, DeRosario, & Conteiro, 1989), and dissociative disorder patients (Putnam, Guroff, Silberman, Barban, & Post, 1986). Repetitive self-cutting has been correlated with histories of childhood sexual abuse (Briere & Runtz, 1988; Himber, 1994; Shapiro, 1987; van der Kolk, Perry, & Herman, 1991; Wise, 1989), and is by far the most common kind of self-harm seen in adolescents and adults with abuse backgrounds. Either delicate or substantial cuts to the arms, abdomen, breasts, genitals, legs, throat, or face (in approximate decreasing order of frequency) are used as repetitive tension-reducing mechanisms. A variety of similarly destructive behaviors seem to be variants on this behavior, including burning or abrading the skin; repetitive banging of the hands, arms, head, or feet; swallowing objects such as razor blades, glass, and pieces of metal; and inserting objects or foreign bodies into body orifices (most commonly vaginally) or into the flesh or veins. This kind of self-harming behavior may seem horrifying and perplexing, but it is widespread among patients who experience explosive inner tensions and who cannot access support from others. In most cases, these self-harmful activities are considered to be parasuicidal and not truly attempts to kill or endanger the self. (One dramatic example was a young woman who repetitively swallowed broken razor blades but became concerned and immediately sought help about her medical condition after swallowing them.)

The primary gain for many self-harming behaviors is an immediate relief of tension. Patients use self-cutting to change internal states—to induce a pleasurable state or at least a kind of numbness, or to end painful dissociated states (Grunebaum & Klerman, 1967; Himber, 1994). Most patients act in a way that is stereotypical and consistent over time; that is, most patients seem to choose certain forms of activities, e.g., cutting in specific places with certain kinds of sharp objects. There is usually little pain associated with the behavior. Prior to cutting or other similar behavior, patients often describe experiencing an intolerable sense of inner tension that may include anxiety, dysphoric dissociative states, or anger, which is immediately alleviated after the self-harmful behavior. In the particular behavior of cutting, it is often seeing the blood that results in the feeling of relief from tension (Himber, 1994). Thus, repetitive self-harming acts are prompt and effective solutions for self-soothing in patients who cannot obtain comfort or support from others.

In addition to tension relief, self-cutting and other similar behaviors are often an acting out of patients' deep-seated sense of defectiveness and self-hate. Some patients describe the need to "get the bad blood" out, or the impulse to cut out something bad from inside of them (Grunebaum & Klerman, 1967; Himber, 1994). Although repetitive self-cutting results in substantial psychological and physiological gains, it almost always is associated with shame and secrecy. Patients are generally aware that self-cutting is aberrant and that others react to this behavior with horror and disgust. Some patients also describe their cutting as compulsive and out-of-control, requiring more frequent or extensive cutting to achieve the desired outcome. This kind of loss of control also leads to increased feelings of shame.

Nonlethal self-cutting or similar behavior has also been described as a mode of communicating distress. Noted psychiatrist Otto Kernberg (1968,

1984) interpreted some acting out through self-harming behavior as attempts to discharge transferential anger, and others have noted the motivation to manipulate others, to gain attention, and to deal with threatened loss (Grunebaum & Klerman, 1967). Some patients may indeed harm themselves for these reasons, particularly in situations of acute distress and explosive anger. When cutting occurs in the context of rage over feeling abandoned, ungratified, or misunderstood, it may convey messages such as "This shows you how angry I am!" "*Now* do you take me seriously?" or "See what you made me do?" However, clinical experience suggests that the central intent of self-harmful behavior is not always about attempts to influence the response from others. After all, most patients began this kind of activity in isolation and secrecy, long before it came to the attention of anyone else. Much self-cutting begins as an inarticulate cry of pain from patients who have no words to adequately describe their distress or who feel repeatedly unheard and unseen. Self-cutting often originates as a solitary act that occurs when patients feel intensely alone, absorbed in their distress, and without a conscious intent to communicate or manipulate.

When revealed in the context of a therapeutic relationship, self-harming behavior may additionally convey unspoken messages. Revealing self-injury is a mute cry for help, but it often also appears to be an invitation for a reenactment of abuse-related scenarios. There is a nonverbal communication of, "Do you see how much I hurt?" as well as an almost defiant statement of, "Do you see how different I am from other people and how I don't need help from anyone else?" The therapist has difficulty knowing how to respond. A response of only concern or sympathy is gratifying for the patient, who then feels heard, but little is gained in terms of promoting direct or verbal communication. A response that ignores or minimizes the behavior increases the patient's sense of being alone and unheard. A response of disgust, frustration, or anger (especially when the behavior violates a therapeutic safety contract) inevitably provokes shame and a confirmation of defectiveness and sets into motion the abuse-related scenario of patients' feeling as though they have been bad and deserve punishment and guilt. Perhaps the best response in these situations is modulated in terms of expressed emotion and expresses concern and interest along with a gentle confrontation concerning the dysfunctional aspects of the behavior: "I can see that you have been in a great deal of pain, and I would like to learn more about your cutting and what leads to it. I am sorry that you have not found another way to let me or other people know about your pain, and that you have had to continue to do something that interferes with your ability to grow and heal." Responding in a matter-of-fact, calm, serious manner with a gentle imperative toward change is essential in transforming the self-harming behavior to direct verbal interpersonal communication and a sense of self-mastery. The therapist also needs to assess the dangerousness of the self-cutting, both in terms of suicide potential (unusual) and physical well-being. Even in the absence of suicidal intent, blood loss, serious scarring, and the potential for serious infection may mandate referral to a physician for ongoing monitoring and treatment.

It is important to make the distinction between establishing safety and extinguishing self-harm. Some patients with childhood histories of neglect and trauma cannot completely stop self-harming behavior until they have developed or restored basic abilities to engage productively with others. However, establishing an alliance around the progressive goal of stopping self-harm is essential. As in the treatment of other addictive behaviors, slips and relapses are common and a sustained commitment to the ultimate goal of abstinence is the most important part of successful treatment. Using an addictions model of treatment, self-harmful behavior should not be regarded moralistically, but as a maladaptive effort at coping that has negative consequences. Emphasis must be placed on the patient to supply the primary motivation to control the behavior, although it must be acknowledged that the patient will require considerable support. As noted by psychologist Judith Himber (1994):

> Establishing an alliance around safety proceeds hand-in-hand with the development of understanding and communication. Although stopping self-cutting is a final goal of treatment, there are useful intermediate steps. If the patient cannot agree to stop cutting, can she identify and agree to goals which will help her recover? Some patients may disavow the seriousness of their behavior or the shame and fear associated with it, insisting that "it's no big deal," not suicidal, and not worth paying attention to. This can set the stage for a struggle between the patient and the therapist. In such struggles, the patient projects her distress and anxiety about self-harmful behavior onto the therapist, and then both attacks and devalues the therapist's interventions. As the patient acts less and less concerned about cutting the therapist may become more and more alarmed and the struggle can escalate. It is important to keep the focus on the patient's responsibility for her own safety and to name her attempts to disavow her own distress. (pp. 629–630)

Clinicians must be careful not to take on one side of this ambivalence (the positive side), which will allow the patient to actually feel less conflicted about the self-harmful behaviors. Clinicians should provide expert advice and emphatic support, but must make clear that patients must carry the primary responsibility for their own behaviors, for ambivalence about the behaviors, and for changing the behaviors. The following case illustrates some of the dilemmas and negotiations concerning the treatment of repetitive self-harm:

> Barbara, a 35-year-old mother of two, was admitted to the hospital for severe depression and suicidal ideation. She reported a 20-year history of repetitive self-cutting, and although she had no major medical problems related to

this behavior, both of her forearms were crisscrossed with hundreds of small scars and more recent wounds. Despite several years of therapy, Barbara was making little progress, which she attributed to both a sense of hopelessness about her own condition and to her outpatient therapist: "She just listens and doesn't actually *do* anything." Barbara reported that she cut herself for a variety of reasons, but mostly when she had intense feelings such as despair, anger, or aloneness. The cutting made these feelings numb. Her outpatient therapist knew about the cutting, and Barbara sensed that she was uncomfortable about it and wanted it to stop. A number of safety contracts had been established, but Barbara continued to cut secretly and somewhat defiantly: "I know she wants me to stop, but it's my body and she doesn't understand how much I need it." Barbara's hospital therapist asked about details of the cutting and the circumstances in which it occurred. She also underscored both the adaptive role of the cutting and its impact on Barbara's life: "I know that cutting has been a kind of friend to you over the years in helping you cope with intolerable feelings and circumstances. You know that I think that you need to find a way to stop cutting or you will not be able to find more adaptive ways to express your feelings and move on in your treatment. However, only *you* can decide when you are ready to stop cutting. Rather than placing the responsibility on your outpatient therapist to 'make' you stop cutting, I think you should remember that the cutting makes you feel ashamed and out-of-control at times and has interfered with your treatment." After considerable discussion, Barbara agreed to try to find ways to stop the self-cutting. She used a number of grounding techniques to control dysphoric dissociative states and followed through with a plan to talk to others when she had the impulse to cut. When she had the impulse to cut, she began rubbing her forearms with an ice cube, which produced a numbing sensation that reduced the need to cut. Finally, Barbara devised a unique solution. Using wooden beads, she painted the name of each of her sons on each of two large beads, which she then fashioned into bracelets. Subsequently, when she would find herself looking at her arms for a place to cut, she would see the bracelets and recall that she had made a commitment to herself and her family to try to stabilize her life. This proved effective and she was able to stop cutting for the first time in decades. Two weeks after discharge from the hospital, the outpatient therapist noticed fresh scars on her arms. Barbara shamefully admitted, "I guess I've been forgetting to wear the bracelets." Barbara and her therapist were then able to discuss Barbara's essential role in controlling the self-cutting and were able to devise a new strategy for addressing this issue in the context of her treatment.

SUICIDE

The specter of suicide is often present in the early treatment of severely traumatized patients. Many patients who have survived extensive early abuse have made suicide gestures or attempts, and nearly all such patients chronically contemplate suicide as a potential relief from their intolerable experiences. The management of true suicide risk should be relatively straightforward. First, truly suicidal impulses and behavior must be distinguished from the parasuicidal behaviors involved in self-cutting or other self-harming behaviors. Second, clinicians must insist that the threat (or implied threat) of suicide not be used as a form of communication or negotiation. Third, therapists and patients must agree that the possibility of suicide is a crisis situation and that any and all interventions can be used. Fourth, although both therapists and patients together may help to determine the risk of suicide, therapists have the ultimate perogative for acting in a crisis situation to preserve patients' lives and well-being. These principles are central to managing chronic suicidal threat and necessary for the sanity of both patients and therapists. They cannot be compromised, and clear limits must be set concerning any violation of these principles (see Chapter 10). Interpersonal conflict and struggle are often inherent in the therapeutic relationship. It is a safe therapeutic strategy to set clear limits concerning the principles about suicide from the outset and to permit the inevitable conflict and negotiation to occur in other, less lethal areas. Without patients' agreement on these principles, treatment may be therapeutically untenable, with little hope for a positive outcome and a greater likelihood of stalemate or even death through completed suicide.

The difference between suicidal and parasuicidal behavior is determined best by direct discussions with patients regarding the motivations and goals of their behavior. Patients are often able to be clear that there is no suicidal intent in certain self-harming activities. However, there are often areas of ambiguity such as patients who hurt themselves in ways that might or might not be lethal, or in behavior that is not intended to be suicidal but may result in serious injury or death (e.g., repeated driving while intoxicated). Because of the extreme consequences of this kind of ambivalent behavior, therapists should err on the side of safeguarding patients' well-being if there is any substantial question of personal safety.

Patients' hints or threats about suicide can be a form of communication or negotiation. Statements such as "I'm not sure I can keep myself from hurting myself" are often a disguised way of asking, "Do you recognize that I am in pain and feel desperate?" or "What will you do for me if I don't kill myself?" Therapists should confront such implied communications directly and ask if the patient is trying to communicate the intent to suicide—or some other message. Because unresolved questions concerning suicide are likely to result in hospitalization or other unwelcome outcomes, the burden is then on patients to try to clarify the underlying message in their statements. Frank and direct discussion about suicide is the best deterrent against self-endangering behavior. If patients and therapists are unable to engage is such direct discussion, suicidal behavior may even increase. For example, the patient who says "I've been thinking about killing myself," as a way of asking, "Do you care about me?" may actually feel impelled to act if the question is not clarified and the patient feels disappointed or upset by the therapist's response.

Agreements that the patient will not attempt suicide, so-called *safety contracts*, can be effective, particularly because many patients have a personal, rigid commitment to adhere to their promises ("I always keep my word"). The best safety contracts are made face-to-face with direct eye contact and with therapists sensing a sincerity (although often with reluctance on the patient's part) about the agreement. Safety contracts also have limitations. For example, it is almost impossible to devise a formal safety contract without loopholes, and patients may stick to the letter of the agreement but may find ways to violate its substance, for example, "I said I wouldn't overdose, but I didn't agree not to drive my car off the road," or "I agreed to be safe until out next appointment, but you canceled it and rescheduled it." Furthermore, safety contracts are usually time-limited because few patients can agree to long-term or indefinite contracts not to attempt suicide. As such, safety contracts must be renewed and any failure to do so will be seen by the patient as an invitation to engage in self-endangering behavior, as in the following example:

> June, an adolescent with a history of severe childhood abuse had made several serious suicide attempts in her young life. She began working with a therapist who helped her decrease her self-destructive behavior through a series of safety contracts that were established on a session-by-session basis. June and her therapist took seriously these contracts, including detailed provisions in the contracts concerning not only the time period of the contracts but various prohibitions against all sorts of self-harming and risk-taking behaviors. Following a therapy session approximately 18 months into the treatment, the therapist recalled that she had gotten an emergency telephone call near the end of the session and had neglected to renew the safety contract. After some thought, she decided that given the trust that had developed in the relationship, and by precedence set by previous agreements, a continued safety contract was clearly implied and she did not act further. June, on the other hand, was acutely aware of the absence of the safety contract and was convinced that this was a clear message from her therapist that the therapist had finally gotten tired of her and wouldn't mind if she killed herself. She took an overdose of all her medication and was subsequently admitted to a hospital after being found by her roommate.

Although safety contracts may be useful, the patient's commitment to continue to struggle to stay alive is much more important. As with safety contracts, this commitment must be repeatedly discussed and reaffirmed.

As is the case with most self-harming behavior, traumatized patients have intense ambivalence about suicide. After all, those who unambivalently wish to die have unfortunately already committed suicide. Many abuse survivors have intense internal conflict about being alive. When patients are unable to tolerate the pain of their own intense conflicts, therapists may find themselves assuming one side of the ambivalent feelings, again, usually the good, or positive, side. Unfortunately, this sometimes permits patients to be negative about this complex issue. Therapists and patients may find themselves battling over the issues involving actual survival rather than recognizing them as the projections of the patient's intrapsychic conflict:

> Deborah, a 36-year-old woman, entered therapy with the goal of wanting to feel "less tortured." She began to describe fragments of memory that suggested horrific physical, sexual, and emotional abuse in a highly chaotic family environment. As the therapy progressed, she became more aware of the extent of her abuse and more overwhelmed by feelings of depression, despair, and loneliness. Her suicidal ideation and self-destructive impulses increased. In therapy, Deborah claimed that she could no longer be responsible for her own safety and that the therapist had to "hold the hope" for her. This resulted in many instances in which the patient would persuasively argue that her life had become a constant torture and that the therapist should understand and allow her to kill herself. The therapist would then counter with reasons why she should live, including hopes for the future and the value of her life for herself and for others. The patient rejected all these arguments as false reassurances. The therapist became increasingly anxious that Deborah might attempt suicide. Finally, following consultation with a colleague, the therapist was able to say, "I understand that you wish to die and that life is a torture for you. However, I think you may be oversimplifying the situation to yourself. I think you have mixed feelings about living and dying. Although you desperately wish to die, you have a remaining small hope that life might get better. Although you know that *I* want you to live, it is much more important for *you* to know that you both want to die and still have the hope to live. I cannot convince you to live, but I can help you sit with the very uncomfortable feelings about not knowing what to do." Deborah acknowledged the validity of these observations, and the therapy continued in a more stable manner.

Specifically concerning the issue of suicide, the therapist may need to temporarily assume responsibility for maintaining the patient's safety, for example, arranging hospitalization when the patient is unable to commit to safety. However, any such stance should be short lived because the therapy itself is untenable unless patients assume the burden of working out their own conflicts about living.

Remaining alive is a prerequisite for therapy. This simple fact is often overlooked by desperately tortured patients and their well-intended therapists. Patients may often be so filled with their own pain that they ignore the fact that they have a basic responsibility in any relationship: They must be alive to participate in the relationship, and that this expectation is a prerequisite for expecting that anyone else will make a commitment to them. Therapists may be afraid to bring up this issue of the patient's responsibility to remain alive because of the principle that therapists should not let any of their own feelings contaminate the therapy. However, even the therapeutic relationship depends on the most basic contract—that both parties agree to make a commitment to continue working together. Thus, another effective intervention is often the therapist confronting the patient's abandonment of the relationship: "I know that you have many reasons to want to die. However, do you remember that you have often asked me to make a commitment to you? I am glad to do so for the foreseeable future, but it is only fair to ask that you do so too—by making a commitment to remaining alive. I have no wish to take away your ultimate control of the decision to live or die, but I do want to ask you to make a decision for now not to destroy our relationship."

Emergency interventions are required in situations in which patients' lives are in danger. Therapists often feel they are not allowed to pursue critical options. They should never agree to relinquish vital therapeutic interventions, for example, agreeing never to hospitalize the patient ("I'll just be put into restraints and be retraumatized"), to always discussing all options beforehand ("I'll never be able to trust you again"), to never contacting family members ("They'll never let me forget it"). Although it is always clinically desirable to discuss matters with patients and to respect their wishes, a possible imminent suicide is an emergency situation that may require extraordinary measures. Such measures may be necessary to save a life, even at the cost of destroying an ongoing therapeutic relationship.

No matter how well managed a therapy may be, there is always the possibility of broken contracts and attempted or even completed suicides. The burden of living with the sequelae of horrific abuse may be more than some survivors can tolerate. Fortunately, the number of completed suicides is small considering that self-harmful behavior and chronic suicidal impulses are common in severely traumatized patients with complex PTSD and dissociative disorders. In situations in which there is a serious breach of the substance or spirit of agreements concerning safety (and the patient survives), the therapist needs to consider several options. First, is the therapist willing to continue the treatment? A chaotic and anxiety-provoking therapy places a considerable burden on the therapist, and therapists need to consider whether they are able and willing to continue. Therapists must be candid with themselves about this issue because both the patient's and therapist's well-being depends on it. Often, therapists convince themselves that they can continue to treat difficult patients and then subtly act out their frustrations and anger much to the detriment of the treatment. If therapists are willing and able to continue the treatment, they must determine what basic requirements must be met by the patient—for example, agreements concerning safety, behavior, outside supports, attitudes, and so on—and then ask the patient to meet these requirements in order to continue the therapy. A serious suicide attempt is a major breach of the therapeutic relationship and it is incumbent on the patient to demonstrate a willingness and ability to heal the rupture in order to continue the therapy.

REVICTIMIZATION

One common failure of self-care results in the revictimization of childhood abuse survivors. Behaviors in patients with traumatic backgrounds range from a seeming obliviousness to potential danger to repetitive risk-taking that sometimes appears almost addictive. These behaviors result from a variety of different and complex psychological processes that are tied to early abuse experiences, and they place many traumatized patients at considerable risk.

Adults who were severely abused as children, are often revictimized, through physical or sexual assault in a way that seems to mirror the traumatic childhood experiences. Research statistics support this apparent high incidence of revictimization. In Diana Russell's study (1986) of a nonclinical population, women who had been victims of childhood incest had far higher rates of adult sexual assault than women with no incest history. In settings such as emergency rooms and crisis centers, adults with histories of childhood abuse have been shown more likely to be victims of multiple rapes and other kinds of revictimization (Briere & Runtz, 1987; Dutton, Burghardt, Perrin, Chrestman, & Halle, 1994; Follette, Polusny, Bechtle, & Naugle, 1996). In one study of adult female psychiatric inpatients, women who had been victims of early sexual abuse were more than twice as likely as nonabused women to be sexually abused in adulthood, and those who had been physically abused in childhood were 17 times more likely than non-abused women to be physically abused as adults (Chu & Dill, 1990). Even in psychotherapy, patients with a history of childhood sexual abuse are more likely to be the victims of therapists' sexual misconduct (Feldman-Summers & Jones, 1984; Kluft, 1989c, 1990). Therapists who have sexually exploitative attitudes or who are repeat sexual offenders pose serious risk to all patients, but particularly to those who have previously been victimized (Schoener, Milgrom, Gonsiorek, Luepker, & Conroe, 1990).

The repetition compulsion in relation to childhood trauma is one of the key factors in revictimization. In his discussion of the repetition compulsion, Freud (1955) postulated the "need to restore an earlier state of things" and a need for the person to rework the original experience, specifically taking an active versus the previous passive role, as a way of gaining a sense of mastery over the experience. He also noted that repetitions of repressed experience allowed the repeated expressions of affects associated with the experience, particularly sadism and hostility. These two last dynamic issues—the active mastery of prior passive unpleasant experiences and the expression of affects associated with past experiences—are important in understanding the repetition compulsion in the revictimization of survivors of childhood abuse. The compulsion to repeat may involve persons taking active (although unconscious) measures to reenact prior traumatic events, as in the following case example:

Susie, a 27-year-old married woman with a childhood history of extreme physical and sexual abuse, was being treated for chronic dysphoria and self-destructive behavior. Frequently, when overwhelmed by her feelings, she felt compelled to hitchhike at night on deserted country roads. Susie was unable to understand why her therapist objected to this behavior, saying that she only wanted someone to pay attention to her and that she knew how to take care of herself. After an episode in which she was picked up and assaulted, she withheld this information from her therapist, feeling angry that the therapist would probably say "I told you so."

Perhaps the clearest examples of attempts at mastery through the repetition of early sexual trauma come from reports that have linked prostitution with childhood sexual abuse. Studies of prostitutes have shown extremely high levels of childhood sexual abuse (Silbert & Pines, 1981) and levels of both incest and rape that are far higher than in control groups of normal women (James & Meyerding, 1977). Herman (1981) documented both promiscuity and victimization in women who had been sexually abused. It is in clinical situations that the elements of this type of repetition are clearly evident. One patient who frequently prostituted herself remarked, "When I do it, I'm in control. I can control them through sex." Her contempt for the men who used her was evident, and she was only minimally aware of how she was being exploited. This situation is a clear attempt to have active control of a previously passively experienced victimization, and a great deal of the affect (contempt and hostility) associated with previous sexual abuse is expressed.

The repetition of past abusive experiences might result in favorable outcomes if persons were able to master past aversive experiences through reenactments. Unfortunately, these attempts usually seem doomed. The inherent interpersonal betrayals of childhood abuse frequently lead adults to avoid supportive alliances. Hence, when they are confronted with overwhelming repetitions of past abuse, they have only their own resources to draw upon and are frequently again overwhelmed, retraumatized, and revictimized. Moreover, the venting of bitterness and anger often results in further disruption of the interpersonal ties that might otherwise help protect and support. In this way, the childhood interpersonal arena is recreated and reexperienced, leaving its victims unprotected and exploited and ultimately leading to isolation, helplessness, and despair.

Trauma-related symptomatology is another key factor related to revictimization. When overwhelming life events are repressed and dissociated, individuals are not only compelled to repeat the events, but may also experience a number of additional post-traumatic syndromes that place them at risk. As Kluft (1989c) noted:

They often have dissociative defenses that cloud their perceptions and leave them with a discontinuous experience of themselves and their mental con-

tents. . . . Their defenses leave their sense of self and identity fragmented, and
experience becomes more compartmentalized than integrated. (p. 487)

Such persons, who are unable to bring their full experience to bear on a potentially dangerous situation, may act with poor judgment, leading to revictimization. The symptoms of chronic PTSD, with the classic biphasic
response of periods of intrusion alternating with periods of avoidance and
numbing, are evident in many survivors of childhood abuse in adult life.
During periods of intrusion, individuals experience recurrent intrusive reexperiences of the traumatic events, along with the associated affect. Individuals who are actively reexperiencing abuse are unlikely to be revictimized; in
fact, they may be hyperreactive even to circumstances that hold no real
threat. However, during the numbing phase when patients avoid recalling
their abuse, have markedly constricted affect, and are detached from others,
they are at high risk for revictimization. Past traumatic events and the associated affects (including fear and anticipatory anxiety) are dissociated from
conscious awareness. Thus, an individual might be in a threatening situation
and seem to be unaware of potential danger, as in the following example:

> Nancy, a young woman in treatment for the sequelae of extensive childhood
> physical and sexual abuse, was accustomed to taking long walks through the
> woods around her home. She found these walks to be soothing and particu-
> larly helpful in allowing her to block out painful memories of her childhood.
> One evening, while walking along a trail, Nancy found her path blocked by a
> young man riding a motorcycle and dressed in Army fatigues—he was appar-
> ently from a nearby Army base. With no qualms, she stopped and allowed
> herself to be engaged in conversation and accepted a ride on his motorcycle.
> She was shocked when he subsequently made sexual advances and raped her.

Dissociative symptoms and unavailability of normal anticipatory anxiety
are most marked in patients with severe dissociative disorders. Their rigid
compartmentalization of experience and identity place them at substantial
risk for revictimization. Not only are traumatic experiences dissociated
from consciousness, but many dysphoric affects (including anticipatory
anxiety) are split off into separate self-states or alter personalities, resulting
in increased vulnerability of revictimization.

One other post-traumatic phenomenon is of note. The model of inescapable shock described by van der Kolk and colleagues (van der Kolk,
Greenberg, Boyd, & Krystal, 1985; van der Kolk, 1987) is based on situations
in which the victim of trauma is helpless to prevent or escape the aversive
events. Inescapable shock leads to an impairment of the ability to learn how
to escape from new aversive experiences. Thus, when persons with childhood abuse histories are faced with potentially threatening situations, they
may feel extremely constricted in their choices and helpless to escape. Not

only do they have difficulty conceptualizing new ways to deal with traumatic circumstances, but they often feel overwhelmed by the return of the helpless feelings associated with the original abuse that is triggered by the current trauma. This is often manifested in patients' description of going limp, freezing, or becoming automatically submissive in the presence of a powerful, threatening, and abusive person.

The absence of nurturing interpersonal attachments in childhood is another powerful factor in revictimization. Disturbances of attachment, particularly separation and disruption of early childhood nurturing relationships, leave individuals vulnerable to being overwhelmed both in childhood and later as adults (Bowlby, 1984; Rutter, 1987). Thus, children who are subjected to traumatic experiences within the context of inadequately protective social environments are at greatest risk for psychological damage. Many investigators and clinicians have noted the presence and effects of relational disruption of abusive families on ongoing ability to relate to others (Briere & Runtz, 1987; Browne & Finkelhor, 1986; Browning & Boatman, 1977; Courtois, 1979; Dutton et al., 1994; Finkelhor & Browne, 1985; Herman, 1981, 1992; Meiselman, 1978; D. E. H. Russell, 1986). Family research psychologists David Finkelhor and Angela Browne (1985) summarized the relational effects of traumatic childhood abuse, citing betrayal as a major dynamic issue:

> Sexual abuse victims suffer from grave disenchantment. In combination with this there may be an intense need to regain trust and security, manifested in the extreme dependency and clinging seen in especially young victims. This same need in adults may show up in impaired judgment about the safety of other people. (p. 536–537)

The deficits associated with disruption of early relationships predispose individuals to revictimization. Individuals with a history of massive relational disruption may be drawn to adult relationships that recapitulate the abusive nature of their early attachments. Investigation of such "traumatic bonding" suggest that prolonged exposure to intermittent abuse predisposes persons to form powerful emotional bonds to abusers and later to others like them (Dutton & Painter, 1981). Thus, survivors of early abuse may remain in abusive adult relationships, caught in a repetitive scenario of abuse and dependency. For such persons, the choice may seem to be either remaining in a battering relationship or being doomed to an endless state of aloneness. For many persons who lack a basic sense of self-efficacy and self-sufficiency, the logical choice may be to opt for continuing abuse.

There are also particular difficulties with individuals who have negative self-images. Individuals who have been subjected to abuse and victimization and who have not received positive reinforcement and validation are likely to have extremely negative self-regard and to view themselves as powerless (Bagley & Ramsey, 1986; Carmen, Rieker, & Mills, 1984; Courtois, 1979; Dutton & Painter, 1981; Gelinas, 1983; Herman, Russell, & Trocki, 1986; D. E. H. Russell, 1986; Shapiro, 1987; Summit, 1983; Swanson & Biaggo, 1985). Feeling responsible for the abuse that they suffered and seeing themselves as loathsome and defective, these persons cannot conceive of situations in which they would be regarded with esteem and respect. Hence, it is not surprising that persons who hate themselves often allow themselves to become revictimized. The role of victim, although painful, is familiar and consistent with their self-image.

Therapists should take certain psychotherapeutic stances with patients with histories of childhood abuse and patterns of revictimization. Therapists should acknowledge the traumatic antecedents of revictimization, but should be sensitive to the risks of exploring the early abusive experiences. Premature exploration increases dissociative and post-traumatic symptomatology that places patients at risk of further harm from self or others. Because of the powerful unconscious dynamic factors that predispose abuse survivors to revictimization, therapists are responsible for educating patients about their vulnerability and confronting potentially self-damaging or dangerous behaviors. An emphasis on relational issues is particularly important because a solid therapeutic relationship and an interpersonal support network may be the most effective way of helping patients avoid revictimization. Finally, every effort should be made to identify situations, internal emotional states, and triggers that are connected to revictimization, and to be aware of important protective defenses such as anticipatory anxiety.

Although therapists must insist that patients take responsibility for their own safety, patients are not to blame for being revictimized. An understanding of how persons with histories of early abuse are intensely vulnerable to subsequent revictimization should serve to underscore the responsibility of a perpetrator who intentionally inflicts harm on another. Similarly, the availability of vulnerable persons does not absolve predators who often search out those they can exploit. Although abuse survivors need to understand the mechanisms through which they may be exploited and to control any behaviors that leave them more vulnerable, they cannot be held responsible for the sadistic and often illegal actions of others. To blame childhood abuse survivors for their own vulnerability and for causing their own subsequent exploitation may be another form of revictimization.

CHAPTER 8

Controlling Post-Traumatic and Dissociative Symptoms*

THE CONCEPT of stage-oriented treatment for survivors of childhood abuse mandates that basic ego-supportive psychotherapy is the first order of business prior to exploration and abreaction of traumatic events. This is a formidable task, given the pervasive symptomatology that many traumatized patients bring to treatment. Florid post-traumatic and dissociative symptoms create chaos in patients' lives. These experiences include reexperiencing of past abuse and numbing responses (e.g., flashbacks), out-of-control state changes such as personality switches in patients with dissociative identity disorder (DID), and the discontinuity of experience seen in partial or complete amnestic events (Braun, 1990; Braun & Sachs, 1985; Briere, 1992; Briere & Conte, 1993; Briere & Runtz, 1988; Coons, Cole, Pellow, & Milstein, 1990; Donaldson & Gardner, 1985; Herman, 1992; Kluft, 1984b; Putnam, 1985; Ulman & Brothers, 1988; van der Kolk & Kadish, 1987; van der Kolk & van der Hart, 1991). All these symptoms can be severe and intolerable to patients, and they must be modulated or stabilized to reduce the level of crisis in patients' lives.

PSYCHOEDUCATION IN A COGNITIVE–BEHAVIOR PARADIGM

Much of the understanding of the effects of childhood abuse is founded on psychoanalytic and psychodynamic principles. Psychologists Laurie Anne Pearlman and Karen Saakvitne (1995b) observed:

---

*Elizabeth Benham, R.N., M.A., E.T. contributed to the sections "Coping Strategies for Post-Traumatic and Dissociative Disorders" and "Crisis Planning" in this chapter, and portions of these sections are adapted, as noted, from her article "Coping strategies: A psychoeducational approach to post-traumatic symptomatology" (Benham, 1995).

Much if not most of our fundamental premises about insight-oriented psychotherapy with trauma survivors—what it is, how it works, and why it works—are originally psychoanalytic in origin. . . . The fact that current relationships are influenced by internalized objects and object relationships is a fundamental psychoanalytic concept essential to understanding transferences and reenactment in trauma therapies. . . . This relatively simple idea elegantly incorporates a developmental perspective and sets the stage for the recognition of the roles that unconscious processes and early relationships play in adult functioning and identity. (pp 43–44)

Traumatic experiences in childhood disrupt the normal formation of psychic structures that are gradually formed over the course of development. Thus, severe and persistent early abuse strongly affects ego capacities and defenses, self-regulatory mechanisms, and concepts of the self and others.

Although trauma theory derives extensively from psychodynamic and psychoanalytic perspectives, effective treatment interventions draw on an eclectic variety of perspectives, including not only psychodynamics, but cognitive–behavioral, object relations, self-psychology, and family/systems theories. The overall treatment of trauma survivors is consistent with psychodynamic principles: understanding the role of past experience, making conflicted unconscious processes conscious, and integrating repressed and dissociated experiences (Matthews & Chu, 1997). However, early in treatment, when the control of symptomatology is a priority, cognitive–behavior interventions are particularly useful. Clinicians trained in this modality may have particular expertise, but the basic principles involved in a cognitive–behavioral approach should be understood by all clinicians treating patients with complex post-traumatic and dissociative disorders.

The basic paradigm for therapeutic interventions used to contain dysphoric or dysfunctional symptomatology has two parts. The *cognitive* component involves setting out a psychoeducational framework and conceptualizing approaches to achieve behavioral goals, and enlisting the patient in an alliance to work toward these goals. The *behavioral* component consists of instituting and rehearsing interventions, and then repeating or modifying interventions until the behavior goals are attained. This type of cognitive–behavioral approach not only is pragmatic, but also tends to minimize the often overly intense transferential aspects of the therapeutic relationship. It offers a task on which both patient and therapist can focus and alleviates the common pitfall of struggles about whether the patient or the therapist is going control the agenda of the therapy. As can often be said to patients, "It isn't a question of doing it *my* way or *your* way. These are the ways that have been shown to help persons like yourself overcome the difficulties that you experience."

The cognitive and psychoeducational component is by far the more important part of this therapeutic agenda. Educating patients about the necessary and possible goal of controlling post-traumatic and dissociative symptomatology is essential to collaboration around this task. Without an alliance concerning symptom control, no interventions or techniques are likely to be effective, e.g., ("I've tried that and it doesn't work"). Conversely, with such an alliance, many interventions may work, and patients themselves are often able to devise specific techniques that are effective for their particular symptoms. The educational process is difficult because forming and maintaining an alliance with traumatized patients is a major undertaking, given that pervasive mistrust is a hallmark of persons with extensive childhood abuse. Moreover, one of the essential qualities of post-traumatic and dissociative experiences is that they are out-of-control. That is, patients experience these symptoms as happening *to* them, often resulting from triggering events in their environment over which they have no control. Few patients easily accept the idea that they can have much control over the flashbacks and state switches that are part of their daily lives, and it is often difficult to engage them in this task. One way to approach this dilemma is to clarify that perfect control is not the goal and is not expected. Rather, the expectation is only that patients begin to look at these out-of-control experiences in such a way that they can begin to have even a minimal impact on them: "I know that you feel as though your flashbacks are totally out of control, and that you have no way of knowing when they will hit and how you can get out of them. However, if you are willing to work with me and other members of your treatment team, we may be able to find some small ways of altering the experiences to some degree. Do you think it might be possible to get even as little as 5% more control over these difficulties?" When the process is presented in this way, patients are more easily able to see it as incremental advances in control over the symptoms that are inherently experienced as uncontrollable.

Even some of the most uncontrollable post-traumatic and dissociative symptoms can be contained through extraordinary patient effort. The following case illustrates both the possibility of controlling post-traumatic and dissociative symptoms and the difficulties of such control in traumatized patients. The patient was treated some years ago, and at the time, her symptoms were not recognized as probably being post-traumatic in nature:

Mary, a 38-year-old married woman and mother of two was hospitalized in 1978 in an inpatient teaching hospital for problems with depression and difficulty functioning. She was known to have a background of considerable trauma, but her difficulties were characterized as "pseudo-neurotic schizophrenia," which implied a kind of surface functioning over a core of schizophrenic-like psychosis. Her symptomatology included periods of acute decompensation—then described as transient psychosis but now more easily recognized as reexperiencing of the trauma—in which she would become paralyzed with fear and act in a very young and regressed manner. Her clinical course was prolonged (even by the standards of the pre–managed care era) because of the fragility of her condition. Despite sophisticated psychotherapy and use of medications, Mary had frequent decompensations, which made it difficult to see how she could be discharged to home. Nonetheless, it was eventually decided to begin the transition process to home, and Mary was put on a bus for a home visit and an appointment with her outpatient therapist. The bus headed down a major highway toward her hometown, only to be snowed in by the Northeast blizzard of 1978 and stranded on the highway miles from any help. Somewhat surprisingly, Mary did not decompensate. Rather, she rallied both herself and the other passengers on the bus, leading them in camp songs (such as "100 Bottles of Beer on the Wall") to help keep their spirits up, and in melting snow for drinking water. Eventually, after being rescued by the highway police, she abruptly decompensated and was brought back to the hospital in a disorganized and helpless state.

A similar clinical situation occurred a few years ago with a dissociative disorder patient whose seemingly out-of-control symptoms were brought under control by external circumstances:

Jill, a thin and athletic young woman with DID, was being treated for suicidal impulses and aggressive acting out. Despite her frightening history of florid post-traumatic and dissociative symptoms and self-destructive and violent behavior, she presented as cooperative and articulate for the most part, but only during the day. As the evening progressed, she began to have episodes of apparent personality switching and flashbacks. During these periods she appeared to be reliving physical and sexual assaults (which had originally occurred during the evening). She would become agitated, panicked, and angry, striking out at anyone who approached her. This behavior continued daily over several weeks, often necessitating the use of restraints. Restraining the patient was particularly traumatic for all involved because while in restraints Jill apparently reexperienced her childhood assaults and sexual molestation. Her screams were piteous and she could not be reassured or soothed. The hospital staff was divided about how to intervene. While some staff members believed that Jill was manipulatively trying "to get attention," others felt that she had no ability to control the episodes and would continue to need this level of external support. The uncontrollable behaviors escalated to the point that the patient began to throw heavy furniture and injured a staff member. This incident produced a consensus among the staff, and Jill was told that if the episodes continued for more than 3 more days, arrangements would be made for her transfer to another facility. The patient had made strong attachments to various members of the staff and was panicked at the thought of transfer. The violence never reoccurred, but it was obvious that the patient had to exercise intense efforts to maintain control in the evenings and was able to utilize a high level of support and numerous verbal interventions from staff.

Although both patients in these examples were highly symptomatic and in states of decompensation, they also were quite regressed. Feeling helpless and exhibiting passivity, they seemed to expect others to assume control of their behavior. The post-traumatic symptoms they both experienced were powerful, and they usually felt unable to control the changes in their experiential states. However, under fairly dire conditions that made it necessary to exercise more control, both patients were able to do so, albeit using an extraordinary amount of personal resources and drawing on the support of others. A kind of medical analogy may be apt here. Many persons with viral gastroenteritis suffer from vomiting and diarrhea. These unpleasant events cannot be suppressed beyond a certain point, but with some effort, a person can influence how and when they occur. Similarly, post-traumatic and dissociative symptoms have a powerful urgency, and yet patients can utilize their own resources (and the resources of others) to help bring them into control. Frequently, if there is an alliance between the patient and the therapist around this task, the patient can consciously work toward the goal of control and make substantial progress over weeks and months. In some circumstances, however, external control may be necessary and the use of hospitalization and/or sedating medication is indicated. Persisting, ongoing, uncontrolled symptomatology makes therapeutic gains impossible and eventually destroys the therapeutic process. As a result, such seemingly drastic measures as ending or suspending therapy, hospitalization, or transfer to other forms of care are logical consequences of the failure to *begin* to establish control.

COPING STRATEGIES FOR POST-TRAUMATIC AND DISSOCIATIVE SYMPTOMS

Most of the coping strategies for patients who experience post-traumatic and dissociative symptoms fall into the category of *grounding techniques*. One of the most basic strategies for enhancing grounding—maintaining contact with current reality—is to ensure good ambient illumination. Whether in the office or hospital or at home, this means using adequate lighting and encouraging patients not to sit in dark or dimly lit environments when they feel anxious and vulnerable to reexperiencing or dissociative state changes. Maintaining good lighting often means that patients must oppose their internal impulses. When frightened or disorganized, many patients feel compelled to hide in their beds, closets, or other dark and confined spaces. Seeking safety in such places facilitates dissociative processes through the lack of environmental cues and makes patients more vulnerable to the intrusion of thoughts, feelings, and events associated with past traumatic experiences.

Maintaining visual contact with cues in the environment is also crucial. In many ways, the syndrome of so-called ICU psychosis has similarities to loss of control post-traumatic and dissociative symptoms. In intensive care units, severely ill medical or surgical patients are placed in an unfamiliar environment that is dimly lit with few cues as to date or time of day, and they are in contact with many unfamiliar people. Under such conditions, some ICU patients become disorganized and disoriented. The solution is often simple. Adding extra lighting, a clock, and calendar, and ensuring contact with familiar people and objects often restores patients' orientation and equilibrium. In a similar way, patients who tend to get lost in dysphoric dissociative states benefit from focusing on their physical environment and on familiar and comforting objects. Psychiatrist nurse and expressive therapist Elizabeth Benham published a description about some of these kinds of interventions in a hospital setting (1995):

> It is by example that we first teach patients how to ground themselves. When a patient is experiencing florid dissociative symptoms, . . . we approach the patient and call her by name and identify ourselves. We tell the patient where she is and what month, day, and year it is. We repeat this information over and over in reassuring tones. If the space . . . is darkened, we illuminate the area by turning on the lights, or opening the drapes. We ask the patient to open her eyes if they are closed, so that the patient can see where she is and who we are. We also ask the patient to try and move her eyes so as not to be in a daze; as this seems to keep patients locked into a dissociated state of flashback. We encourage the patient to look at our faces so that eye contact can be made. . . . We tell the patient we know she is frightened, but that she is safe. We ask her to begin naming what she sees in the room such as the color of the rug, or chair, how many chairs are in the room. We might ask her to identify what color her shirt is, the color of our clothes, or even how many shoelace holes are in her sneakers. If we know the patient well enough, we might remind her of significant others such as a child or a spouse. Instructing patients to feel their own weight in the place they are sitting is also useful, as is having them sense where their other body parts are touching. For example, we ask, "Can you feel your elbow on the chair?" "How about the glasses on your nose?" "What about the rings on your fingers?" or "Can you feel your watch on your wrist?" Once the patient is alert enough to recognize us, it is helpful to have the patient reposition the posture that is held during the dissociative or flashback experience. Having her stand up and walk with us allows the patient to connect with the ground . . . As we walk with the patient, the patient continues to identify the surroundings. If she is not alarmed by our suggestion, we encourage her to look in a mirror, so that she can see she is an adult and not a child in a traumatic situation. (p. 33)

This description of interventions with post-traumatic symptoms contains several critical elements. It is particularly important that although the patient's affective state is induced by reexperiences of early abuse, there should be only limited exploration of the etiologic traumatic experience. That is, patients are asked to find ways to cope with the dysphoric experiences, and not to deepen them. The tone of voice that is used is also important: It should be reassuring, but it must not be hypnotic or trance-inducing.

A calm tone of voice with a near-normal level of pitch and volume that avoids rhythmic cadences will help orient the patient better than a tone that is very soft, soothing, and rhythmic. This latter way of speaking may promote more dissociative experiences, but even if effective, may be overly reassuring in terms of patients' secondary gain.

In an interpersonal situation, eye contact is enormously effective. In fact, direct and focused eye contact makes it impossible for patients to remain in dysphoric dissociated states. Inherent qualities in eye contact produce a powerful interpersonal connection that is enormously grounding. Many crisis situations have been resolved simply by the therapist being quietly and firmly directive, asking the patient to look at him or her, to focus on the therapist's face, and to make eye contact. Some traumatized patients have difficulty with direct eye contact, perhaps fearing the anger or hatred seen in the eyes of abuse perpetrators. Even when asked to look directly, some patients may be so fearful that they cannot, or they gaze blankly in a kind of terror. In these situations, the therapist may direct the patient to look around at other objects in the room or even at parts of the therapist's body that are less threatening, for example, legs, hair, shirt, and so on. Aside from being effective as a grounding technique, eye contact demonstrates that some kind of interpersonal connection can be helpful and not hurtful as it was in the past.

Using grounding techniques in an office or a hospital setting provides the opportunity to learn more about the internal emotional events that precede loss of control. Flashbacks and state switches are experienced as happening abruptly and unpredictably, without any warning. However, careful monitoring of emotional states often shows that dysphoric post-traumatic or dissociative states are often preceded by certain specific kinds of internal emotional states that escape the awareness of most patients. Practicing grounding in a treatment setting offers an opportunity to learn about these internal states, as in the following example:

Jane, a young woman with a history of severe emotional abuse, was prone to flashbacks of being berated and humiliated by her father whenever she began to feel too close (and hence vulnerable) to another person. Shortly after beginning therapy, the therapist noticed that Jane wasn't able to maintain eye contact and seemed to drift away into some internal state. She seemed oblivious to efforts to attract her attention, and then appeared frightened and seemed to be fending off blows. After considerable efforts on the part of both Jane and her therapist, Jane was able to maintain visual focus on a small ornamental horse that was part of the office decor. After several months of work on grounding, she was even able to look at the therapist briefly for a few seconds at a time. During this process, the therapist asked about Jane's internal emotional experience: "I wonder if you can tell me what you are feeling inside when you begin to have trouble looking at me? Is there some feeling or sensation that you are experiencing during those times?" Eventually, Jane was able to identify levels of increasing anxiety that she experienced as a tightness in the pit of her stomach. She and her therapist recognized that whenever that feeling became worse, she was beginning to lose contact with her current reality. They were then able to devise various relaxation techniques, including simple measures such as taking a series of deep breaths, which tended to reduce the feelings and sensations associated with the anxiety.

Therapists familiar with cognitive–behavioral techniques may also wish to use formal mood monitoring to help patients track the specific emotions they experience and the intensity of particular emotions that call for therapeutic interventions. This kind of attention to internal emotional states may be extremely helpful for patients to be more aware of their emotional functioning and more able to have control over them.

The use of formal relaxation techniques, hypnosis, and guided imagery have an important adjunctive role for therapists skilled in these modalities. It should be emphasized that early in the treatment process these techniques are used for stabilization, containment, and relaxation, *not* for exploration of traumatic experiences. Hypnotherapeutic techniques such as age regression, affect bridges, and various forms of visualizing traumatic experiences are usually contraindicated until stabilization is achieved. All such techniques need to be used skillfully and cautiously since some of the altered states or trance states induced by these techniques can have adverse results, as in the following case:

> Steve, an adolescent young man, repetitively suffered from painful dysphoric states in which he relived the beatings that he received as a child. After identifying some of the emotional cues that seemed to presage these reexperiences, he and his therapist used some visual imagery to help him relax. Because Steve was fond of swimming and the ocean, his therapist helped him visualize sitting in warm tropical waters and feeling the waves wash over his legs and lower body. This technique worked well, and the therapist encouraged Steve to try this technique at home. That evening, when starting to feel anxious, Steve was successfully able to visualize the ocean scene, but quickly panicked when he lost control of the scenario and experienced being pummeled by crashing waves and being drawn out into the ocean and deeper waters.

Despite the pitfalls of using hypnosis and guided visualization, relaxation in the office and outside the office (with careful instruction and practice) can be achieved. Specialized techniques, such as being able to "lock up" painful experiences or feelings in a room or box, can help to pace the therapy. Some particularly skilled hypnotherapists have described a procedure in which patients can learn to manage dissociative symptoms, using techniques that control depth of trance (Deborah Block, Ph.D., personal communication, 1995). Patients can be taught exercises such as visualizing having control of an elevator that represents the depth of dissociative experiences, thus helping the patient gain a sense of mastery over these painful and difficult symptoms.

CRISIS PLANNING

Therapeutic efforts in the office or hospital setting are crucial, not only for their immediate impact, but also as rehearsals of the interventions that patients can adapt for use out of the office. Most crisis situations happen at inopportune times. For example, patients with PTSD and dissociative disorders often report that they become most panicked and develop dysphoric symptoms in the evening or at night. The timing of these symptoms is due to the lessening of visual cues in the environment and the loss of control that results from fatigue. In addition, some patients identify evening as the time when sexual abuse occurred, and they become more anxious as the day progresses. Thus, unless therapists and patients ascribe to the view that therapists should be available at any hour of the day or night to provide therapeutic support, every patient must develop a crisis plan for use at any time.

A crisis plan is a simple strategy or list of activities or interventions to be used in situations in which patients feel anxious or overwhelmed. Some interventions are applicable to a wide variety of patients. These interventions include turning on lights or pulling up blinds and opening curtains, turning on the television or radio, and calling friends or other supportive persons. Other interventions are more specific to individuals and may include such activities as relaxation exercises, reading or looking through art or picture books, expressive modalities including painting or singing, taking a warm bath (or cold shower), calling a hotline, doing physical exercise such as jogging or walking, or playing with pets or comforting objects such as stuffed animals (Benham, 1995).

A crisis plan should also include a regular structure to support grounding and self-care, especially during periods of predictable stress (Benham, 1995). For example, if evenings are consistently difficult, routine activities such as drawing the curtains, turning on lights, and engaging in specific activities are important for ongoing containment and stability. Patients may also create "safe places" in their environment such as well-lit, comfortable areas with soothing objects where they can go when feeling especially frightened or impulsive. Therapists can facilitate such self-soothing interventions through the use of transitional objects, such as notes or letters from the therapist, tape recordings of the therapist's voice, or even actual objects from the therapist's office. If patients are able to engage in the process of formulating a crisis plan, they are often able to provide some very individualized or unique solutions. One married woman was able to use her wedding ring as a comforting and grounding object that reminded her that she was an adult and not being abused as she was when she was a child. Another patient, described by Benham (1995), who loved to cook and bake, used these activities to provide relaxation. Because it was too difficult to organize a baking activity when panicked, she prepared kits of premeasured ingredients packaged in shoe boxes along with recipe cards. When she began to feel overwhelmed, she simply opened a box and began to cook.

All the interventions in the crisis plan may need considerable practice and rehearsal. As Benham (1995) aptly pointed out:

> These interventions have a cumulative effect. The patient will not necessarily feel immediate relief the first time that the intervention is tried. Over time and with practice, the interventions become progressively more effective. Most patients initially see their only choices for relating to their emotions as either "stuffing it" as they did in their painful past[s], or losing control, which usually leaves them with a poor self-image. With practice, the patient finds that she can process feelings without being overwhelmed by them or letting them take over her life. (p. 33)

Patients' abilities to achieve a measure of control over their post-traumatic and dissociative experiences has enormous benefits. They begin to have a sense of being empowered in areas that formerly left them feeling helpless and traumatized. They can begin to limit the intrusion of traumatic thoughts and feelings to times when such experiences are useful and appropriate, such as in the therapy sessions. Even in treatment settings, patients can use their new-found abilities to limit regression, putting away overwhelming experiences until the next session. This ability is crucial to maintaining a balance between therapeutic work and functioning, and is essential in order to limit regression while attempting to resolve the effects of traumatization. Well-developed skills in containing and controlling symptomatology are prerequisites for the effective abreaction, working through, and integration of the experiences of past abuse. The process of learning control may be difficult and time-consuming. There are few shortcuts, but patients and therapists who invest the time and energy to achieve these fundamental skills are able to rely on them to facilitate the process of recovery.

CHAPTER 9

The Therapeutic Dance: Relational Issues in the Treatment of Survivors of Childhood Abuse*

T HE SURVIVORS of the battlefields of childhood abuse carry the scars of family wars. Having been repeatedly victimized and defeated, they remain wary; they fear attack and are prepared to retreat, mistrust alliances and expect betrayal from others, and are alienated from the rest of the world. Many investigators and clinicians have described these difficulties that impair the relational capacity of chronically traumatized patients (Briere, 1992; Briere & Runtz, 1987; Browne & Finkelhor, 1986; Browning & Boatman, 1977; Chu, 1992c; Courtois, 1979; Davies & Frawley, 1994; Finkelhor & Browne, 1985; Herman, 1981, 1992; Janoff-Bulman, 1992; Meiselman, 1978; D. E. H. Russell, 1986). The experience of this interpersonal world is vividly communicated by abuse survivors themselves through their relationships with others, including the relationships with the clinicians that treat them. Their unarticulated feelings and behaviors based on fear, anger, and despair speak with mute torment about their past relationships and the harshness of interpersonal world that they continue to inhabit. It is only by entering this interpersonal world—and by even briefly sharing the experience of the chronically abused patient—that clinicians are able to understand their dilemmas and to be effective in treating the distress that they experience.

---

*Portions of this chapter are adapted from the article "The therapeutic roller coaster: Dilemmas in the treatment of childhood abuse survivors" (Chu, 1992c).

ASSUMPTIONS CONCERNING BASIC TRUST

Many survivors of severe interpersonal abuse experience intense internal conflict about their relationships with others. Despite having been abused, exploited, controlled, betrayed, and abandoned, many still have a persistent wish to engage with others in ways that might alleviate their pain. Yet even these wishes are influenced by their early experiences and their own sense of disempowerment. They see other persons only through the lens of victimization. Having little sense of their own self-worth or self-efficacy, they cannot engage in relationships that are partnerships between equals. Rather, they see others as powerful potential rescuers who may also become powerful abusers. In this sense, relationships provide little gratification and perpetuate uncertainty, conflict, and fear.

Psychologist Ronnie Janoff-Bulman (1992) wrote about the shattered assumptions of trauma survivors. She noted that most people hold basic assumptions about the world as benevolent and meaningful, and about themselves as worthwhile. In contrast, persons who have been severely and chronically abused assume that their interpersonal world will mirror their abusive past experiences:

> The traumatic experience is apt to become fully incorporated into the child's inner world; the basic building blocks of this world are still in the developmental stage, and the victimization is likely to define the world and self-assumptions of the child. These children are apt to have negative assumptions in all domains, for core beliefs are less likely to be disentangled at an early age. The trust and optimism, the sense of safety and security, the feeling of relative invulnerability that are afforded the person with positively based assumptions are absent in the psychological world of these children. Instead, their world is largely one of anxiety, threat, and distrust. (p. 86)

It is the failure to understand the abuse survivor's interpersonal assumptions that most frequently leads to empathic failure on the part of therapists and other clinicians. Clinicians often bring their own set of assumptions about the world—usually intact assumptions about the benevolence of others and their own sense of self-empowerment and self-worth—that are often at considerable odds with patients' assumptions about the malevolence of others and their own vulnerability. In fact, in order to maintain a normally optimistic set of assumptions, therapists frequently exercise a kind of self-preserving denial concerning the experiences of abused patients, and are startled at times by the reactions of their patients, as in the following clinical example:

> Tracy, a 16-year-old girl, had a lifetime of pervasive abuse. In her infant and toddler years, she had been brutalized by her father and neglected by her im-

paired mother. She was subsequently removed from her home by a social service agency and was brought up in a series of foster homes and group homes that ranged from grossly abusive to distantly caring. Following placement in a residential school setting, Tracy appeared withdrawn and angry and had difficulties with both her school work and her social interactions with peers. She was referred for therapy with a well-meaning psychiatric resident. During an initial period of several weeks, Tracy was rather quiet. Although she responded with only silence or monosyllabic answers, she seemed willing to come to the therapy sessions. As the therapist continued to express interest in Tracy's current and past experiences and pressed her to express her feelings, Tracy became more withdrawn in sessions. Although she continued to reliably show up for her therapy, she appeared more and more uncomfortable. When pressed by the therapist about the cause of her anxiety, the patient finally blurted out, "What do you want from me? Everybody wants something from me." Panicked by her own outburst, she then tried to run out of the room. The therapist quickly rose from his chair and went toward Tracy, who was blindly struggling with the door handle. She recoiled and cried out, "Please don't hit me!"

It can be difficult for clinicians who have always trusted in the benevolence of the world to understand the vulnerability that patients experience in interpersonal relationships. A longed-for sense of interpersonal connection and increased intimacy—particularly in the therapeutic relationship—causes heightened anxiety rather than being soothing. Even if a therapist is able to get through the interpersonal defenses of a patient and to be seen as kind or helpful, the patient is thrown into more internal conflict, trying to juggle the fragile sense of therapist as benevolent with the certainty that the therapist will soon become hostile, exploitive, or abandoning. This kind of conflict can be intolerable to patients and may lead to a classic type of negative therapeutic reaction. Panicked by intimacy, patients may regress in therapy or even sabotage the therapeutic process following periods when the therapist feels that there have been positive developments in the treatment such as increased interpersonal connection, more sharing of information, or more expression of feelings.

One of the most primary developmental tasks, as described by the developmental psychologist Erik Erickson (1968), is the development of basic trust. Based on experiences from the earliest years of life, children come to expect that fundamental needs for nurturing and care will be met. When such needs are not met, or are subsequently denied through pervasive victimization, children have no sense of basic self-worth and no sense of basic trust or interpersonal safety, beliefs that they carry into adulthood, described by Janoff-Bulman (1992) as the "fundamental schemas of their assumptive world, their core psychological structures" (p. 87). How can clinicians who have not experienced childhood abuse begin to understand the deficits in trust and interpersonal assumptions of their traumatized patients? Perhaps an analogy through an imagined professional situation might be useful:

> A therapist sought consultation from a senior and respected supervisor. In a departure from the usual methods of consultation, the supervisor took the therapist to the roof of a very tall building and made the following suggestion: "In order to provide you with a new kind of learning experience, I am going to help you to demonstrate something wonderful and dramatic about the power of the human mind. We will both spend a minute or two concentrating on believing that we are as light as air, and when I give the signal, we will join hands and step off the edge of the building and float lightly to the ground." The therapist voiced considerable trepidation about this plan of action, which the supervisor seemed to understand. The supervisor attempted to reassure the therapist, and finally even demonstrated that the unimaginable feat was possible. To the therapist's amazement, the supervisor concentrated, then stepped off the roof of the building and floated to the ground, landing softly and completely unhurt. The supervisor then said to the therapist, "Now you try!" After only a moment of hesitation, the sensible therapist turned around and went down by conventional means using the stairs.

This is the kind of challenge that we offer traumatized patients when we say, "Trust me." This seemingly innocent suggestion is perceived by patients as an invitation to participate in their own self-destruction. Many traumatized patients have accurately observed that others around them have been able to safely participate in trusting interpersonal relationships. However, such relationships seem to present an impossible risk for them, further reinforcing their beliefs about their own defectiveness and their sense of alienation from others.

In the early 1980s it was often suggested that the first step in the treatment of traumatized patients involved establishing trust. For survivors of pervasive childhood abuse, this kind of recommendation now appears naïve because a stable sense of basic trust is often not established until well into the later stages of recovery. Nonetheless, this difficult task must be addressed from the outset of the therapy and requires much time and patience on the part of both therapists and patients. For example, a patient in her fourth year of therapy remarked, "Do you remember all the clever things we were trying to do in the first two years we worked together? I now realize that what I was really doing was doing my best to sit in the same room with you and to cope with the vulnerability and terror of your actually *seeing* me." There are inevitable disruptions in the therapeutic relationship when patients become frightened, flee from the relationship, or try to undo the work of the therapy. Misunderstandings and miscommunication on the part of the patient or therapist and mistimings and even errors by the therapist are an inherent part of the substance of the treatment. As the conflicts that result from these events are resolved, the patient gradually builds an interpersonal history with the therapist that becomes the foundation for future growth and recovery. This process is almost never easy or predictable. Even attempts to empathize and expressions of caring can be misunderstood by patients who have grown up in environments of pervasive victimization. For example, a patient whose mother had caused her to suffer daily public humiliation recoiled from her therapist's labeling such behavior as abusive and accused the therapist of being patronizing.

THERAPEUTIC STANCES

Although a psychodynamic and psychoanalytic understanding concerning early traumatic experiences is valuable in the therapy of abuse survivors, certain aspects of the psychoanalytic stance are not. Traditional psychoanalytic distance (i.e., the therapist as "blank screen") is contraindicated in work with many of these patients. Given patients' backgrounds of abuse and their lack of a sense of basic trust, intense passivity and withholding on the part of the therapist allow traumatic transferences to flourish. Patients often find themselves unable to articulate their concerns and feelings, and therapists' inactivity results in long periods of silence. For patients with backgrounds of healthy attachments and who have benevolent interpersonal assumptions, the therapist's inactivity might be interpreted as respectful or perhaps challenging. For patients with backgrounds of interpersonal abuse, silence is commonly misinterpreted as a sign of disapproval, hostility, or repugnance. Such transferences have their origins in a past reality and can rapidly become functionally psychotic. They frequently become the basis for reenactments of abusive situations and can be a source of retraumatization in the present relationship. Traditional psychoanalytic distance is designed to encourage transference distortions that are useful in breaking through the armor of well-defended persons in order to examine underlying feelings and attitudes. In contrast, many abuse survivors have only brittle defenses that shield against overwhelming and disorganizing underlying affects. Thus, therapy with abuse survivors should generally attempt to *minimize* transference distortions. Therapists' active verbal involvement in therapy sessions is essential, and therapists must monitor periods of silence in the therapy and determine whether the silence is perceived by the patient as respectful or disorganizing.

Maintaining strict therapeutic neutrality with abuse survivors is at times both difficult and inappropriate. Such patients routinely have fixed and skewed negative beliefs about themselves and others, and such beliefs are likely not to change if unchallenged. For example, survivors of sexual abuse may fail to understand that the sexual involvement of adults with children is wrong. Or, even if they understand the concept, they may feel that it was permissible in their particular circumstances. Abuse survivors—even those who are bright, articulate, and educated—almost universally accept the blame and responsibility for their own abuse; their belief that they somehow caused the abuse allowed them to have a sense of control over their own helplessness and powerlessness. Therapists must be unequivocal about the idea that the exploitation of children is wrong and that children do not cause their own abuse even in circumstances in which they were provocative or took an active role. Strict therapeutic neutrality concerning such basic issues is inappropriate and damaging to the therapy as it is seen by patients as collusion with their own negative beliefs.

An attitude of caring and willingness to engage on an interpersonal level is important in any effective psychotherapy, but is particularly essential in the therapy of most abuse survivors. While persons with healthy interpersonal assumptions assume that others are interested in their experience and are able to empathize with them, patients who have been interpersonally abused assume that others are disinterested and do not understand their experiences. Therapists must sometimes make extra efforts to demonstrate that they comprehend their patients' difficulties with interpersonal connections. For example, therapists might reiterate that they have heard or understood the patient ("Do I understand you correctly that you are trying to tell me . . . ?" or "I understand how difficult it is for you to tell me this"), or even acknowledge that the patient has evoked an emotional response in them ("I can feel how painful this is for you").

Therapists who treat patients with backgrounds of severe abuse need to be actively involved in the therapeutic relationship as participants and not just as observers. Thus, it is normal for therapists to feel much more personally involved both in the therapy and with the patients themselves. As a result, therapists' overidentification—not too much distance—is a major hazard in the therapeutic relationship. Such therapists (particularly those who view their role as reparenting their patients) are prone to becoming so involved in empathizing with patients' experience that they lose their sense of therapeutic perspective. Uncritical acceptance of patients' helplessness and their subjective sense of being overwhelmed can lead therapists and patients to a shared sense of immobilization in the treatment. Therapists in this situation commonly also feel that others do not adequately understand their patients' pain and disabilities. They find themselves at odds with their colleagues—particularly in settings such as inpatient units, where team treatment is necessary—and defensively reject consultation. Therapists in this position may take extraordinary measures to alter the external environment for their patients, as in the following example:

Karen, a patient with a dissociative identity disorder, was admitted to an inpatient unit after a suicide attempt. She remained extremely isolated, refusing to interact with various staff members whom she claimed were controlling and demeaning to her. She demanded that all the staff address her by the names of her various personalities as they appeared from time to time. She also superficially cut herself repeatedly when anxious or angry. When confronted with her dysfunctional behavior, Karen angrily referred staff to her therapist so that the therapist could tell them how to manage her: "You better talk to Dr. Smith. *She* knows how to work with me!" The therapist was, in fact, confused and angry at the situation. She called the unit director and complained that the staff were too impatient with Karen and did not understand the difficulties with dissociation. She also demanded that Karen's self-cutting behavior be accepted since it was clearly not lethal and she had no other way to express her feelings. When a consultation was suggested, the therapist responded by questioning the clinical competence of the unit staff. The patient then signed out of the hospital with the agreement of her therapist.

Therapists working with abuse survivors need to maintain a dual role. While on the one hand they must actively participate in the therapy and empathize with the patient's experience, they must also maintain a sense of therapeutic perspective and direction. They must recognize that although patients feel overwhelmed and helpless, there are ways to achieve mastery over these feelings. Therapists must empathically confront patients' demands that the external world adapt to their disabilities and ask patients to make efforts to make changes in order to deal with the world—a task that may initially feel overwhelming and impossible. Rather than becoming enmeshed in their patients' helplessness, it is essential that therapists reiterate that patients have the ability to make choices. It is helpful for the therapist to understand patients' despair, but to also express the conviction that the therapeutic process can help patients ameliorate or overcome their difficulties. In this way, therapists model the expectation that it is necessary not only to respect patients' intolerably tortured inner world, but to also maintain a well-grounded awareness of the demands of the external world.

REENACTMENTS OF CHILDHOOD ABUSE

Survivors of childhood abuse not only bring their abusive experiences to the therapeutic arena, but they make them part of the therapeutic relationship itself. That is, they compel the therapist to assume a role in the reenactments of their traumatization. It is crucial to understand that this process is inevitable. Given their traumatically based interpersonal assumptions, traumatized patients must see all their adult relationships as mirroring their abuse. These powerful assumptions transform any intense relationships—particularly the therapeutic relationship—into reenactments and recapitulations of their early experiences. However, this process is not simply a pitfall to be avoided or side-stepped; it is an intrinsic part of the treatment of these patients. The therapeutic dance, with its endless repetitions of disruptions and reengagements in the early stage of therapy, provides a model of interpersonal connection, conflict resolution, and collaboration. If recognized and skillfully managed, the interpersonal reenactment of the abuse offers an opportunity to provide the experience of a relational world that is positive and growth producing, enabling patients to learn new relational skills.

Psychologists Jody Messler Davies and Mary Gail Frawley described the major roles that are recapitulated in the therapy of abuse survivors (1994). Patients repeatedly take on and reenact the roles of abuser, victim of abuse, indifferent or neglectful parent, and idealized rescuer. Because therapists are involved by necessity as active participants in the therapeutic relationship, they assume similar and complementary roles. These abuse-related interpersonal dynamics are extremely powerful, as are patients' projective identifications that compel therapists to experience many confusing and overwhelming countertransferential feelings and impulses. Certain relational positions may be recurrently assumed or even become the predominant relational dynamics during phases of therapy. However, these relational positions may be quite fluid, changing frequently and abruptly as they mirror and reenact the kaleidoscope of the malignant interpersonal disturbances that characterized the childhood abuse. As has been observed by a number of experienced clinicians and investigators (e.g., Chu, 1992c; Davies & Frawley, 1994), therapists must both allow themselves to be engaged in these reenactments and maintain perspective and clarity concerning the process in order to allow a benign resolution. Again, it is the therapeutic dance, the cycle of abuse-related difficulties in the therapeutic relationship with repeated resolutions involving healthier relational experiences, that eventually allows patients to leave behind their trauma-based assumptions and emerge into a more benevolent world.

Davies and Frawley (1994) described a series of transference–countertransference positions that commonly occur in the therapy of abuse survivors. *Transference–countertransference* is a remarkably apt description because these interpersonal dynamics are dependent on both the patient's abusive past and the therapist's own experiences. It is important that therapists be reasonably free of any major relational pathology of their own in order to work with abused patients. Even "normal" personal characteristics of the therapist are heightened and distorted by the powerful interpersonal forces of the therapy, for example, caring evolving into rescuing, facilitation becoming control, personal restraint transformed into withholding. Serious interpersonal pathology on the part of the therapist—for example, problems with aggression, major narcissistic or social deficits—will almost certainly result in therapeutic impasses, serious boundary violations, or harm to both patient and therapist. One scenario deserves special emphasis. Many clinicians are drawn to mental health professions in response to their own backgrounds of abuse or deprivation. The resulting countertransference need to rescue patients, provide caretaking, or compensate for past abuse must be strictly examined and limited. The dynamics of the therapy must be largely driven only by patients' past experiences, and becoming a kind of interpersonal Rorschach that elucidates and expresses the nature of the patient's past interpersonal experiences.

Interpersonal dynamics in the therapy of traumatized persons are as varied as the individual circumstances of the abuse itself. Perhaps the most common interpersonal scenario occurs as the patient reenacts the position of being abused. This abused child role includes many characteristics: helpless and devastated, angry and manipulative, appeasing or caretaking, or demanding and entitled. Each of these roles produces a complementary response in the therapist. The patient who reacts in the therapy by becoming a helpless and devastated victim often induces a rescuing response and even overidentification, but may also elicit anger or distance in response to the patient's passivity and dependence. Patients' hostile and angry stances frequently produce withdrawal or retaliatory rage in the therapist. Idealization or caretaking from patients may induce therapists to become passive recipients who collude with avoiding or seeing the covert agendas in a reenactment of hidden abuse. And patients' demands often produce attempts to placate or rescue, or they produce anger at the patient's narcissism.

The roles of the patient who defensively takes on the position of abuser are similarly varied. Patients may be overtly hostile and demeaning, covertly intrusive and invasive, distant and uninvolved, or seductive and insidiously ingratiating. Such interpersonal positions also elicit specific responses from therapists. Rageful attacks often produce attempts to appease or placate, interpersonal withdrawal, or retaliatory hostility. Covert intrusion concerning personal boundaries induces therapists to feel helplessly violated or angrily defensive. When patients become uninvolved in their therapy as if it is the therapist's job to make the treatment occur, therapists may find themselves either redoubling their efforts or angrily withdrawing. And seductive responses can cause therapists to become troubled and passive—replicating and reexperiencing the confusion of the abused child—or angry and rejecting.

All these interpersonal positions have the potential for either providing invaluable information about the patient's experience or resulting in impasses and foundering of the therapeutic process. Resolution of these conflictual transference–countertransference positions depends on an accurate understanding of the dilemma, clarification and interpretation, reality testing, and patience. As in any effective interpersonal psychotherapy, therapists must learn to examine their own responses as a way of understanding their patients' dilemmas. Therapists must not be afraid to acknowledge to themselves dysphoric feelings of enmeshment, coldness, hostility, sadism, or even sexual arousal that can be evoked in the therapy of severely trauma-tized patients. Such feelings enable therapists to make clarifications and in-terpretations that allow patients to understand the confusing interpersonal world that their abuse continues to evoke. Therapists must also be prepared to maintain personal and therapeutic boundaries and to set appropriate lim-its (see Chapter 10). Out-of-control aggression or violation of therapists' personal boundaries are not helpful to the patient or therapy and should not be tolerated. Therapists must ask patients to examine their relational pat-terns in the context of their early abusive experiences. This process is often long and difficult: To patients the dysfunctional relational dynamics are real, not transferential, and therapists must use all their patience and skill to move toward mutual and collaborative relationships and healthy interper-sonal perspectives. The following clinical example illustrates some of the vi-cissitudes involved in the shifting interpersonal reenactments of past abuse:

> Joan, a 42 year old divorced woman, was hospitalized following a difficult se-ries of events in which she was intrusive in the personal life of her therapist, Dr. White. She had initially begun to ask questions about the therapist's life "in order to feel more equal—like a friend and not just a patient," and made frequent telephone calls to the therapist's office and home in states of crisis. Joan appeared to become increasingly preoccupied with her therapist, and made personal comments in ways that made him uncomfortable ("You dress so nicely, but you know you really shouldn't wear brown shoes with that suit."). Dr. White felt unable to bring up any of these intrusions in the therapy because he knew that Joan would feel upset about his rejecting her. Instead, he became distant in sessions, even to the extent of falling asleep on one occasion. Joan then accused Dr. White of not wanting to be involved with her, and re-doubled her efforts to find out more about him, even following him home and covertly watching him and his wife, children, and visitors to the house. When she finally confessed to this last activity, Dr. White became angry and threat-ened to terminate the therapy if such behavior ever recurred. Joan became in-tensely ashamed and begged him not to abandon her. Later that night she called Dr. White and confessed to having taken an overdose of a tranquilizer that he had prescribed, and was hospitalized. When the inpatient case man-ager introduced herself, Joan seemed angry and withholding. After being asked about her life and daily activities, Joan blurted out, "I know you think I'm pathetic because of my involvement with Tom—I mean, Dr. White—but I am somebody, too! You therapists all think you're something special." The case manager, becoming angry, controlled her wish to say something demean-ing and instead commented on Joan's anger, "You seem enraged with me as if I have insulted you. I want to make it clear that I have no preconceived no-tions about you, and I am just trying to understand how you have come to be involved in this very uncomfortable situation." After further discussion, Joan became less defensive and was able to discuss her distress about her relation-ship with Dr. White. Although she was aware that her behavior was pushing him away, she felt exposed in the therapy and felt compelled to find out more about him both to feel closer and to "get something on him." Dr. White also admitted to the case manager that he was feeling trapped in the relationship,

and although he genuinely liked the patient and was committed to helping her, he felt uncomfortable about the relationship. After some discussion, it became clear that the patient was reenacting the dynamics of the relationship with her father, who was generally demeaning and neglectful, and only became attentive and seductive during times leading up to his sexual abuse of her. When Dr. White broached this subject with Joan, she responded angrily, "So you're saying that my feelings for you aren't real and that I can't tell the difference between you and my father! I thought you were nice. My father's a bastard!" However, after discussion and explanation concerning abuse-related relationships, the patient was able to calm down as she at least felt less blamed for the problems, although she remained unconvinced about the basis of her relational difficulties. Joan and Dr. White were able to renegotiate some basic agreements concerning their relationship and the treatment. She was discharged from the hospital to continue the long process of working with her therapist to try to understand and cope with assumptions and effects of her incestuous past.

MANAGING COUNTERTRANSFERENCE REACTIONS

Countertransference responses in the treatment of abuse survivors are complex and cause considerable difficulties for therapists. One particular difficulty has been called *vicarious* or *secondary traumatization* (Pearlman & Saakvitne, 1995a), in which a therapist's assumptions about the benevolence of the world are disrupted by understanding the abuses perpetrated on patients. The brutality, callousness, sadism, and diabolical ingenuity that characterize malevolent abuse are indeed overwhelming, especially for therapists who have no previous exposure to such experiences. Therapists may have their own post-traumatic responses to hearing about the terrible details of patients' abuse. Shock, disbelief, confusion, and even a pervasive sense of their own vulnerability can afflict therapists who then struggle to regain a sense of safety and stability. Such reactions are common, and clinicians must use their own personal interpersonal support—friends, colleagues, consultants, or therapists—to help regain their equilibrium. Fortunately, most clinicians are generally able to adjust to even new and horrifying knowledge, to integrate such information, and even reinstate some healthy denial and dissociation in rebuilding a new and workable set of assumptions about the world.

Overidentification and overprotection of patients are common countertransference difficulties. In addition, fascination is a particular difficulty, especially with the rather dramatic symptomatology of multiple personalities (Chu, 1994; Kluft, 1989b). However, the most common countertransference problem in working with abuse survivors may be unacknowledged therapist discomfort. The level of involvement that is necessary to work with traumatized patients, and the need to recapitulate abusive interpersonal relationships places significant emotional strain on therapists. In addition, the extraordinary psychological pain experienced by patients frequently causes them to be narcissistically preoccupied and unable to have a sense of the experience of others around them, including their therapists. In relationships with patients, therapists often feel that their experience is disregarded or invalidated, and, given the slow pace of many treatments, patients' gratitude for sometimes lengthy and extraordinary services may be long delayed.

Many patients go through episodic crises, endanger their own lives, wrestle with their intolerable conflicts and unbearable experiences, and have numerous regressions in which they are unable to take responsibility for themselves or control their experiences. As a result, therapists are often placed in positions where they feel anxious, confused, and burdened. However, therapists are frequently unable to acknowledge the extent of their own discomfort or even anger with both the therapeutic process and with patients themselves. Instead, it is usually much more ego-syntonic to acknowledge only compassion for the patients' pain and sympathy for their struggle to overcome their past abuse. Moreover, many patients give both direct and indirect messages for therapists not to be upset, frustrated, or angry. Patients perceive the all-important and sustaining interpersonal bond between them and their therapists as fragile and fear that it would not withstand the therapist's dysphoria or anger. Many patients have previous experience with anger as out-of-control and destructive, and fear any manifestation of therapists' discomfort in the therapy. Moreover, many patients are unable to integrate their own conflictual feelings and are unable to see their therapists as being complex and multifaceted. Thus the patient sees any indication of frustration or anger as being the therapist's primary affect toward him or her. Therapists' unintentional collusion with patients by not acknowledging their dysphoric feelings (even to themselves) is remarkably common.

Manifestations of unacknowledged discomfort, frustration, and anger vary considerably, and therapists are not immune to utilizing common so-called primitive defense mechanisms. For example, few therapists are overtly hostile, but many find themselves becoming neglectful or distant. This kind of acting out is usually manifested in failure to follow through with commitments, forgetfulness concerning appointments, habitual tardiness, or behaviors such as interrupting sessions to take telephone calls, excessive note taking, or scheduling appointments in an erratic or unpredictable manner.

A more common manifestation of countertransference discomfort occurs through therapists' use of reaction formation. Instead of acknowledging frustration or angry feelings about patients, therapists become concerned about patients and convinced that they need to redouble their efforts. This kind of response can be detrimental to the therapy because therapists avoid bringing up issues that might disturb patients, and they exercise a level of overprotectiveness that does not allow patients to develop psychologically. This overprotective stance is also painful for therapists, causing them to feel anxious, enmeshed, and burdened, as in the following example:

> A respected therapist worked with a survivor of extreme familial neglect and physical abuse for several years. He weathered many difficult periods, most of which were marked by the patient becoming controlling concerning the nature of the therapy and the therapist's responses; in such situations there was always the implied threat of the patient killing herself. The therapist found himself becoming so anxious about the patient that he worried constantly and even his sleep was disrupted. He had frequent emergency appointments with the patient and even called her several additional times a week to make sure she was safe. In a consultation meeting with a trusted colleague, he found himself highly anxious and tearful, and began to describe his fears about the patient, the burdens he felt, and his uncertainties about the therapy. After being able to discuss his concerns and to acknowledge his anger about being manipulated, the therapist was able to gently confront the patient on an ongoing manner about the nature of the therapy, and to set reasonable limits. After a period of turmoil, the therapy become more stable and contained. The therapist's level of anxiety and sleep returned to normal.

The most painful form of countertransference reactions occurs when therapists are unable to acknowledge their countertransference anger and project their own anger and sadism onto their patients. In the therapist's eyes, the patient then becomes a seemingly real and substantial threat. Not infrequently in such situations, the therapist may actually develop a mild form of PTSD, complete with unwanted intrusive thoughts, nightmares and disturbed sleep, avoidant responses, and even startle responses (such as to the ring of the telephone when the patient might be calling). The therapist begins to feel threatened by the patient and to dread sessions or other interactions. Furthermore, the therapist feels as though he or she cannot abandon (or escape from) the patient, and feels impotent to make any kind of positive change in the therapy. This kind of therapist reaction, although extreme, is understandable in the context of the patient's dilemmas. It is yet another recapitulation of the patient's unresolved early abuse. In the setting of the therapeutic relationship, the patient becomes the real or imagined abuser. In response to patients' cues, therapists become enmeshed in relationships in which they are highly emotionally invested and from which they feel they cannot exit. They feel dysphoric, panicky, despairing, and limited in their options and choices. In short, they have assumed the position of the abused child in a reenactment of the abuse. It is essential for therapists in this position to directly address these issues by acknowledging and working through their personal difficulties. This type of reenactment must be understood and interpreted as needed in the therapy, and patients and therapists must move back into mutually respectful and collaborative relationships.

Professional support through ongoing consultation, continuing education programs, and support from colleagues is an essential part of working with patients with complex post-traumatic and dissociative disorders. Given the intensity of the patient–therapist relationship, the powerful affects related to traumatization, and the slow pace of treatment, therapists often get little or intermittent gratification. Clinicians must use their professional and personal support networks to help maintain their own equilibrium and to hone their professional skills. Especially in situations of transference–countertransference enmeshment, therapists must practice what they preach: Interpersonal connection and support are an essential part of human experience and are particularly necessary in times of difficulty or stress. Traumatized patients are often astute in observing their therapists, and patients' dilemmas cannot be resolved until therapists are able to understand and to model that they are able to resolve relational impasses.

CHAPTER 10

Good Fences Make Good Neighbors: Establishing Boundaries and Setting Limits*

THE ABUSE of children is an inherent violation of limits and boundaries. Physical and sexual abuse are clear violations of familial roles as children are exploited for parental needs, and pervasive neglect represents a profound abrogation of parental responsibility. All these kinds of abuse also ignore the limits of coping capacities of children, overwhelming them repeatedly with stimuli that they are unable to tolerate. In treatment, many patients who have experienced childhood abuse replicate the enmeshment and violation of their early experiences, breaching boundaries and challenging limits. Effective treatment must confront these recapitulations of abuse and help patients establish reasonable boundaries and limits within the therapeutic relationship, providing a safe and respectful framework for both the patient and the therapist.

Establishing a safe structure for treatment is an essential task with patients who are survivors of severe childhood abuse, and is an inherent and essential part of the treatment (Briere, 1992; Chu, 1992c; Courtois, 1988; Davies & Frawley, 1994; Herman, 1992; Pearlman & Saakvitne, 1995b). Particularly in the early stages of therapy, many patients have frequent crisis situations such as repeated and unpredictable reexperiences of traumatic events accompanied by despair and panic. They also experience intense impulses, often of a de-

---

*Portions of this chapter are adapted from the articles "The therapeutic roller coaster: Dilemmas in the treatment of childhood abuse survivors" (Chu, 1992c), and "Empathic confrontation in the treatment of childhood abuse survivors, including a tribute to the legacy of Dr. David Caul" (Chu, 1992a).

structive nature, that feel compelling and overwhelming. These crisis situations often lead patients to seek increasing amounts of reassurance and time from their therapists. Interwoven with these crisis situations and demands for more from the therapist is the tendency for traumatized patients to reenact abuse-related interpersonal dynamics in the therapeutic relationship. As the intensity of the therapeutic relationship heats up, therapists may begin to find themselves responding to frequent calls, increasing the frequency or lengths of sessions, and coping with intrusions into their personal lives. In these kinds of situations, therapists must understand the need for maintaining boundaries and setting appropriate limits.

ESTABLISHING A TREATMENT FRAME

A treatment frame, the ground rules of the therapy, is one of the foundations of treatment. Therapists must be clear about issues such as the frequency and length of sessions, the availability of the therapist outside the office, and the roles of both patient and therapist. The treatment frame serves somewhat different functions for therapists and for patients. Therapists must establish a treatment frame that minimizes the anxiety and confusion that comes from feeling consumed by enmeshed relationships and reduces unwarranted intrusions into their personal lives. Patients need to learn that limits and boundaries are a part of mutually respectful relationships, that they provide safety and predictability.

Therapists must be explicit about the treatment frame and should not assume that patients will inherently understand the norms of relationships. Many patients from abusive backgrounds may not even understand the need for a treatment frame. Patients may actually invite boundary violations that feel normal to them (e.g., wanting the therapist to be more of a friend in order to feel more secure, or even inviting the therapist to engage in a sexual relationship as a way of experiencing "safe" intimacy). Although setting limits and establishing boundaries may frustrate patients' wishes, a strong treatment frame ultimately allows patients to feel safe in a relationship where the rules are mutually understood and respected.

Struggles with the treatment frame often seem to occur around the issue of therapist availability. A certain amount of therapist availability is helpful, and some patients are able to make use of brief telephone contact to feel comforted and contained until the next session. However, constant or extraordinary availability is problematic for at least three important reasons. First, escalating demands for therapists' availability ignore the real human limitations of therapists and therapists' legitimate need to maintain their own separate lives. Second, constant availability leads to increasing dependence on the therapist to provide reassurance rather than encouraging patients to find their own internal mechanisms of containing dysphoric affects and providing self-soothing. Finally, the expectation that therapists can always provide soothing and reassurance early in therapy is unrealistic. Both patients and therapists need to accept that throughout the early stage of treatment patients may encounter overwhelming pain, and that an important aspect of therapy is learning to find nonharmful ways of managing and tolerating psychological pain.

Therapists must establish clear limits based on both their own needs and their judgment of patients' needs and abilities. Exactly where the limits are set is a function of what is tolerable for the therapist and what is helpful for the patient. For example, some therapists are willing to accept evening and weekend calls, and others are not. Some patients require someone to be available on evenings and weekends, and others need to be challenged to find ways of coping on their own during these times. If there is a clash between therapist and patient needs, such as the patient who needs out-of-the-office contact and a therapist who is not willing to be available, some other solution must be found, for example, hotlines, a walk-in emergency center, or other supports. However, the basic principle is not so much exactly where (within reason) the boundaries and limits are set, but that there is a need for a clear and reasonable treatment frame. Therapists who avoid setting and maintaining a clear treatment frame are likely to become exhausted and then either to abandon the therapy or to renege on explicit or implied promises. Although periodic renegotiation of the treatment frame is common, it is important to avoid situations in which too much is promised since retrenching is likely to result in patients feeling abandoned, betrayed, or abused. The following clinical example illustrates some of the relevant issues concerning limit setting:

> An experienced therapist, who prided himself on being able to meet even the extreme needs of his patients, became involved in the treatment of several patients with a history of sexual abuse. As a successful product of medical education and training, the therapist believed that he should be able to respond at any hour, day or night, even at the cost of his sleep, health, mental stability, and family. He found himself awakened frequently at night by phone calls, often to participate in long discussions about suicide. He learned to dread the ring of the telephone and slept poorly, expecting to be awakened. The introduction of a new puppy into his household, and the responsibility of getting up at dawn to walk the puppy, brought him to the brink of exhaustion. Violating his teachings not to talk to his patients about his own needs, the therapist told each of his patients that he retired early and that he expected each of them to respect his sleep. He emphasized that he did not enjoy late-night calls and would permit calls only for serious emergencies after 8 p.m. All of the therapist's patients became upset at this limit. One patient retorted, "Fine! Then I'll just kill myself!" to which the therapist responded that a condition of the therapy was for the patient to call if seriously suicidal at whatever time. However,

he was clear that such a call would only involve negotiations for hospitalization and not a long discussion concerning suicide. Another patient became distant and panicky, and then called later, just before 8 p.m. to be reassured that the therapist still wished to work with her. After a stormy period of patient protest and anger, evening and night calls decreased dramatically to only one or two calls every month. One patient later explored that she had been acting out her anger by sadistically calling him repeatedly at home. Another acknowledged that the limits made it easier for her: "Since I know I can't call you, I just make myself shut down, instead of fighting with myself whether or not to call."

The guidelines in this discussion may seem rather obvious, but many otherwise competent and experienced therapists have made major errors in permitting violation of the treatment frame. Such therapists have tried to become friends with patients, have engaged in activities such as extensive touching, holding, and even bottle feeding, have entered into business arrangements, and invited patients to live with them. What leads therapists to fail to set adequate limits and to participate in these boundary violations? Several common patterns occur. Therapists may lose their therapeutic perspective and come to believe that their only alternative is to gratify patients' demands. They may recognize patients' own limited internal resources and fail to understand the need to help patients find ways of developing internal coping mechanisms. Therapists may also come to believe that survivors of childhood abuse deserve and need a radically different kind of treatment than other psychologically injured patients. They may then proceed to implement a treatment based primarily on patients' perceived needs such as schemes to reparent or to allow unlimited regression. Perhaps one of the most difficult scenarios involves therapists who have promised never to abandon the patient no matter what the patient does. Although this promise may give patients a certain amount of security, it also permits some patients to engage in uncontrolled scenarios of appalling and sadistic reenactments of past abusive interpersonal interactions. There is little evidence that providing this unconditional love is helpful to patients. In contrast, a therapy that is based on the patient adhering to the treatment frame and achieving maximal personal growth is ultimately more reassuring and safer.

Forensic psychiatrist Thomas Gutheil (1989) has witnessed many therapeutic misadventures as an expert witness in legal cases where patients have sued their therapists for engaging in boundary violations (e.g., for engaging in a sexual relationship). He described the phenomenon of a kind of "bubble" that can separate the patient and therapist from the realities of the external world. Within this bubble, the therapist empathically enters the intrapsychic world of the patient, where the needs of the patient are intense and compelling. Separated from the perspective and judgment of others, the patient and therapist then proceed on a course of action that may seem to make sense within the patient's frame of reference, but that lacks any kind of wider or longer-term perspective, and that almost inevitably damages both patient and therapist. Therapists in this situation are at least somewhat aware that the course of treatment they are pursuing might be questionably regarded by other professionals, and they often hide their activities. Therapists who find themselves in this position should immediately seek consultation with a trusted senior clinician.

Patients' reactions to their therapists' interventions are powerful determinants of therapists' behavior. Patients' responses often seem alternately idealized (e.g., "You are the first therapist who really understands me") and devaluing (e.g., "You have no idea what I am feeling and can't help me"). This pattern of responses creates a system of partial gratification, having both positive and negative reinforcers, that is remarkably effective in molding therapists' behaviors. Thus, therapists may tolerate a pattern of slowly escalating demands and only become aware of the consequences when they find themselves overwhelmed by them. The intensity of patients' experiences also causes therapists to make premature and ill-considered decisions. Patients' needs to be reassured, to be rescued, to be touched, and to be soothed are all too human and often intensely compelling. These needs are often combined with an atmosphere of crisis, with the implied threat of patients' decompensating or suiciding, and are conducive to ill-considered decisions. Therapists should remember that the qualities of predictability and consistency, rather than extraordinary therapeutic interventions, provide containment. In particular, touch and physical contact are problematic with traumatized patients, and therapists should be conservative regarding such matters. In general, any major changes concerning limits and boundaries should be carefully considered. No such decisions should be made against the therapist's better judgment because of a crisis situation. Therapists must take the responsibility for making decisions that maintain the treatment frame, keep the structure of the therapy intact, and promote patients' healthy psychological growth.

THERAPEUTIC RESPONSIBILITY

The issue of therapeutic responsibility is another area that involves boundaries and limits. The locus of responsibility for achieving treatment goals or even remaining alive may seem obvious, but often becomes unclear in the roller coaster ride of the therapy of severely traumatized patients. It is common for therapists who begin treating an abuse survivor to find that the direction of the therapy changes dramatically after only a few months. For example, the therapy may begin with some general agreement that the work is to improve the quality of the patient's life. However, therapists may soon find themselves attempting to convince the patient to remain in therapy or not to attempt suicide. Clearly some major shift has occurred in the therapy. Understanding this shift involves recognizing the conflicts and profound ambivalence of abuse survivors.

Abuse survivors are exposed to experiences that lead to conflict in almost every major aspect of their lives. The intensity and circumstances of the childhood abuse lead to these seemingly irreconcilable psychological conflicts. For example, the child who is sexually abused by a parent often carries the incompatible feelings of love and hate for his or her father. The intensity of the intrapsychic conflicts leads to the use of dissociative defenses so that the conflicted feelings can be repressed and forgotten, or even apportioned into different parts of the self, as in the case of dissociative identity disorder. As discussed in Chapter 7, abuse survivors are conflicted concerning self-harm. They also have ambivalent feelings about virtually all major issues in their lives: I am worthwhile/I am worthless, I was abused/the abuse never happened, I was loved/I was hated and exploited, I was powerless and victimized/the abuse was my fault, I can have a life/I'll never have anything, I want therapy/I'm afraid of therapy, I trust my therapist/I hate my therapist, and so on. These sorts of ambivalent feelings and beliefs are unbearably painful. Particularly when overwhelmed, patients humanly ignore one side of their ambivalence.

When patients are unable to tolerate the pain of their own intense conflicts, therapists may find themselves assuming one side of the ambivalent feelings—usually the positive side. Unfortunately, this allows patients to be unambivalently negative about these complex issues. This shift of therapeutic responsibility results in the therapist being placed in an untenable therapeutic position. Therapists and patients find themselves battling over these conflicts (some of which involve actual survival) rather than recognizing them as the projections of the patients' intrapsychic dilemmas. The untoward effects of such situations are the assumption of additional burdens for therapists and a foundering of the therapeutic process, as illustrated in the following example:

> Barbara, a woman in her late 40s, entered therapy for long-standing interpersonal problems. Despite having difficulties with coping and almost no close friends or other interpersonal supports, she took pride in having held down a good job and having functioned at a high level. However, with the retirement of her boss, Barbara felt inexplicably betrayed. She began to increasingly dwell on the emptiness in her life and her failed marriage, and to vividly recall details of a neglectful and abusive childhood. She began to abuse alcohol on a regular basis, often becoming more depressed and calling her therapist at night for comfort and reassurance. These calls were initially brief and helpful. However, over time the calls became more frequent and less productive as she became more depressed and seriously thought about suicide. The therapist became progressively more frantic, redoubling his efforts to help Barbara have

hope for the future. He reminded her of her past accomplishments and considerable strengths, to no avail. Barbara began to talk about quitting therapy, because she could not bear to hurt the therapist by killing herself while being treated by him. Finally, she was found unconscious by her ex-husband after ingesting excessive tranquilizers and alcohol; Barbara was hospitalized. The therapist was able to use the hospital staff as consultants for his dilemma. After perceiving how he was the impetus for Barbara's treatment, he was able to approach her to renegotiate the treatment contract, saying, "You and I have struggled about an issue that primarily concerns your mixed feelings. Although I want you to stay in therapy and live, my feelings don't really matter. You have to make the commitment to cope with these issues and not depend on me to provide you with the reasons to go on. If we are to continue to work together, you will have to decide that you are willing to wrestle with the issues of your own welfare, learning ways to cope instead of expecting me to always be there to convince you to live." After prolonged discussion, Barbara was able to commit to certain safety measures, including abstinence from alcohol and taking on the responsibility of working out a crisis plan. Much later in her treatment, she was able to recognize how much she wanted the therapist to be the encouraging father she longed for and to take over and manage the burdens of her life.

Therapists of abuse survivors need to encourage and help patients to carry the weights of their conflicts. It is not that therapists should avoid making their stances clear (e.g., about suicide or the value of treatment), but they should help patients take on the responsibility of wrestling with these issues rather than projecting them onto the patient–therapist relationship. Interventions regarding therapeutic responsibility need to be made with empathy and sensitivity because it is easy for therapists to use the issue of responsibility punitively and to effectively abandon patients. These difficulties are often caused by the immense psychological distress of conflictual feelings, not by lack of motivation or weak moral fiber. Therapists should demonstrate that they understand patients' dilemmas, and offer their assistance in trying to work out conflicts (e.g., "I know that you have very mixed feelings about therapy. I would like to help understand both your hopes and fears about therapy rather than your feeling that I am 'making' you attend therapy."). Obviously, the principle of expecting patients to assume primary responsibility for their lives and treatment does *not* extend to emergency situations in which patients are acutely at risk of suicide or possible serious self-harm. In particular, confrontation concerning matters of personal safety should *not* be made during emergency telephone contacts. In such circumstances, clinicians must do whatever is necessary for the patient's safety and welfare (e.g., hospitalization). Once safety is assured, the issue can be directly addressed in subsequent face-to-face meetings. In these situations, the issue of therapeutic responsibility should be the primary issue discussed until some resolution is reached.

Another area of therapeutic responsibility that abuse survivors often have difficulty maintaining is basic interpersonal relatedness. Abuse survivors often have histories of being treated like objects to be exploited rather being related to. Thus, abuse survivors may have only minimal awareness of what is necessary to sustain a normal mutual relationship. This difficulty may be recapitulated in the therapy because such patients may have little understanding of their personal responsibility in the therapeutic relationship. Compounding this circumstance is the valid therapeutic view that the therapy is primarily for the patient's benefit, and the therapist's needs should only minimally interfere with the process. This view may lead both patients and therapists to overlook the need for patients to maintain their part of the relationship. Patients should recognize that they must share the commitment to the relationship and to the therapeutic process, the commitment to try to resolve interpersonal difficulties, and the commitment to maintain shared therapeutic goals. The following example illustrates this issue:

> After 3 years of therapy, Patty, a 44-year-old single woman, began to despair of ever achieving closeness with others. Despite considerable gains in self-care and vocational matters, she still experienced intense fear when trying to make friends or to function in social situations. In therapy she became angrier and angrier, until virtually every session was a combination of stony silence and diatribes about the inadequacies of the therapist and the therapy: "I don't know what you expect of me. *You* have a life and a husband and a baby and a house. *I* have nothing! I hate you for that! You think this therapy is so great. What has it done for me? My life is over. I'm in a lot of pain and I have to pay attention to giving myself the relief that I need. You think I should continue to live, but you don't have to live my life! You just want me to go on suffering. Well, see if you can stop me. I can kill myself whenever *I* choose!" The therapist tolerated Patty's anger for many sessions. The therapist recalled that during a period of her own personal therapy she had been angry at her therapist, and that expressing this anger had allowed her to eventually come to terms with some important feelings. However, the angry attacks seemed to intensify and not to result in any new insights or gains. Finally, the therapist sought consultation. After hearing the story, the consultant observed that the patient was caught up in a near-psychotic transference, so consumed by her rage that she was effectively destroying the therapy. The consultant made several suggestions about setting limits on the patient's behavior. The therapist subsequently was able to say to Patty, "I understand that you are truly tortured. However, I cannot allow you to continue to attack me. I think you have forgotten that I have spent years trying to help you and that I am not your enemy. Even though you feel tormented, you are still in a relationship with me, and you continue to have a responsibility for maintaining our relationship. You have frequently asked me to not to abandon you. You now seem to be saying that you have the right to destroy and abandon our relationship. We cannot have a workable therapy if I'm constantly on the defensive or terrified that you might kill yourself." Patty responded with genuine surprise, "I didn't know therapists had feelings!" She controlled her attacks (initially with reluctance), and was later able to examine how she repeatedly found herself angrily challenging persons in her life with whom she felt vulnerable.

One other issue involving therapeutic responsibility has arisen as attitudes have shifted from widespread disbelief about patients' reports of childhood abuse to too-easy acceptance of *any* such reports. Patients have sometimes asked therapists to validate or deny the reality of their past abuse when patients themselves do not have adequate information to make such a determination. It seems appropriate for a therapist to acknowledge or even raise the issue of abuse when the history seems relatively clear, but given the vagaries concerning the nature of traumatic memory, it is difficult to respond to all inquiries of "Do you believe me?" In situations where patients are uncertain about the reality of past events or when memories are clearly not credible, therapists should respond to these inquiries by acknowledging only the painfulness of uncertainty and being able to know the realities of what actually happened. Patients and therapists together should assume the responsibility of sifting through known facts, likely conclusions, fantasy, and conjecture until such time as patients themselves can be reasonably clear about their personal realities.

EMPATHIC CONFRONTATION

Patients with trauma-based disorders frequently have worthwhile ideas concerning the course of their therapy, guided by a kind of internal road map. However, it is also common for patients to advocate unwise treatment strategies or to cling to dysfunctional but ingrained behaviors. For example, patients may vigorously advocate for premature abreactive work without having established the psychotherapeutic foundations for safe exploration. Similarly, patients may insist that they have no control over their posttraumatic and dissociative symptoms, may persist in self-destructive and revictimizing, risk-taking behavior, or may demand inordinate therapist availability and reassurance that result in boundary violations. When such issues emerge in psychotherapy, patients often manifest extraordinary resistance to change. Many of the dysfunctional patterns of behavior have long served as coping mechanisms, and no matter how unpleasant, are more familiar than the well-intentioned but unknown treatment course advocated by therapists.

Setting limits on patients' dysfunctional behavior involves confrontation and is often a difficult task. Patients with severe childhood abuse and a lifetime's experience of abandonment and betrayal may have a tenuous sense of alliance with their therapists. Hence, therapists are often afraid to confront patients even with important therapeutic issues because they fear patients' likely reactions of withdrawal, anger, and regressive and self-destructive behavior. However, confrontation of unsafe and dysfunctional patterns *must* be a part of the therapy, not only to guide the therapy in a positive direction, but also to prevent the therapist from becoming an unwitting enabler of continued destructive behavior.

Confrontation in psychotherapy has been considered an important part of treatment to clarify resistances in therapy and to facilitate change (Greenson, 1967; Myerson, 1973), and as a mode of teaching (Mann, 1973). Two papers by psychoanalytic psychiatrists Daniel Buie and Gerald Adler, from an era prior to acceptance of trauma as an important common etiology of adult psychopathology, described confrontation in the treatment of patients with borderline personality disorder (Adler & Buie, 1972; Buie & Adler, 1972), and are highly applicable to work with traumatized patients. For example, confrontation was seen as sometimes necessary to help patients recognize "(1) the real danger in certain relationships; (2) the real danger in action used as a defense mechanism; and (3) the real danger in action used for discharge of impulses and feelings" (Buie & Adler, 1972, p. 101). The authors felt that confrontation of patients' denial allows the therapist "(1) to help the patient become aware of his impulses, so that he need not be subject to action without warning; (2) to help him gain temporary relief through abreaction; and (3) to help him gain a rational position from which he can exert self-control or seek help in maintaining control" (Buie & Adler, 1972, p. 103). In discussing the misuses of confrontation, the authors stressed patients' vulnerability to harm from confrontation due to their propensity to feel abandoned, their intense impulses and inadequate defenses, and their tenuous capacity to form a working alliance. They noted that the therapist often misuses confrontation due to countertransference "rage and envy when he feels he must rescue his helpless, demanding patient and then finds his efforts met by increasing demands and regression" (Adler & Buie, 1972, p. 109).

Many of the observations noted are surprisingly apt in the context of the sometimes decidedly nonanalytic treatment of survivors of childhood abuse. However, it is normative that confrontation is also difficult in the psychotherapy of patients with severe childhood abuse. The need for confrontation may be obvious, such as in cases involving danger to the patient, therapist, or therapeutic relationship, or behaviors that are out of control or sabotage the therapy. However, therapists may be reluctant to confront the patient either due to countertransference difficulties (Chu, 1992c; Comstock, 1991) or simple concern that confrontation will be misunderstood and make the patient feel abandoned and betrayed. In fact, therapeutic confrontations *are* often initially misunderstood, but patience in reiterating concern for the patient and for the therapy often allows the confrontation to eventually be heard and understood as intended. The model of empathic confrontation offers a way of intervening that is effective in helping patients ally with therapists in a direction that is positive and therapeutically sound.

When making a confrontation, the demonstration of empathy for the patient's position is essential. With survivors of extensive childhood trauma, particularly early in the therapeutic process, it should never be assumed that there is a firm therapeutic alliance. Traumatized patients repeatedly lose a sense of connection, sometimes actively pushing away a dangerous sense of vulnerable intimacy or retreating to views of the therapist as threatening or abusive. Thus, if no empathic resonance is established prior to making a confrontation, the patient is compelled to hear the intervention as simply an attempt of the therapist to control, abuse, exploit, or deprive the patient.

The model of empathic confrontation is based on the need to establish empathic resonance as a part of making a confrontation or other intervention that is painful to the patient (Chu, 1992a). That is, it is crucial to reestablish some sense of alliance before saying something that will result in the patient feeling attacked, defensive, guilty, or shamed. In practical terms, empathic confrontation often takes the form of a two-part statement. The first part strongly communicates that the therapist understands the patient's position, feelings, and experience. This can often be done in a few sentences. The second part (often connected to the first part by a *but* or *however*) contains the confrontation concerning the patient's behavior. Two examples are illustrated here:

> Kay, a 24-year-old woman who had been brutally sexually abused throughout much of her childhood, chronically cut her arms and legs with a razor. She tended to cut herself whenever she was overwhelmed with feelings, particularly when angry or ashamed. Despite the urgings of her therapist, she continued to self-mutilate, claiming that she found the cutting helpful, and that it was only her therapist who found it objectionable. Moreover, Kay argued convincingly that the cutting was not intended to be lethal, and that she had no other ways to cope with her feelings. Her therapist gently confronted her on this behavior, saying, "I understand that you don't want to give up cutting yourself and that the cutting has helped you survive. In fact, your cutting yourself was an ingenious solution when you didn't have anyone else to rely on. However, unless you begin to work together with me on this, you will not find other ways to deal with your feelings, and your therapy will not be successful." Kay responded by angrily accusing her therapist of trying to control her, to which the therapist responded, "I know that it has been crucial for you to have a sense of your own control in your life, especially when others have hurt you. I know you have often been controlled by other people, but I'm asking you to do something that will be helpful in your therapy, not to do something my way." After some discussion, Kay was able to acknowledge the need to find a way to control her cutting and noted, "When people used to try to get me to stop, I always felt that they thought I was bad and didn't want anything to do with me."
>
> Cheryl, a 35-year-old woman with dissociative identity disorder, was hospitalized because of frequent flashbacks of horrendous childhood abuse. In the

hospital she continued to be out of control, frequently having flashbacks late in the evening, during which she was so agitated that she needed to be physically restrained. When asked to control her behavior, she angrily claimed to have no control over the flashbacks, and, in fact, didn't remember them since *she*, Cheryl, wasn't "out." Her therapist said, "I know that it feels as though the flashbacks just take over and that you have no control. I also understand that you feel separate from the other parts of you that were out of control. I know it is a core issue of your difficulties to feel alienated from the other parts of you. However, unless you can work very hard with me to *begin* to establish some control and to communicate with your other parts, the therapy will not work, and neither I nor the hospital will be able to help you." After a period of angry denial, Cheryl was observed to be exercising extraordinary efforts to maintain control, pace the therapy, and promote internal communication.

Work with adult survivors of severe childhood abuse can be challenging. It is crucial that therapists maintain attitudes that are empathic but also based on solid psychotherapeutic tenets, such as maintaining a solid treatment frame and confronting patients' dysfunctional behaviors. A pioneer in the treatment of patients with dissociative identity disorder and a fine clinician skilled in empathic confrontation, psychiatrist David Caul (Chu, 1992a) wrote:

The therapist should be willing to exhibit appropriate respect for the patient . . . respect, not indulgence. Respect does not preclude firmness and insistence on working together for progress. Respect does not preclude normal differences in feelings of the therapist with recognition that a wide variety of feelings toward the therapist will be forthcoming, especially early in therapy. . . . There has to be an element of cooperation that is woven as a thread throughout the course of therapy. The fact that a patient keeps coming back for sessions may be the main indication (even if unspoken) of cooperation by the patient. The therapist should always be willing to listen and accept suggestions and workable ideas. Sometimes it is difficult for a therapist to acknowledge the exquisitely sensitive nature of this "two-way street." Continue to emphasize the fact that productive therapy will require some sort of partnership between the parties. . . . The therapist should be able to distinguish between candor and sometimes cruel hostility. Remember that these people are very sensitive and very vulnerable. I suppose candor might be described as being truthful in addition to being caring, considerate, and concerned. The therapist should not be afraid to appropriately admit that there are difficulties in the treatment and should attempt to openly discuss them. All attempts should be made to do this in a positive way and to relate it to the therapy, and not direct it toward the patient. . . . It will remain for the therapist to use whatever energies there are toward good judgment and careful consideration in providing therapy for this phenomenon that is of such magnitude that it will require all the help that we can get. (pp. 101–102)

PART THREE

SPECIAL TOPICS IN THE TREATMENT OF TRAUMA-RELATED DISORDERS

CHAPTER 11

The Rational Treatment of Dissociative Identity Disorder*

O VER THE PAST decade, there has been a dramatic increase in professional awareness concerning dissociation as a response to childhood trauma. As a consequence, many more patients have been diagnosed as suffering from dissociative identity disorder (DID) and related disorders. The accurate diagnosis of DID and dissociative disorders has proved to be of benefit to many patients. However, in many instances, the particular nature of DID and dissociative symptoms appears to have led some professionals to engage in poorly considered therapeutic practices. Even experienced therapists have struggled with difficulties in understanding and treating DID and dissociative disorder patients. Many of these difficulties are generic to patients with histories of extensive childhood abuse and are described elsewhere in this volume. This chapter examines the specific areas of difficulty commonly encountered with DID and dissociative disorder patients.

The manifestations of DID are often dramatic and difficult to manage. The switching of personalities, the dissociative and amnestic barriers, and the complexity of internal psychic structures and identity are often bewildering to clinicians first encountering DID. In addition, the periodic intrusions of reexperiencing phenomena, including flashbacks, nightmares, overwhelming affect, and even somatic sensations lend a sense of chronic instability. Furthermore, comorbid characterologic difficulties including patients' intense interpersonal disturbances, affective instability, and impulsive and self-destructive behavior add to the sense of ongoing crisis and chaos. It is in this context that many clinicians seem to ignore the estab-

---

*Portions of this chapter are adapted from the article "The rational treatment of multiple personality disorder" (Chu, 1994).

147

lished principles of traditional psychotherapy and engage in practices that appear to respond to the immediate clinical situation but may be ill-advised in terms of the therapeutic process.

DID and the difficulties that are suffered by patients who have histories of severe childhood abuse sometimes *do* require therapists to make thoughtful modifications of certain psychotherapeutic stances. However, therapists should adhere to the basic principles of psychotherapy that have been established and tested over generations of patient–therapist interactions. Not to do so results in potential therapeutic impasses and negative outcomes. Treatments that are not founded on traditional psychotherapeutic principles risk becoming out of control and detrimental not only to patients, but to therapists as well. This discussion describes specific treatment for DID patients and those patients with similar, severe dissociative disorders that do not quite meet the criteria for DID (e.g., patients who experience themselves as fragmented but retain a single identity). Four areas of therapeutic difficulty that are common in the treatment of DID and dissociative disorders are highlighted: differential diagnosis, treatment staging through establishing proper psychotherapeutic foundations and pacing the therapy, understanding severe dissociative disorders as a system of personalities or self-states representing a fragmented sense of self within a single person rather than as a group of autonomous individuals, and working with the patient who has DID without undue focus on DID phenomenology.

DIFFERENTIAL DIAGNOSIS ISSUES

Prior to embarking on treatment for DID or a similar dissociative disorder, it must be determined that the patient indeed has a dissociative disorder diagnosis. As with any clinical presentation, evidence of DID must be carefully examined in terms of differential diagnosis. Specifically, patients must be examined for evidence of *DSM-IV* criteria (American Psychiatric Association, 1994) including naturally occurring separate internal states, dissociative barriers between states, and amnesia. Etiologic issues concerning the necessary traumatic antecedents must be carefully considered. It should be determined whether there are comorbid conditions such as another Axis I diagnosis of an affective or psychotic disorder, substance abuse, an eating disorder or somatization, and Axis II disorders such as borderline personality disorder. The possibility of self-induced elaboration of symptoms or iatrogenic factors should be considered, and embellished dissociative features and factitious or malingered DID should be ruled out. (For a discussion of these last issues, please see Chapter 14.)

DSM-IV criteria (American Psychiatric Association, 1994) for DID require the following four essential features:

A. The presence of two or more distinct identities or personality states (each with its own relatively enduring pattern of perceiving, relating to, and thinking about the environment and self)
B. At least two of these personalities or personality states recurrently take control of the person's behavior
C. Inability to recall important personal information that is too extensive to be explained by ordinary forgetfulness
D. [The above symptoms are] not due to the direct effects of a substance (e.g., blackouts or chaotic behavior during alcohol intoxication) or a general medical condition (e.g., complex partial seizures) (p. 487)

Psychiatrist Richard Kluft (1996), perhaps the most preeminent investigator of DID in the past two decades, described some of the classic presenting features of naturally occurring DID:

The personalities' overt differences and disparate self-concepts may be striking. They may experience and represent themselves as being different ages, genders, races, religions, and sexual orientations; they may experience themselves as having different appearances and/or hold discrepant values and belief systems. Their awareness of one another may range from complete to nil. Directionality of knowledge is almost always found among some alters, such that alter A knows of doings of B, but B is unaware of the activities of A. . . . Differences in handwriting and handedness, voice and vocabulary, accents and speech patterns, and even preferred languages are encountered. Their facial expressions and movement characteristics, both when neutral and affectively engaged, may show impressive and rather consistent differences. . . . The classic host personality, which usually . . . presents for treatment, nearly always bears the legal name and is depressed, anxious, somewhat neurasthenic, compulsively good, masochistic, conscience-stricken, constricted hedonically, and suffers both psychophysiological symptoms and time loss and/or time distortion. While no personality types are inevitably present, many are encountered quite frequently: childlike personalities, . . . protectors, helper-advisors, inner self-helpers, . . . personalities with distinctive affective states, guardians of memories and secrets, memory traces, . . . inner persecutors, . . . anesthetic personalities, . . . expressers of forbidden pleasures, . . . avengers, . . . defenders or apologists for the abusers, those based on lost love objects and other introjects and identifications, specialized encapsulators of traumatic experiences and powerful affects, very specialized personalities, and those . . . that preserve the idealized potential for happiness, growth, and the healthy expression of feelings. (pp. 345–346)

Kluft cautions that dramatic presentations are not necessary to make the diagnosis of DID. However, many of the features he mentions should be present either in overt or muted form in order to pursue a DID-oriented treatment.

In addition to the symptomatic presence of dissociative fragmentation, patients with dissociative disorder almost universally have historical evidence of trauma (Braun, 1990; Braun & Sachs, 1985; Kluft, 1984b; Putnam,

1985, 1989; Putnam, Guroff, Silberman, Barban, & Post, 1986; Ross, 1989) and long-standing dissociative symptoms. Patients with severe dissociative disorders, particularly early in treatment, have a reluctance to discuss, acknowledge, or reveal both evidence of internal separateness and past histories of traumatization because their difficulties are based on the need to distance and disavow such experiences. Moreover, if the traumatization is due to abuse or victimization, the patient feels deep shame and guilt, and wishes to hide these experiences from others. Any clinical presentations that do not have these characteristics should be examined closely for evidence of an atypical dissociative disorder that requires special treatment, another psychiatric diagnosis masquerading as a dissociative disorder, or a factitious or malingered dissociative disorder (Brick & Chu, 1991; Chu, 1991a; Kluft, 1987c).

Comorbid diagnoses must be recognized. As described in Chapter 12, any prominent Axis I diagnosis must be actively treated prior to instituting treatment for a dissociative disorder. Disorders such as depression, bipolar disorder, or psychoses will inevitably exacerbate and perpetuate any existing dissociative symptoms. Major substance abuse, eating disorders, or somatization should also be an initial focus of stabilization. Axis II disorders, such as borderline personality disorder, are common in dissociative disorder patients (Horovitz & Braun, 1984) and must be recognized because the patient's deficits in affect tolerance, behavior control, and relational ability will have enormous impact on the emphasis and pace of treatment.

TREATMENT STAGING

Perhaps the most common difficulty in the treatment of severely traumatized patients (and DID patients in particular) has to do with failure to stage the treatment and pace the therapy. Concerning DID patients, Kluft (1989a) observed:

> A common experience of the sophisticated therapist is to have difficulties with regards to issues of dosage in treating DID. The patient often experiences therapy as a guided tour of his or her personal hell without anesthesia. When a therapist fails to pace the treatment to the tolerance of the patient, the patient may become overwhelmed over and over. (p. 88)

All the caveats concerning work with traumatized patients are particularly relevant with DID patients and those with similar disorders. Premature efforts to abreact past traumatic events generally result in regression and retraumatization. Therapists treating dissociative disorder patients should be aware of and respect the need for establishing the necessary and proper psychotherapeutic foundations prior to engaging in exploratory and abreactive work. The major principles in treating severely traumatized patients, including the SAFER model—which calls for the development of skills concerning self-care and symptom control, acknowledgment (but not extensive exploration) of traumatic antecedents, functioning, appropriate expression of affect, and maintaining collaborative and supportive relationships, as a preliminary stage prior to exploratory work—are described in Part II of this volume. Unless patients master these skills, any attempt at abreactive work may result in patients becoming overwhelmed and attempting to cope through dysfunctional isolation and regressed, self-destructive behavior. The profound difficulties that DID patients often have in establishing a sense of safety and mastering the various tasks of early-stage therapy may mandate a long period of preliminary work prior to active focus on the etiologic abuse.

Failure to adequately pace treatment is also seen in premature attempts at integration and fusion. Therapists often attempt to pursue integration prior to adequately working through underlying conflicts and traumatic events. Such misguided efforts often entail therapists' heroic efforts in the form of prolonged sessions, special techniques, and constant monitoring of patients. The integrations usually either quickly disintegrate or new personalities appear to take on the functions of those who have been merged. Patients and therapists who are invested in this kind of practice often seem to persist in working in this manner, convinced that the next integration will result in therapeutic gains and stability. Unfortunately, there is usually only a downhill spiral of regression, chaos, and exacerbated symptomatology.

As with other traumatized patients, therapists working with DID and dissociative disorder patients should recognize that patients frequently do not have an understanding of the need to pace the therapy. Many patients, particularly those who have severe reexperiencing phenomena, may wish to purge themselves of their toxic past experiences and are only minimally aware of the danger of overwhelming themselves with premature abreactions. Patients may also present with little control over post-traumatic and dissociative symptoms, may persist in ingrained self-destructive and risk-taking behaviors, or may demand inordinate therapist availability, which may result in boundary violations (Fine, 1989; Kluft, 1989b). Therapists must address issues concerning limits, boundaries, control of behavior, control of symptomatology, and therapeutic collaboration. It is part of the early stage of therapy for the therapist to help the dissociative disorder patient learn to respect the treatment frame, to assume the therapeutic responsibility to collaborate in treatment, and to learn the basic coping skills to control destructive behavior and symptomatology (Greaves, 1988; Kluft, 1988).

One particular area of difficulty in the early treatment stages concerns working with the various personalities. Often after the acknowledgment of the existence of DID, personality switching begins to escalate, with the appearance of an increasing array of different personalities, most commonly child, depressed/suicidal, and angry/self-destructive personalities. Therapists may soon find the process out of control as patients present a parade of personalities. Moreover, the dissociative barriers allow patients to ignore their own sense of interpersonal vulnerability and prematurely expose intensely private aspects of themselves. Patients then experience negative therapeutic reactions after showing aspects of themselves that invoke feelings of shame, repugnance, or fear. The following clinical example illustrates this scenario:

> Cathy, a 23-year-old woman with DID, entered therapy with a long history of interpersonal instability and several failed past therapies. In therapy she was cautious about exposing herself to her therapist, aware that she was not yet ready to cope with forming an intense attachment to her therapist. However, outside the office she began to write in a journal that she gave to her therapist to read. In the journal, various personalities began expressing strong feelings about the therapy and therapist and began disclosing details of past abuse. During the next several weeks, Cathy appeared more frightened in the therapy and was either mute or made angry verbal attacks toward the therapist. The therapist finally realized that Cathy was exposing too much about herself in the journal and was feeling vulnerable, and that she could not tolerate having her writings discussed in the sessions. Cathy and her therapist then agreed that the journal writing would be limited in amount and the content would be restricted to only material that could be discussed in sessions. The therapy then proceeded in a useful manner.

Excellent texts have been written about the treatment of DID by psychiatrists Frank Putnam (1989) and Colin Ross (1989). These texts describe specialized techniques in the treatment of DID, such as identifying the various personalities understanding their origins, characteristics, and functions, and "mapping" the personality system. These suggestions and techniques are helpful, but the authors do not imply that they be used indiscriminately; these techniques should be used only when it is clinically appropriate to do so, and therapists should realize that it is often only quite late in the treatment course that a reasonably complete understanding of the personality system is known. In fact, it is normal for therapists to have only an incomplete knowledge of the patient's personality system and to lack a detailed chronology of the patient's history until well into the course of treatment. The practice of actively eliciting personalities (sometimes assisted by hypnotic interventions) when patients are reluctant to bring them into the therapy is potentially destructive. Therapists can appropriately help patients overcome resistance, but the psychological dissection of DID patients is questionable. After all, when working with non-DID patients, most therapists would not consider extensive exposure of hidden aspects of the patient until therapeutically appropriate.

TREATING THE DID SYSTEM

The presentation of patients with dissociative disorders may be confusing to many therapists. How many personalities should be a part of a given therapy session? Is it necessary to call hidden personalities forward into the therapy? Many of these kinds of questions can be answered by attempting to conceptualize the DID presentation as a conflict model. The various parts and personalities of dissociative patients remain relatively separate because of the intense psychological conflicts engendered by past traumatic experience. Thus, an understanding of the inherent conflicts in a given situation will suggest which personalities must be a part of working through the current dilemma. At any time in the therapy of DID patients, the therapist should be working with a relatively small number of personalities that represent the current issues to be resolved. The particular personalities working in the therapy will change as issues are resolved and the therapeutic process progresses. The following clinical example illustrates these principles:

> Marjorie, a 35-year-old married nurse, entered treatment for treatment of sexual dysfunction and depression. Over the first few months of treatment, it became clear that she had a DID diagnosis. Marjorie had a long history of periods of amnesia, unexplained activities, and marked changes in her mood, appearance, and functioning, as well as a known history of brutal childhood abuse. Marjorie had been able to deny the significance of her symptoms and background until her therapist began to gently inquire about them. Several alter personalities emerged in treatment, including a number of child-like personalities that asked to be able to play with toys in the therapy "because we were never allowed to play when we lived with our parents." Over the course of a few weeks, the therapist played with the child personalities in therapy, and no adult personalities appeared except at the very end of sessions, when they seemed confused and disoriented. Finally, Marjorie's husband called the therapist to complain that Marjorie was on probation at her job because of her absenteeism, that she had been withdrawn and angry at home, and that she had driven off the road coming home from a therapy session, presumably because a child personality had emerged while she was driving. After some consideration, the therapist realized that she had unwittingly permitted the patient to focus on only gratification of her infantile wishes to be cared for, at the cost of balancing the demands of work and adult functioning. Moreover, the increased intimacy seemed to interfere with Marjorie's ability to engage in and tolerate intimacy in her marriage. The therapist then tried to explain the situation to the child personalities, and despite their tearful recriminations, insisted that adult personalities appear regularly in sessions and use the time to solve problems concerning the current realities of Marjorie's life. Balance then seemed to be restored to both the therapy and Marjorie's outside life.

Therapists treating dissociative disorder patients commonly find themselves highly involved (and sometimes overinvolved) in the emotional experience of their patients. Patients' difficulty with maintaining a sense of interpersonal connection, and their vulnerability to feeling abandoned and abused, often makes it necessary for therapists to be more active in the therapeutic relationship and to demonstrate their empathic understanding of patients' experience. This necessary level of involvement has some potential untoward effects in that therapists are vulnerable to becoming so empathically identified with their patients that they lose therapeutic perspective. With DID patients, it is not uncommon for therapists to be so aware of the patient's sense of internal separateness that they accept the patient's various alter personalities as virtually independent, autonomously functioning entities. In this situation, therapists begin to treat the alter personalities, rather than treating a single person with a fragmented sense of self, as in the following clinical example:

> Stacie, a 32-year-old woman with DID, progressed well in her therapy for over a year. She struggled to understand her diagnosis and worked productively with her therapist to develop appropriate skills to stabilize her life. She began to have more of a sense of an internal alter personality whom she called the "Evil Father." Stacie was terrified of this personality, which appeared to be angry and persecutory and which apparently made Stacie lacerate her arms and genitals. The therapist was similarly alarmed by this personality, which seemed to be the personification of Stacie's sadistic and abusive father. The therapist tried to help Stacie with strategies to block the behaviors of this personality, but to no avail. Finally, the therapist used a hypnotic intervention and managed to induce the Evil Father to emerge in a session. This personality did emerge and insisted that he needed to teach the other personalities to behave through his behavior. The therapist pointed out the destructiveness of his behavior and urged him to cease such behavior. Stacie then returned and reported amnesia for the previous several minutes. That evening, she again lacerated herself, and the Evil Father wrote a threatening note in Stacie's journal, challenging the therapist to try to control his actions.

This kind of interaction ignores the psychological validity of the father introject, as well as the functioning of the personalities as part of a system. It also assumes that it is primarily the therapist (rather than the patient) who should have the omnipotent position of dealing with difficult alter personalities, a task that is both grandiose and therapeutically untenable.

The outcome of these kinds of clinical dilemmas depends on the therapist's ability to understand the psychodynamic underpinnings of the clinical presentation, to help the patient negotiate the resolution of the inherent conflict, and to insist on the active involvement and collaboration of the patient. In working with difficult alter personalities, the therapist must understand the psychological development and role of each personality and must respect the validity of each. The whole personality system must work toward resolving the conflict that the difficult personality represents since it is the conflict that made the dissociative splitting of identity necessary. Finally, the therapist should engage other personalities in working with the difficult personality.

The conceptual model of family/systems theory is of great assistance in negotiating difficult DID dilemmas. In family/systems theory, the family, rather than any particular family member, is seen as the patient. For example, in a family situation involving an adolescent who is acting out, the family as a whole is asked to look at family conflicts rather than focus on the adolescent. Are there issues between parents or other members of the family, or projective identifications from parents, or major disturbances among other family members that are driving the acting out behavior? The family as a whole takes on the responsibility of understanding, resolving, and containing the behaviors of each family member. In DID patients, family/systems theory is applicable to the inside family of alter personalities or parts. Using this framework, there are no bad personalities, only personalities that are compelled to behave in a particular way because of past events and because of the actions and behaviors of other parts of the personality system. Increased interpersonality communication, collaboration, and empathy are the key elements of this kind of family/systems work with dissociative disorder patients.

The psychopathological process in DID depends on the separation of apparently irreconcilable conflicts through fragmentation into alternate personalities. Hence, patients are understandably resistant to increase interpersonality communication because this process intensifies awareness of intrapsychic conflict. As a result, patients cannot be expected to be comfortable about promoting internal communication and often will not provide the primary impetus for resolution of intrapsychic conflict. However, the therapist can provide reasons for increasing communication, can suggest safe mechanisms for doing so, and can point out potential positive gains and the negative consequences of not doing so. In the case of the patient Stacie, the impasse was resolved as follows:

Following consultation, the therapist approached Stacie somewhat differently. She said to her, "I know you are frightened of the Evil Father, who seems to represent much of what you haven't been able to accept about your father. However, you must begin to understand that this Evil Father is part of you. I know you will find this hard to accept, but this part of you actually helped you survive by becoming like your father." The therapist went on to underscore the survival value of identification with the aggressor, as well as the potential value of being able to express aggression, albeit in a more controlled manner. The therapist then suggested a type of bargain or truce: "If I help you to understand this part of yourself that you are so frightened of, I would like to ask that the Evil Father stop hurting your body. I have no way of forcing this to happen, but if you, Stacie, are willing to work hard at accepting and understanding, perhaps safety can be maintained." When the Evil Father emerged, the therapist said, "I know you have played an important role in the past, and that you are upset at not being recognized. I will work with the other parts of you so that they will acknowledge you, and will begin to bear the burden of your angry feelings. I hope you understand that some of your threats and destructive behavior are not necessary or productive, and if you can work together with me and the other parts of yourself, we may be able to avoid more extreme measures such as hospitalization." After a considerable period of negotiation, internal stability was restored.

It is not always necessary to have important underlying personalities immediately emerge in the therapy as in this example. The technique of talking through to underlying personalities can be useful in allowing the patient control over the timing of exposing previously hidden parts. All that is usually required is for the therapist to make it clear that he or she is addressing all parts that are relevant to the situation, for example, "It is very important that all parts involved in the current problem listen to what I have to say."

A therapist working with the personality system as a whole must keep in mind that his or her role is as facilitator, not peacemaker. The primary impetus for internal cooperation must come from the patient, particularly from the host personality. In the traumatically driven psychopathological process, the host personality dissociates overwhelming or unacceptable events, affects, impulses, and behaviors. To the extent that these experiences remain disavowed, they begin to take on autonomous functioning in the form of separate personalities. Somewhat paradoxically, if the host personality is able to begin to acknowledge and accept disavowed experiences, these experiences can be more controlled and integrated into the self as a whole.

The recent crisis in the former country of Yugoslavia offers an interesting analogy to a DID system. Under authoritarian rule of president Marshal Tito, Yugoslavia functioned as a single entity, albeit with considerable repression of personal freedom for its citizens. This political situation is not unlike some trauma survivors who function in a state of rigid control in a chronic benumbed state with marked constriction of affect and social interaction. However, when the control breaks down, there is an irreversible fragmentation similar to the reemergence of the Balkan states following the fall of Communist Europe with renewed conflicts, hostilities, and destruction. Peacemaking efforts with the states of the former Yugoslavia failed, and an uneasy truce was only restored when the warring parties agreed to peace, with NATO forces acting only to facilitate their agreements. In a similar fashion, no therapeutic efforts can bring about internal agreements within the conflicted personality systems of DID patients unless the patient as a whole is motivated to do so.

Work with personalities that present as young children often brings a different kind of vulnerability to making errors in the psychotherapy. Therapists are frequently confronted with situations in which child alter personalities ask to be cared for, held, or nurtured by the therapist. Some child personalities are able to present in such a believable and disarming manner that the therapist sometimes loses sight of the fact that the child personalities exist as only a part of an adult patient. Therapists should keep in mind that child personalities need to conform to the constraints of reality, including the reality that the patient must function as an adult for the most part, both outside the therapy and frequently in therapy sessions as well. Child personalities cannot rely on their therapists as the primary source of gratification and nurturing. In practical experience it seems inevitable that therapists have some role in providing care and nurturing for the child personalities of the patient. However, any such nurturing should be viewed only as modeling to help patients begin to take care of themselves. Extensive "reparenting" schemes are almost always ill advised and have questionable therapeutic value. Any kind of reparenting should be predominately from within the patient (Greaves, 1988; Putnam, 1989). Internal soothing and nurturing is often difficult as the adult personalities in DID patients are often resistant to internal caretaking of child personalities. Early abusive experiences often seem to have resulted in patients having to disavow and dissociate their identities as children and their legitimate infantile needs. Often the DID system reinforces this separation. For example, it is common to find angry and persecutory personalities that punish child personalities in order to teach them that it isn't safe to want nurturing and to trust others. Therapists must insist that adult personalities begin to have empathy for the distress of internal child parts and to care for and nurture them as part of learning self-care and self-soothing.

A focus on personalities rather than the personality system also allows the patient to maintain split ambivalent feelings. The intense ambivalence of childhood abuse survivors about important issues (e.g. wanting to live/wanting to die, wanting to trust/fearing relationships, remembering the past/blocking out the past) may be apportioned to the various personalities in DID patients, with dissociated parts holding radically different views and feelings. It is easy for therapists to forget that they are dealing with only a part of their patient at any given time, and not to consider the omnipresent internal ambivalence and conflict. Thus, therapists may find themselves understanding the patient with a very narrow perspective and advocating certain stances that are at odds with the patient's interests as a whole. This kind of situation is frequently aggravated by the patient's understandable wish to keep conflict and ambivalence out of the therapy, as in the following example:

Anita, the host personality of a patient with DID, began arguing persuasively for more aggressive exploration of past traumatic experiences. The therapist sensed that exploration was premature and was reluctant to pursue such a course. Anita became angry and accused the therapist of blocking her psychological healing, of not wanting to hear about her abuse, and of not being able to handle the stressful emotional consequences of the abuse. Although he denied this, the therapist himself began to wonder if this were true. However, after some consultation, he said to Anita, "I know you feel strongly that you want to get to the abusive events of your childhood. However, are you aware that there may be other parts of you that would almost certainly be completely overwhelmed by these memories, and that other parts of you would be frightened and angry by having the memories at this point? I will be much more comfortable working on the memories when you have better internal communication and an overall better sense of safety and stability."

In the treatment of DID patients, increasing internal communication is a crucial task. The amnestic and dissociative barriers are significant liabilities. These barriers not only preclude a sense of continuous awareness, but also predispose patients and therapists to make decisions without an awareness of the full range of the patient's thoughts and feelings. Thus, even from the beginning of treatment, the therapy must encourage and reinforce the relationship of various personalities to the personality system as a whole (e.g., "I know you have the experience of just going away, but I want to encourage you to stay and feel painful feelings or to try to stay close when other parts of you emerge"). The patients must see themselves as a kind of family system (albeit dysfunctional) that must find a way to act in harmony without exploiting, scapegoating, or attempting to destroy any member of the family. Of course, the need for helping the DID "family" system to achieve some sense of cohesion and harmony is particularly urgent since ultimately this family cannot literally separate or split up.

DID PHENOMENOLOGY

DID can be dramatic in its presentation and has proven to be a fascinating phenomenon (Kluft, 1988, 1989b). Even to sophisticated professionals, DID is fascinating as a model of the human psyche. In DID, one sees the separation of psychic structures, where hypothesized phenomena such as introjects and the punitive superego present as distinct entities. DID is also a model for understanding how overwhelming life events affect the human mind and how dissociative mechanisms can provide at least temporary adaptive protection. In addition, the changeability of DID patients or the extraordinary circumstances of their backgrounds arouses the voyeuristic traits of virtually all persons. However, excessive fascination or preoccupation with DID phenomenology can also have a number of untoward effects, including prolonging the patient's use of dysfunctional dissociative defenses and a tendency to overdiagnose DID.

Overt therapist fascination about DID phenomenology leads to considerable secondary gain for patients in terms of maintaining the attention of the therapist. The therapists who, in past years, have appeared on television or radio, or who have written books with their DID patients, may have allowed their patients to develop and solidify a primary identity as DID patients, which is hardly an ideal outcome. However, even more subtle preoccupation with the phenomenon of DID can sidetrack or obscure the main work of the psychotherapy, as in the following example:

> Katie, a 21-year-old woman with DID, was admitted to the hospital. The outpatient therapist informed the inpatient team that the patient had a total of 76 alter personalities. He was able to describe the personalities in detail, citing differences in appearance, age, gender, mannerisms, and other characteristics. Katie showed frequent and precipitous personality switches on the ward and was generally out of control, with flashbacks and other dissociative symptoms. The inpatient treatment team introduced a treatment regimen to help the patient achieve a sense of control over her behavior. As her behavior stabilized, it became clearer that Katie had focused on her personalities as a way of ignoring her continuing frequent contacts with her father, who had been a perpetrator of abuse. She and her outpatient therapist were urged to focus on issues of personal and psychological safety rather than on the manifestations of DID. Although both Katie and therapist were somewhat resistant to this idea, they were eventually able to find a way to work with the patient's personalities in the context of rational overall treatment goals.

The various manifestations of DID are at the extreme end of a dissociative continuum (Bernstein & Putnam, 1986; Braun, 1986). Although DID may be more prevalent than previously thought, less severe syndromes of dissociation are even more common. In two studies, severe dissociative symptoms were found in approximately 20% of psychiatric inpatients, and full-blown DID was apparent in approximately 5% of inpatients (Chu & Dill, 1990; Ross et al., 1990). This suggests that three quarters of patients with significant dissociative syndromes do *not* have DID. This group of patients can easily be confused as having DID, and therapists' preoccupation with DID phenomenology can lead to their overdiagnosing DID (Chu, 1991a).

There is considerable evidence against the notion of iatrogenesis of DID in patients who do not already have dissociative symptoms (Braun, 1984, 1989; Ross, Norton, & Fraser, 1989). However, patients who have dissociative symptoms but do not have DID may consciously or unconsciously exaggerate their symptoms. Particularly in inpatient settings and outpatient groups, an identity as a DID patient, with distinct, well-defined, and dramatic symptomatology, may seem appealing. Therapists must help patients to understand and cope with existing symptomatology and must not even subtly encourage patients toward greater degrees of dissociation. For example, therapists should not label ego-state phenomena (Watkins & Watkins, 1989) as "personalities." Therapists should use unifying language consistent with the least degree of fragmentation that the patient is able to accept; for example, "part" and "aspect" are preferable to "personality" or "person." Therapists should also avoid naming of personalities that do not already have names. Overall, careful attention to the needs of the patient should be a priority with the clear therapeutic intent of decreasing the level of dissociative fragmentation.

Various specialized treatment interventions can be found in a variety of papers and texts (e.g., Putnam, 1989; Ross, 1989). However, the use of any specialized treatment should conform to the following criteria:

1. The use of any treatments must adhere to the general principles of understanding and treating traumatized patients.
2. Clinicians must be skilled in any modality utilized (e.g., hypnosis, expressive therapy, psychomotor therapy, EMDR).
3. Principles of good psychotherapy must be respected.

Clinicians must be clear that the majority of the interventions used in the treatment of DID and complex dissociative disorders involve the same fundamental skills that are used with all patients. Only a relatively few specialized perspectives and interventions are essential in the treatment of dissociative disorder patients.

SUMMARY

The successful treatment of DID patients depends on a thoughtful and rational approach. As with all severely traumatized patients, dissociative disorder patients must be encouraged to build solid coping skills before moving on to abreaction and eventual integration. Premature abreaction has little value other than venting dysphoric affect. Until patients can control dysfunctional behavior, tolerate intense affect, and maintain good collaborative relationships, they cannot work through traumatic events, and premature abreaction is largely retraumatizing. Therapists must also respect the need to proceed carefully in the process of uncovering personalities. DID patients' intense interpersonal vulnerability should be respected, and therapists should use good clinical judgment to guide the therapeutic process.

The rational treatment of DID must always primarily focus on the treatment of the patient who has DID and not on the personalities or DID phenomenology. The various personalities should be acknowledged, and the therapist needs to be skillful in working with them. However, the various personalities must always be considered as part of an overall family system, and the goals of the work should be toward increased communication, cooperation, and integration. Therapists should keep in mind that excessive fascination or preoccupation with DID may interfere with patients' treatment or even encourage the development of further fragmentation.

An important teacher in the modern study of DID, the late David Caul, M.D., observed, "Therapists should always remember that good basic psychotherapy is the first order of treatment regardless of any specific diagnosis" (Chu, 1992a). This sage advice should be heeded by all therapists involved in the treatment of dissociative disorders. The treatment of patients who have survived profound childhood abuse is challenging for even experienced therapists, and the difficulties that these patients present can lead to serious pitfalls and impasses. However, good clinical judgment and the use of sound psychotherapeutic practices permit rational and productive treatment for even the most challenging DID patients.

CHAPTER 12

Hospitalization, Acute Care, and Psychopharmacology*

SEVERELY TRAUMATIZED patients maintain a tenuous homeostasis between numbing and intrusion, control and dyscontrol, and interpersonal connection and alienation. They often have brittle defenses that shatter in the face of stress or changes in the external environment. Current traumatic events or reminders of a past traumatic event may result in powerful intrusive symptomatology. For example, an assault or even a prolonged and painful childbirth may trigger memories of past sexual abuse. Therapeutic efforts may increase intrusive symptomatology. Overly intensive psychotherapy or self-help groups that focus on traumatic experiences may bring on intrusive thoughts, feelings, and recollections, as well as autonomic arousal in the form of heightened anxiety, irritability, and nightmares.

Changes in the patient's external environment are frequent precipitants to the decompensations that require acute care, such as hospitalization or partial hospital treatment. The loss of supportive relationships or important external supports, either temporarily or permanently, often lies behind increases in symptomatology. The breakup or deterioration of relationships (including dysfunctional relationships); the sudden lack of availability, departure, or death of a friend; the loss of a job or other regular activity; and the vacation of a therapist are frequent etiologies of decompensation. These events tend to trigger the dysphoria, anger, panic, helplessness, and despair associated with previous traumatic experiences. Unfortunately, as a result of the relational patterns that derive from their early abusive experiences,

---

*Portions of this chapter are adapted from the articles "Trauma and dissociative disorders" (Chu, 1997b) and "Inpatient treatment of dissociative identity disorder" (Chu & Terk, in press). Karen Terk, R.N., M.S., contributed to the section in this chapter titled "Hospital Treatment for Trauma-Related Disorders."

patients often are unable to turn to others for support. They feel isolated and overwhelmed, and often resort to ingrained dysfunctional solutions. Many of these solutions—including self-destructive or suicidal behaviors, risk taking or addictive activity, and aggression or other kinds of acting out—can result in the need for acute psychiatric care. Traditionally such care was provided in a hospital setting, but is now often provided in residential or partial hospital settings.

One particular situation merits special emphasis. Patients' flight into isolation from others results in a profound experience of aloneness. While such a course may seem safest to patients, it leaves them with only themselves and their self-hate. Behind many complicated scenarios of decompensation in traumatized patients lies a simple formulation. Patients who are left alone with their own self-blame and self-loathing often turn to self-destruction or other dysfunctional behaviors as a way of alleviating an intolerable internal experience.

ASSESSMENT

It is crucial to evaluate psychiatric decompensation with post-traumatic and dissociative symptoms in the context of psychosocial issues and the patient's external environment. Given the common formulation of psychosocial stressors resulting in increased symptomatology and dysfunctional attempts to cope, comprehensive treatment must be focused not only on the symptomatology itself, but also on ameliorating the stressors that precipitated decompensation. For example, a patient may present with symptoms such as traumatic nightmares or flashbacks. In addition to attempts to contain and alleviate these symptoms, attention must also be directed toward their precipitants, such as the loss of an important supportive relationship or a current abusive relationship that repetitively threatens the patient. The following case illustrates some of the complexities of assessment:

> Lucy, a 27-year-old married woman with dissociative identity disorder (DID), was admitted to the hospital in crisis. She internally heard the voice of a personality that threatened to hurt her. She also was having nearly constant flashbacks of sexual molestation that occurred when she was a teenager. Lucy was initially uncommunicative on the ward and had to be physically restrained on two occasions when she was having flashbacks and began banging her head into a wall. She reacted angrily to the restraints and accused staff members of being abusive. She convinced her inpatient therapist that she needed to work through her adolescent rapes. However, after a week of tumultuous and frightening abreactions, Lucy appeared to be more regressed and was acutely suicidal. Because her treatment did not appear to be helping her, the treatment team carefully reviewed her circumstances. It was eventually ascertained that an incident of somewhat aggressive sexual contact with her husband prior to

admission had frightened her. Lucy told her outpatient therapist about this in the next session, after which the therapist announced he would be going on vacation. It was at this point that the acute, symptoms began. In reviewing the events prior to admission, it was felt that Lucy's decompensation had been triggered by the sexual interaction with her husband, which was then compounded by the therapist's vacation (perceived as abandonment). In view of this information, the treatment team shifted approaches. The outpatient therapist was brought in as part of the treatment team, and the husband was engaged in a series of couples meetings to negotiate safety at home. On the ward, active efforts were made to help the patient with grounding techniques to control her florid dissociative symptoms. Aftercare arrangements were a focus of the treatment, and the patient was discharged without incident in several days.

A dual focus is particularly important when working with patients with severe dissociative disorders. Their intriguing and shifting presentations may often hide the mundane realities that cause their current distress. In many ways, such therapeutic difficulties are not surprising. After all, post-traumatic and dissociative defenses are utilized to distance and disavow stressful events; the patient's psychological gain is in *not* attending to them. However, any successful resolution of a crisis situation necessitates both symptomatic control and restoration of a safe and stable external environment.

Another important area is the ongoing outpatient treatment. Acute intensive treatment such as hospitalization offers the opportunity for consultation to such treatment. Such consultations must be performed with great sensitivity, as there appear to be particular characteristics of severely traumatized patients and their therapy that normatively result in painful clinical dilemmas (Chu, 1988; Kluft, 1988; Pearlman & Saakvitne, 1995a). As a result, ongoing treaters often find themselves beleaguered, emotionally drained, and uncertain and defensive about what they are doing. Issues regarding the pacing of the therapy, transference–countertransference binds, defining treatment goals, setting limits, and maintaining boundaries are all common dilemmas in ongoing treatment. Given the similar dynamics generated by the patient in both inpatient and outpatient settings, the inpatient therapist is in a unique position to be able to empathize with the dilemmas posed by the patient and to consult with the outpatient therapist. If this kind of consultation is done sensitively, supportively, and effectively, the beneficial effects of inpatient hospitalization on the patient's treatment may extend well beyond the hospital stay.

DIFFERENTIAL DIAGNOSIS

In any situation necessitating acute care, the therapist should carefully examine the differential diagnosis between post-traumatic and dissociative disorders and other psychiatric conditions. The therapist must also consider the development or exacerbation of a comorbid condition as a reason for acute decompensation. Comorbidity of post-traumatic disorders and other *DSM* Axis I disorders is common, with a number of studies showing comorbidity in the range of 60–99% (Breslau, Davis, Andreski, & Peterson, 1991; Kessler, Sonnega, Bromet, Hughes, & Nelson, 1995; Kulka et al., 1990; Shore, Vollmer, & Tatum, 1989). These findings may make sense in that features of trauma-related disorders may be similar to the symptoms of other syndromes. Post-traumatic and dissociative disorders have sometimes been described as "umbrella disorders" because a wide variety of symptoms may be understood as part of a traumatically based syndrome. For example, the dysphoria, emotional constriction, and social withdrawal of post traumatic stress disorder (PTSD) may be similar to symptoms to depressive disorders. The illusions of post-traumatic flashbacks and the hallucinations and thought insertion associated with severe dissociative disorders are easily confused with psychosis. The National Comorbidity Study (Kessler et al., 1995) found that traumatic events often preceded the development of other Axis I disorders, suggesting that the post-traumatic disorders are often primary umbrella disorders.

The differential diagnosis of post-traumatic disorders from mood disorders can be subtle. Time-limited assessment of patients may fail to distinguish between traumatized patients and those with more biologically oriented major depression. One study comparing *DSM-III* criteria for depression between a group of patients with a history of childhood physical or sexual abuse and a group of nonabused patients with a diagnosis of major depression failed to show significant differences between the two groups—including no differences in neurovegetative signs (Chu, Dill, & Murphy, 1990). There were subtle distinguishing features in that members of the traumatized group were more likely to report being afraid to go to sleep (afraid of loss of control) and had more awakenings during the nights and more anxiety upon awakening.

The switches in self-states often seen in severe dissociative disorders may mimic the mood changes of bipolar disorder. In general, dissociative switches are more rapid than the cycling of bipolar disorder. And although sleep disturbance is common in both post-traumatic and dissociative disorders, total sleep time is maintained at a minimum of 4 hours per night. Sleep disturbances that persist at levels less than 2 or 3 hours per night are more consistent with mania or hypomania, particularly in the presence of high energy upon awakening.

Symptoms of some post-traumatic and dissociative disorders also may mimic psychotic symptomatology. Chu and Dill's (1990) study of adult psychiatric patients with histories of childhood abuse demonstrated an elevated level of psychotism on the MMPI, which might be explained by the observations of some investigators that symptoms such as hallucinations and even Schneiderian "first rank" symptoms of schizophrenia frequently occur in severe dissociative disorders (Kluft, 1987a). Recurrent brief reactive psychoses should be examined to determine whether they represent post-traumatic flashbacks or dissociative state switches. Intense visual, auditory, somatic, and olfactory illusions or hallucinations are frequent components of flashbacks, and auditory hallucinations are common in severe dissociative disorders as dissociated self-states talk to other parts of the self. Differential diagnosis concerning auditory hallucinations may be enhanced by the characteristics of the hallucinations. Dissociative hallucinations almost always are heard as coming from inside the head and are generally a familiar set of voices over time. Psychotic auditory hallucinations tend to be more bizarre (e.g., voices from the radio or TV), heard from both inside and outside the head, and are variable over time.

Other Axis I disorders may offer ways of coping with the dysphoria of post-traumatic conditions. A history of traumatization, particularly childhood abuse, is high in patients with substance abuse (Kessler et al., 1995; Loftus, Polonsky, & Fullilove, 1994; National Victim Center, Crime Victims Research and Treatment Center, 1992), eating disorders (Hall, Tice, Beresford, Wooley, & Hall, 1986; Welch & Fairburn, 1994), and somatization (Barsky, Wool, Barnett, & Clearly, 1994; Morrison, 1989; Pribor & Dinwiddie, 1992; Pribor, Yutzy, Dean, & Wetzel, 1993). The psychological numbing of substance intoxication eases the distress of post-traumatic numbing and isolation and may ease awareness of disturbing symptoms such as amnesia or state switches. Moreover, intoxication may offer an opportunity for persons to release internal tension by acting out intense feelings associated with traumatic events. Eating disorders and somatization are avenues in which persons can focus away from past distressing events and can structure their lives around preoccupation with bodily concerns.

Differential diagnosis is further complicated in situations in which there is true comorbidity (i.e., two or more disorders, not simply one disorder mimicking another). Very often, a patient presents with pronounced post-traumatic symptoms rather than clear evidence of the other disorder. One hypothesis for this kind of presentation is that because PTSD and dissociative disorder are responses to stress, the onset of another disorder such as mood disorder or an acute psychosis results in more stress to the individual, thus increasing post-traumatic responses. In virtually all situations in which there is true comorbidity of Axis I disorders, the trauma-related disorder has *secondary* importance in the hierarchy of treatment. That is, any acute mood disorder or psychosis, out-of-control substance use, or eating disorder should be treated prior to embarking on treatment for the post-traumatic or dissociative disorder. The following case illustrates this principle:

> Esther, a 53-year-old single woman, was admitted to a psychiatric hospital with florid PTSD symptoms. She almost continuously had intrusive thoughts

about known physical and sexual abuse that had occurred when she was abandoned as a child and raised in a series of foster homes and institutions. She was particularly fearful at night, having flashbacks and seeing images of menacing men outside her window. A closer examination of her symptoms suggested that Esther was suffering from major depression with psychotic features. She showed extreme psychomotor retardation, barely moving from her bed or chair, had sustained a recent 20-pound weight loss, and spoke of feeling that her insides were decaying. A brief course of electroconvulsive treatment, followed by medication, brought about a remarkable change. She recompensated with both an improvement in her mood and PTSD symptoms. Although she still thought about her early abuse, the thoughts did not overly disturb her and she was able to return to her previous level of functioning.

Therapeutic efforts must be directed at any active biologic processes. Little progress will be made in treating experiences of traumatization in the presence of a major affective or psychotic disorder. Additionally, the biologic expressions of PTSD (including heightened reactivity, chronic severe anxiety, disturbed sleep, and explosiveness) must be addressed. These difficulties are intensely distressing and may interfere with the psychological management of other symptoms. In addition to the use of medications, other strategies such as relaxation training and self-soothing techniques can be utilized in efforts to reduce autonomic overactivation.

Finally, comorbid personality disorder characteristics are almost inevitably present in hospitalized patients with post-traumatic and dissociative disorders because these characterologic difficulties predispose patients to decompensation. The presence of borderline personality disorder or traits has major implications for inpatient treatment. Patients with borderline psychopathology are likely to have extreme difficulty engaging in new relationships, including the therapeutic alliances necessary for treatment. Such patients are likely to approach new relationships with mistrust engendered by abusive past interactions. This understandable mistrust complicates inpatient treatment because patients hold on to their isolation and dysfunctional ways of coping rather than engaging in supportive alliances. Many borderline patients find the intensity of the therapeutic relationship with a single therapist anxiety provoking, and the prospect of having to engage with multiple members of an inpatient treatment team may seem extremely threatening.

PSYCHOPHARMACOLOGY

The careful pharmacological treatment of patients with trauma-related disorders can be beneficial. A variety of psychotropic medications have been proposed as effective treatments for PTSD. Antidepressants have been the most studied agents in the treatment of PTSD: Investigations have shown efficacy of MAO inhibitors (Kosten, 1992), tricyclic antidepressants (Davidson et al., 1993; Davidson et al., 1990; Kosten, 1992; Reist et al., 1989), and selective serotonin reuptake inhibitors (Davidson, Roth, & Newman, 1991; Klein, 1994; Nagy, Morgan, Southwick, & Charney, 1993; van der Kolk et al., 1994). Studies also have suggested that anticonvulsants (Fesler, 1991; Lipper et al., 1986; Wolf, Alavi, & Mosnaim, 1988), propranolol (Famularo, Kinscherff, & Fenton, 1988; Kolb, Burris, & Griffiths, 1984), and clonidine (Kinzie & Leung, 1989; Kolb et al., 1984) may be helpful. One open trial suggested that use of the benzodiazepine clonazepam may be helpful for controlling post-traumatic symptoms in dissociative identity disorder (Loewenstein, Hornstein, & Farber, 1988). However, the use of medication in treating dissociative disorders has been much less systematically studied, and there is cautious agreement that medications should not be the primary therapeutic interventions (Putnam, 1989; Ross, 1989). Despite evidence from the studies cited here, the usefulness of medications for the treatment of trauma-related disorders remains unclear. A number of these studies were open trials, and most investigated specific traumatized populations (e.g., combat veterans). Further investigations that control for chronicity of traumatization, severity of symptomatology, and premorbid adjustment will clarify the role of medications in treating post-traumatic and dissociative symptoms.

Many patients with post-traumatic and dissociative disorders have significant dysphoria, mood lability, disturbed sleep, and hyperarousal that do not readily respond to standard antidepressant treatment. In practical clinical experience, however, antidepressants often are used for PTSD and dissociative disorders, even in the absence of an independent major depression. Although these agents rarely eliminate depressed mood and dysphoria, some clinicians have observed an increase in energy with the use of activating tricyclic antidepressants such as nortriptyline and desipramine, MAO inhibitors, or selective serotonin reuptake inhibitors. Similarly, benzodiazepines commonly are used for both panic attacks and chronic anxiety. However, if possible, benzodiazepines should be used acutely rather than routinely because they carry the risks of tolerance and habituation and may disinhibit destructive impulses and behavioral dyscontrol. Patients' anxiety usually cannot be completely resolved, but medication can help reduce panic so that patients are able to work psychologically.

Disturbed sleep also is common in traumatized patients. As noted previously, patients are likely to fear going to sleep and to wake up repeatedly with high anxiety and/or nightmares. Benzodiazepines are usually of limited effectiveness over time. Proper sleep hygiene (getting out of bed and staying awake during the day) may be of some help, as are other practical measures such as getting adequate exercise. Trazodone, a sedating antidepressant, has been used in doses of 25 mg to 200 mg. Zolpidem (Ambien), a non-benzodiazepine hypnotic, has a reduced risk of habituation, but the effects of long-term use remain unclear.

The use of neuroleptic or antipsychotic medications is controversial. Some patients are so overwhelmed by constant flashbacks, intense dysphoria, and intrusive thoughts that they appear to benefit from the use of low-dose neuroleptic medications (Saporta & Case, 1984). However, the question of whether neuroleptic medication should be continued on a long-term basis should be carefully reviewed with the patient, especially considering effects on mental alertness, cognitive abilities, and the risk of tardive dyskinesia. The newer generation of antipsychotic medications, particularly risperidone, may offer some of the advantages of neuroleptics but a reduced risk of anticholinergic and Parkinsonian side effects (and perhaps less risk of tardive dyskinesia). Recent clinical experience with risperidone, given as a bedtime dose of 0.5 mg to 3 mg, has shown promise as an effective medication for post-traumatic conditions as it appears to help with sleep and to reduce autonomic overactivation on the following day.

HOSPITAL TREATMENT FOR
TRAUMA-RELATED DISORDERS

The post-traumatic and dissociative symptomatology of traumatized patients are often difficult and challenging problems to professionals who work in inpatient settings. In addition, the atmosphere of crisis and the involvement of many members of the inpatient treatment team usually complicate an already complex treatment. In order for treatment to be productive, the philosophy and structures of inpatient hospitalization must be clearly understood, and some of the potential pitfalls presented by severely traumatized patients should be recognized and addressed.

THERAPEUTIC PHILOSOPHY

A general acceptance of trauma-related disorders is essential for the successful hospital treatment of patients with post-traumatic and dissociative disorders. Hospital administrative support is necessary (Kluft, 1991; Ross, 1989) to provide the resources for the sometimes intensive treatment interventions. In addition, the risks involved in treating patients who are chronically self-destructive and impulsive must be understood. The senior clinical staff of the unit, specifically including the medical director and nurse manager, must be supportive and knowledgeable about the treatment of trauma-related disorders. Without such support, the treatment team will be unable to sustain the treatment approaches and staff cohesion that are necessary for productive treatment. The professionals on the treatment team who provide the psychotherapy for individual patients must also have a high level of acceptance about trauma-related disorders as well as sophistication about treatment. In the case of DID, it is not essential for each member of the staff to believe in the diagnosis, as long as there is agreement to pursue a unified and coherent treatment approach (Kluft, 1991; Steinmeyer, 1991). This kind of approach is crucial because the potential for conflicts in the treatment teams of DID patients is high. In fact, without active efforts to maintain a unified and coherent treatment approach, it is common for the treatment to flounder as the treatment team begins to reflect the projected internal fragmentation of the patient.

In addition to accepting the diagnosis, the ward therapeutic milieu must place a high value on respect and collaboration, as opposed to authoritarian attitudes and control. In actual practice, this type of philosophy is difficult to maintain. The out-of-control behaviors of many traumatized patients often invite more than the limit-setting needed to stabilize the treatment. Often, inpatient unit staff members find themselves responding to dysfunctional patient behaviors with an ever-increasing array of rigid rules and policies that eventually make flexibility or collaboration impossible. Basic unit rules concerning important treatment issues are essential, but care should be exercised to avoid the tendency to collude with patients' compulsion to reenact the abusive relationships of their childhoods in the milieu.

Interpersonal relationships should have high value in the treatment of traumatized patients. In addition to relationships between patients and their inpatient treatment teams, important relationships include those between patients and community therapists, families, partners, and other persons who provide social support. The treatment of traumatized patients should include all important individuals in the patient's outside life. Specifically, anyone living and interacting with the patient should be involved in the treatment, and the unit should make active efforts to involve community therapists and to foster and maintain outside therapeutic relationships.

Personal responsibility should be a hallmark in the philosophy of inpatient treatment of patients with post-traumatic and dissociative disorders. Prior to admission, patients are frequently overwhelmed by the burdens of maintaining control, such as refraining from impulsive and self-destructive behavior and modulating symptomatology. Some patients see being in the hospital as a welcome relief from having to stay in control and an opportunity to let down their defenses (Kluft, 1991). This often results in patients letting go of personal responsibility and placing hospital staff in the position of taking care of them. This shift of therapeutic responsibility is untenable, and patients must be willing to assume as much personal responsibility as possible during their hospitalizations. It is unworkable and regressive for the inpatient staff to take full responsibility for such issues as personal safety and behavioral control. Patients should be expected to monitor their own capabilities and seek out help should they need it.

PSYCHOEDUCATION

Psychoeducation about the process of treatment is extremely important in the inpatient treatment of PTSD and dissociative disorder patients. In particular, patients must learn and understand how to pace the therapeutic work. Virtually all traumatized patients admitted to inpatient settings are in early stages of their treatment, and many are attempting to do abreactive work prior to building adequate psychotherapeutic foundations. In fact, the underlying difficulty of many hospitalized patients is that they (and sometimes their therapists) have been attempting to purge themselves of their abusive childhood experiences long before they have built up the requisite relational skills and coping capacities that make productive abreaction possible. The task for most hospitalized PTSD and dissociative disorder patients is to learn how to maintain control—letting go and letting down defenses is rarely a problem.

Current accepted models of treatment staging (Chu, 1992c; Herman, 1992; Lebowitz, Harvey, & Herman, 1993) emphasize that safety, containment, and stabilization are prerequisites for abreaction of trauma, which will most likely occur outside a hospital setting. Any attempts at abreaction of past traumatic experiences during episodes of acute care must be approached cautiously. A few patients who have mastered the tasks of early-stage treatment may benefit from a circumscribed amount of abreactive therapy in the hospital. However, this kind of work should be limited in scope and carefully monitored because patients are extremely prone to again becoming overwhelmed. There are common clinical situations in which patients must be able to discuss some of the memories of past abuse—not to do so would create more problems. In these situations, patient and therapist must share the burden of limiting the extent of work about the traumatic material, and must avoid the trap of believing that just one more piece of abreactive work would result in full resolution of the current difficulties. In past years, elective hospitalization was used to support patients in later stages of treatment during particularly difficult abreactions (Kluft, 1991; Sakheim, Hess, & Chivas, 1988). This kind of support has often been helpful to patients while working through horrendous past experiences. However, given the economic realities of the health care environment, such elective admissions are likely to become increasingly rare.

LIMITS AND BOUNDARIES

Although authoritarian attitudes and controlling stances are not productive in the treatment of patients with post-traumatic and dissociative disorders, clear limits and boundaries are essential to minimize regression and foster therapeutic growth (Braun, 1993; Caul, 1978; Chu, 1992c; Courtois, 1988; Davies & Frawley, 1994; Herman, 1992; Pearlman & Saakvitne, 1995; Putnam, 1989; Ross, 1989; Steinmeyer, 1991). Limits and boundaries are crucial to help maintain the treatment frame, to encourage patients to exercise control of dysfunctional behaviors, and to maintain the hospital therapeutic milieu. Limits and boundaries are particularly important given the intensity of involvement between traumatized patients and staff. These patients often require a high level of involvement with staff members since trauma-related problems, such as management of reexperiencing phenomena and personality switching, require considerable time and effort. The mistrust with which traumatized patients approach relationships may require some additional staff involvement in order for these patients to feel safe. However, there need to be clear limits on the extent of staff involvement both to prevent staff exhaustion and to encourage patients to learn to meet some of their own needs for reassurance and care.

Out-of-control behaviors—including repetitive self-mutilating or self-destructive behaviors, verbal abuse or violence, and prolonged abreactions—should not be tolerated in PTSD and dissociative disorder patients. Patients should be expected to conform their behavior to unit norms as a condition of their treatment. Placing limits on patients places the burden on them to find alternate ways of expressing themselves or to contain abreactions to appropriate settings. Patients must begin to work with the treatment team to achieve control. Intermittent lapses in control are inevitable due to the nature of patients' difficulties and are expectable and understandable. However, lapses due to patients' failure to strive for control are not therapeutically acceptable.

DISSOCIATIVE DISORDER ISSUES

The characteristics of dissociative disorder inpatients predispose their treatment to particular difficulties. As psychiatrist Frank Putnam (1989) noted:

> Once a patient is admitted, perceptions of the hospital can change dramatically and rapidly. Within a short time, most multiples will have alters emerge who experience the hospital as a frightening and traumatizing place. Normal hospital procedures and routines, such as medications, milieu activities, privilege status, pass restrictions, and other unit rules are perceived as coercive and traumatizing. (p. 272)

DID patients who have difficulty building supportive alliances often engage with hospital staff in a way that reenacts the control struggles and abuses of their childhoods. Patients may also project their internal fragmentation onto various staff members, resulting a particularly intense form of "staff splitting" (Braun, 1993; Putnam, 1989; Ross, 1989; Steinmeyer, 1991). Some staff members are viewed as hostile and abusive, and others are seen as nurturing and understanding; this problem is aggravated by the tendency of staff to have markedly differing views of DID patients (Kluft, 1991).

The initial assessment of patients with dissociative symptoms is crucial, particularly for patients with DID symptoms. Historically, relatively few patients were admitted to hospitals with a diagnosis of DID. However, in recent years, it has become necessary to determine both when a patient has DID and when a patient does *not* have DID (Chu, 1991a). It is particularly important to distinguish between patients with full-blown DID and the many patients who have a lesser degree of dissociation or some other kind of post-traumatic disorder. After all, treatment should be designed to decrease dissociative symptoms and should not reify dissociative symptoms that are consciously or unconsciously exaggerated. Clinicians also should consider the possibility of factitious or malingered DID, particularly in a forensic context or where there are compelling secondary gains (Brick & Chu, 1991; Chu, 1991a; Kluft, 1987c).

All therapeutic work with DID patients must be approached as work with a single (although fragmented) person rather than with individual personalities. During a time of crisis such as hospitalization, all work with personalities should emphasize conflict resolution and stabilization. The patient's cooperation must be obtained in this venture, and hospital staff must encourage and reinforce interpersonality communication, understanding, and acceptance.

DID patients must not learn that having DID makes them special. Furthermore, even though the hospital environment buffers DID patients from some of the demands of the outside environment, patients need to exercise control to respond to routine demands of their surroundings. Psychiatrist Colin Ross (1989) had some excellent practical suggestions:

> We expect our patients to follow regular ward guidelines and procedures. They do not have special rooms, they eat with other patients, and the consequences for unacceptable conduct are generally the same as for other patients. (p. 291)

Ross suggested that out-of-control switching should not be allowed in the ward milieu and that child alter personalities should generally be allowed to have executive control only in psychotherapy. As a general rule, DID patients are expected to conform to usual adult standards of behavior in the public areas of the hospital unit.

NURSING PRACTICE

Hospitalized patients with histories of severe traumatization often fear that they will be subject to excessive control and mistreatment. In a hospital setting, members of the nursing staff bear the brunt of this mistrust because of their role in monitoring and managing the milieu and the inherent authority and control over patients' daily lives. Thus, nursing staff members have a major responsibility for establishing and maintaining a therapeutic alliance with patients. Staff members must have a sophisticated understanding of the effects of early abuse and must be able to empathize with patients' difficulties. They should be able to project the therapeutic attitudes of acceptance and respect. They should be skilled in bridging mistrust during control struggles, and in setting limits and establishing boundaries.

The negotiation of the therapeutic alliance begins at the time of admission, when issues such as privileges, rooming arrangements, and unit rules provide areas of potential conflict. Patients should be treated respectfully, but patients must also respect the judgments of the staff and the real limitations of the hospital environment. For example, attempts should be made to accommodate the patient in terms of comfort and privacy (e.g., room location or roommate), but nursing staff members also must be allowed to consider and weigh the clinical needs of all the patients and to make decisions based on their assessments. Similarly, DID patients should be accorded the respect of being called by the names they choose (Kluft, 1984a, 1991). However, it is unrealistic to expect that every staff member will consistently recognize (or even remember) each patient's different alter personalities (Kluft, 1991).

During an episode of acute care, most traumatized patients experience distress from intrusive reexperiencing of past abuse. Patients suffer overwhelming affects such as despair, panic, and rage, and may have impulses to flee, strike out, or hurt themselves. Effective nursing interventions are critical to patients. Daily structure can be helpful for patients who are experiencing intrusive symptoms such as flashbacks and nightmares. Planned activities as well as rest and recuperation are important components of a daily structure. Emotional support and medication also should be provided as necessary. It is helpful if the hospital setting has flexible rules about sleep and rest. Many patients are afraid of sleeping at night in a darkened room, especially if their abuse occurred at night. The use of night lights should be permitted, and patients should be allowed to get out of bed and sit quietly in an area close to staff members for brief periods of time. Patients may need to sleep for brief periods during the day if they did not get sufficient sleep during the previous night, but nursing staff members should be careful not to allow patients to completely reverse their sleep/awake cycles.

The management of flashbacks and other forms of traumatic reexperiencing involves the use of grounding techniques (Benham, 1995). Patients may find it helpful for a staff member to approach them and maintain contact with them until the flashback is over. The staff member should let the patient know that he or she is there and orient the patient to time and place.

Staff members may need to speak firmly and give specific instructions to help anchor the patient in the here and now. The following clinical example illustrates some common grounding techniques:

Ellen, a 26-year-old woman with DID, was found huddled in her closet shortly after admission. She appeared frightened and refused to speak to the nurse who found her, and instead stared at the wall while sucking her thumb. The nurse said, "You look very frightened and very young. You seem to be reliving something very frightening. My name is Sally, and I am a nurse in this hospital. I am here to help you, and I will not let you be hurt. I'd like you to try to understand that you are safe. I'd like you to try to look at me and remember that you know me as a safe person. I'd like you to try to look around and to feel yourself here with your feet on the floor, and to remember that you are safe in the hospital." Ellen was able to engage with the nurse, calm down, and emerge from the closet. She was observed closely for a time, until she could begin to talk about her distress and to reengage in the milieu.

The psychoeducation that patients receive on how to manage their symptoms often occurs through nursing interventions in the milieu. Nursing staff members are often the principal teachers of grounding techniques and other ways to help patients achieve control of dissociative symptoms and to pace the process of abreaction. Nursing staff members can help patients overwhelmed by past abusive events by encouraging containment of painful memories to therapy sessions. Patients can learn to control intrusive thoughts and feelings, rather than feeling controlled by them. In addition to grounding techniques, nursing staff members can use nonverbal means (e.g., visual imagery such as visualizing shutting the door on memories until therapy sessions). When patients become flooded, they can be encouraged to use artwork or journals for brief periods and then put them away.

Nursing staff members are in the unique position of being with patients during periods of crisis—often in the evening or at night. During such times they have the opportunity to reinforce important messages such as, "It wasn't your fault that you were hurt." Nursing staff members are able to participate in helping patients achieve crucial skills in self-care and self-soothing by maintaining adequate food and fluid intake, accessing medical attention, or simply taking a warm bath, reading, watching television, or going on a brisk walk. Nursing staff members also have the critical task of helping patients utilize other people during periods of crisis, especially by making contact with them and urging patients to trust their support.

INDIVIDUAL THERAPY AND CASE MANAGEMENT

Individual therapy and/or case management is critical in the treatment of complex patients with post-traumatic and dissociative conditions. The individual therapist or case manager is the central professional in formulating a dynamic understanding of the patient's difficulties and implementing a productive treatment plan. Therapists or case managers should be given the autonomy and authority to make important decisions about and with the patient during an acute care episode. Patients often are able to better tolerate hospitalization when decisions that affect them are made by someone who has taken the time to develop a trusting relationship, rather than when decisions are based on inflexible and rigid unit rules.

If possible, patients should be provided with individual therapy during their hospital course because some therapeutic gains are best realized in an individual trusting relationship. Therapists or case managers also are able to provide services such as specific interventions (e.g., negotiations between alter personalities in a patient with DID), liaison with outpatient professionals, family work, and aftercare planning. The individual therapy should be well integrated into the remainder of the inpatient treatment, and the work should pursue treatment goals common to the overall treatment plan. Although individual treatment is valuable, much of the therapy during the course of a hospitalization is derived not only from individual therapists but from many other members of the hospital staff, especially the nursing staff.

GROUP TREATMENT

The use of verbal groups in the acute treatment of traumatized patients has been controversial. Although group treatment for post-traumatic disorders has a long tradition (van der Kolk, 1993), the use of groups with dissociative disorders has been discouraged (Kluft, 1984a, 1991; Putnam, 1989). In practice, certain kinds of verbal groups cause regression whereas others appear to be helpful. Traditional psychotherapy groups that focus on relationships within the group and psychoanalytically based groups that tend to mobilize intense affect are contraindicated because they are too overwhelming for patients who have intense relational difficulties and affective instability. Groups that encourage or permit the discussion or details of past abusive experiences are also not useful because patients often are triggered by other patients' stories into reexperiencing their own trauma.

Verbal groups that are focused on particular tasks appear to be useful for many traumatized patients. Some of these groups deal with current symptomatology and the effects of past experiences, but explicitly do not permit detailed discussion of past abuse. These groups have a psychoeducational focus and discuss ways of coping with dissociative symptoms and intense feelings, ways to remain functional, and ways to sustain relationships. Some cognitive–behavioral groups (e.g., assertiveness training, relaxation groups) and gender issues groups (e.g., women's issues) also are helpful. Finally, the role of groups that involve activities is enormously valuable. Certain skill-building, task-oriented, or expressive groups also are helpful for patients whose self-esteem is shattered and who have little ability to use verbal modalities for relief of intense affect. Recreational activities are a welcome relief from the heavy burdens of psychotherapeutic work and are a good reminder that treatment is intended to improve the quality of patients' lives, not to consume them.

FAMILY WORK

Inpatient hospitalization usually brings family issues into the treatment arena. Families and other persons who are part of the patient's social support system almost always should be involved in the treatment. Spouses or partners may need support and education. More often, however, there are significant relationship problems, such as a partner who reenacts an abusive relationship, or conversely, a partner who is overinvolved and overprotective. Children in the home should be assessed to determine whether they are at risk as a result of the patient's difficulties. Although many traumatized patients are exemplary parents, others involve their children in the transgenerational cycle of abuse or neglect because they are self-absorbed in their own difficulties (Kluft, 1987b).

In situations where patients have a history of intrafamilial childhood abuse, contact with families-of-origin is problematic. Premature disclosure of the abuse secret to family members is destabilizing to families' equilibrium and potentially has negative consequences for the patient and family. Most experts in the field of treatment of childhood abuse survivors suggest that disclosure and confrontation of a perpetrator should only occur when it is the patient's clear choice, when the patient can withstand the family's reactions, and when there is no expectation of apologies or reparations. This usually occurs relatively late in treatment—not during episodes of decompensation and acute care (Courtois, 1979; Herman, 1981; MacFarlane & Korbin, 1983; Schatzhow & Herman, 1989).

STAFF SUPPORT

Working with traumatized patients requires considerable staff involvement. Staff members must be willing to extend themselves to empathize with patients and to struggle with them to overcome their difficulties. This can be a psychologically exhausting task. Sometimes just sitting with someone who is reliving a trauma can be painful for staff members, who may have to confront their own overwhelming feelings. In addition, patients bring their intense emotions into the treatment arena, and often reenact the abusive relationships in the hospital setting. The anger and rage that result from childhood abuse can be overwhelming, and patients may displace their anger onto hospital staff members.

Hospitalized patients with PTSD and dissociative disorders are often in crisis. Difficult situations that are common in the hospital include episodes of self-destructive behaviors (including suicide attempts, suicidal gestures, self-mutilation, substance abuse, and eating problems), violence and out-of-control behaviors that may require restraint, and even flight from the hospital. All these kinds of crises create high levels of anxiety, anger, and guilt in hospital staff members. Staff members commonly worry that they should have been able to prevent crises from happening, and they question whether they are competent to treat these patients.

Given that the treatment of traumatized patients subjects hospital staff to stressful experiences, it is essential that there be a supportive environment for all staff, particularly for nursing staff. An important component of support is staff empowerment. For example, it is essential that staff members be given the authority to make decisions in their area of expertise, and they must be supported and guided in their work. In order for staff to communicate and encourage patients' growth, they themselves must also be validated and empowered. This model of staff empowerment must have the full cooperation of the clinical and administrative staff associated with the unit.

Hospital staff must be given permission by the unit leadership to express feelings engendered by work with traumatized patients. In addition to positive feelings, common staff feelings include exhaustion, frustration, anger, and dislike. Such feelings must be expressed in a responsible manner, as opposed to being acted out in the milieu. Staff must learn to differentiate anger about patients' behavior from dislike for patients. Even when staff members dislike patients, they must find appropriate ways to express this dislike privately so that they can continue to work with patients in a nonjudgmental and empathic way. Staff members must also be given the opportunity to express their anger and fear. In order to maintain a safe and supportive milieu, staff members must be able to set limits on inappropriate behavior and cannot be immobilized by their anger or worry excessively about retraumatizing patients.

Periodic staff meetings open to all staff members are essential to maintain unit functioning. Although some of the meetings may be used for unit or hospital business, there should always be an opportunity for staff members to discuss the feelings generated by working with patients. Just as it is important to provide education for patients about their illness and symptoms, it is necessary to provide adequate education for staff. Staff members must learn that it is normal for them to sometimes feel abused, burned out, or used up. Staff members must also learn about the process of the treatment so they understand and appreciate the importance of the work they are doing, how it helps patients, and how it affects them. It is part of the job of unit leadership to provide a sense of mission that can guide and inspire the work of the unit staff.

Informal availability of senior staff members is perhaps one of the most important ways to support and reassure staff. If all therapists and senior clinical staff leave the unit at the earliest opportunity, nursing staff feel burdened and unsupported. It is helpful if senior staff are consistently available to nursing staff (even for brief periods) to help with problem solving and to intervene and provide informal supervision and role modeling. Formal supervision for all staff is also helpful, and staff members should constantly be given the opportunity to learn more about their work and the treatment of PTSD and dissociative disorder patients.

The principles and practices outlined in this chapter are easier to maintain on specialty units dedicated to the treatment of patients with dissociative or post-traumatic disorders. However, patients with dissociative and post-traumatic disorders can also be successfully treated on general, mixed-diagnosis psychiatric units. On general psychiatric units, individualized treatment plans must be implemented for traumatized patients because their treatment may differ significantly from the treatment of other patients (e.g., a psychotic patient may need more control and structure from staff). A treatment team that is particularly knowledgeable about PTSD and dissociative disorders and clear leadership about treatment issues are helpful on a general psychiatric unit.

Many other kinds of patients can be treated alongside traumatized patients. However, two groups of psychiatric patients do not seem to mix well with them. Highly agitated, acutely psychotic, and intrusive patients may be frightening for patients who are already overwhelmed by intrusive reexperiencing of their abuse. Patients who are sexual abuse perpetrators are also problematic, sometimes frightening traumatized patients, but also often engaging them in seductive and abusive reenactments.

The hospitalization of patients with complex PTSD and dissociative disorders often appears to magnify the normative difficulties of outpatient treatment. However, a well-grounded understanding of the principles of treatment, clear and compassionate interventions, and measures to sustain the treaters can make the inpatient treatment a productive and growth-producing experience for both patients and staff.

CHAPTER 13

The "Impossible Patient": Treating Chronically Disempowered Survivors of Childhood Abuse

THE STUDY OF the effects of childhood trauma has had enormous impact on the treatment of many psychiatric patients. A new understanding of early trauma as a cause of a variety of psychological difficulties has added a fresh perspective in the treatment of many patients, particularly patients with post-traumatic and dissociative disorders, and for many others with characterologic difficulties in the borderline/narcissistic range. However, it is clear that there is no singular presentation for persons who have had extensive childhood abuse. The effects of such traumatization range from simple to complex, and functioning can vary from nearly normal to total disabled. Similarly, there is considerable variation in responses to treatment for traumatized patients, depending on the nature of their difficulties. For example, persons who have mild post-traumatic and dissociative symptoms and who have a history of good functioning and intact ego capacities may respond well to outpatient treatment over a fairly brief period. These patients seem to benefit from a combination of validation, support, and some exploration and abreaction of the traumatic events. On the other hand, it is clear that survivors of extensive early abuse who are highly symptomatic and disabled often have a complex, difficult, and protracted course of treatment. These challenging patients require a carefully staged treatment that emphasizes pacing and ego-supportive interventions.

Even among a symptomatic and extensively traumatized patient population, there seem to be subsets of patients who have a more difficult clinical course and whose disabilities appear to be more chronic. At least two groups of patients have this type of difficult and chronic clinical course. Patients in one of these groups have had major *DSM-IV* Axis I disorders in addition to post-traumatic and dissociative disorders. These comorbid disorders have included major mood disorders, psychosis, and substance abuse, and result in a complicated clinical presentation with complex differential diagnosis issues, and often require prolonged treatment (see Chapter 12).

A second group of patients that has a more difficult and chronic course has a clinical presentation that might well be called *chronic disempowerment*. Even among patients with complex trauma-related disorders, these patients present long-standing difficulties that seem impervious to change. They seem to come to treatment with a combination of intense psychological distress and an entrenched sense of despair, hopelessness, and helplessness. These patients represent an extraordinary clinical challenge. They are highly symptomatic and utilize extensive amounts of psychiatric and psychological care. They are prone to severe regression in treatment, which may lead to considerable morbidity and even mortality. And they elicit strong and often negative reactions from their caregivers. Understanding chronically disempowered patients is a clinical necessity, for without expert treatment these patients are likely to remain "impossible patients."

CHRONIC DISEMPOWERMENT

Generations of theorists and investigators of early childhood development have concluded that healthy psychological growth derives from appropriate parent–child attachments and interactions in a protective and nurturing environment. Good parenting requires that parents be attuned to the needs of a child and interact in a way that validates the child's positive sense of self, soothes and protects the child from overwhelming stimuli, and challenges and encourages the child's developing coping capacities. Good parenting allows a child to achieve healthy and mature characterologic development, including a sense of self-esteem and self-efficacy, a stable sense of self in relation to others, a capacity for self-soothing, and an ability to respond to the environment. In contrast, in chronically disempowered patient populations, childhood traumatization leads to a sense of self as hateful and defective, intense difficulties in managing relationships, dependency on others for soothing, and dysfunctional and rigid responses to the environment (Briere & Runtz, 1987; Browne & Finkelhor, 1985; Browning & Boatman, 1977; Carmen & Rieker, 1989; Courtois, 1979; Finkelhor & Browne, 1985; Gelinas, 1983; Herman, 1981; Meiselman, 1978; D. E. H. Russell, 1986; Shapiro, 1987; Shengold, 1989; Summit, 1983).

Many of the patients with post-traumatic and dissociative symptomatology that are seen in the inpatient setting have horrific histories of childhood abuse. For example, in one study of these patients (Kirby, Chu, & Dill, 1993), more than 70% had been first physically and/or sexually abused prior to age 11, and 80% had been abused on multiple occasions, sometimes over years. The effects of this kind of maltreatment on psychological development are profound. As discussed in Chapter 4, early and prolonged traumatization leads to massive disturbances in characterologic development. Not all borderline patients experience long-term disability, but some of these fundamental characterologic impairments can easily evolve into a syndrome of chronic disempowerment. An ingrained sense of self as defective, helpless, and powerless perpetuates the effects of early traumatization and interferes with abuse survivors' ability to take control of their lives. Moreover, profound difficulty in negotiating supportive relationships results in chronic isolation and promotes a tendency toward reenactment and revictimization. In many ways, the cruelest legacy of childhood abuse may be that it can result in dysfunctional and deeply ingrained patterns of thinking and beliefs about the self and relationships with others. These negative thoughts and beliefs can perpetuate shame, misery, and torment long after the etiologic abuse has ended.

The concept of empowerment has become a part of the psychological literature, particularly concerning the psychological development of women. Psychologist Janet Surrey (1991) wrote:

> I define psychological empowerment as: the motivation, freedom and capacity to act purposefully, with the mobilization of the energies, resources, strengths, or powers of each person through a mutual, relational process. Personal empowerment can be viewed only through the larger lens of power through connection, that is, through the establishment of mutually empathic and mutually empowering relationships. (p. 164)

In contrast to this view of empowerment, many persons who have been victims of extensive childhood abuse can be described as strikingly disempowered. Survivors of childhood traumatization often have little sense of freedom to act in a way that asserts a sense of control or autonomy. Rather than be able to engage with others in a mutually empowering fashion, they repeatedly relate to others in ways that recapitulate abusive or exploitative past relationships or flee into dysfunctional isolation.

Views of healthy empowerment have no meaning to victims of chronic childhood traumatization. These victims may even cling to their sense of disempowerment as the only reality they have known. Very often, patients' disempowerment creates dissonance in the therapy when therapists assume that patients share their own assumptions about the world and relationships. When therapists assume that patients naturally understand empowerment and are inclined to move toward feeling more empowered, an impasse often occurs based on therapists' empathic failure. Patients react by becoming more resistant, distant, or angry, and therapists tend to become overwhelmed, frustrated, and blaming. Moreover, because patients only understand their own disempowered world, they may have difficulty articulating what is wrong; they simply feel confused, misunderstood, and not heard, as in the following clinical illustration:

> Janice, an attractive 27-year-old woman, sought psychotherapy after a series of failed relationships. The young and enthusiastic therapist quickly ascertained that Janice had a history of severe emotional abuse and neglect. Janice's mother and father routinely used her as the family scapegoat, demeaning her and blaming her for the failure of the family to get along together, calling her "stupid," "gross," and "ugly." They would punish her by refusing to speak to her for days, denying her food, and even locking her out of the house. Not surprisingly, Janice developed patterns of behavior based on her early experience. She engaged with others in a defensive and angry way, assuming they would grow to hate her. This self-fulfilling prophecy often resulted in her relationships ending with the other person blaming her for all the difficulties they had experienced together. Janice also learned to punish herself for these relational failures, sometimes starving herself, and even taking small overdoses of aspirin. The therapist was horrified by the history of abuse and was determined to help her patient overcome her abusive past. She tried to be positive and encouraging, urging Janice to work on social skills issues and to make practical steps toward meeting others, such as joining a dating service. Janice became progressively less responsive in therapy and began to lose weight and neglect her grooming. When pressed to explain this behavior, she struggled for words, finally saying, "I guess I don't like myself very much." Frustrated, the therapist said, "You're going to have to try to have a more positive attitude about yourself if you're going to get anywhere!" to which Janice responded, "I knew you would come to hate me, too."

DILEMMAS IN THE TREATMENT OF DISEMPOWERED PATIENTS

The treatment of chronically disempowered patients poses a number of painful dilemmas for both patients and therapists. Most therapists have only a minimal number of these so-called impossible patients in their practice, but find that they create a maximal amount of clinical crises, personal distress, and uncomfortable countertransference responses. A number of clinical problems are commonly presented by such patients. Each of these problems must be well understood, and treatment approaches must be well conceived and skillfully implemented.

RIGID AND REPETITIVE REENACTMENTS

Reenactments of past abuse and past abusive relationships are often part of all of the traumatized patients' relationships, including therapeutic relationships. These reenactments are particularly difficult with chronically disempowered patients and tend to be rigid and repetitive. They often seem like scripted scenarios that are resistant to change. From the patient's vantage point, the reenactments feel like familiar but painful interpersonal situations. The therapist may feel pulled into an interaction in which the responses seem prearranged. Such scenarios can vary from repetitious discussions of despair and helplessness that seem impervious to alteration to statements that seem to demand certain responses from the therapist. In many instances the interchanges seem to be predetermined and often have an air of unreality. The therapist may even feel as though the patient is stuck in a drama played out for the therapist as audience, sometimes not even requiring a response, as in the following example:

> Diane, a 38-year-old woman, was admitted to the hospital in crisis and was having flashbacks of sexual abuse and intense suicidal impulses. Although she was advised by her long-term therapist and inpatient treatment team to find ways to contain and stabilize her symptoms, she insisted that the only real treatment was for her to abreact some episodes of childhood abuse. Furthermore, she insisted that the only safe way this exploration could occur was for her to be in physical restraints. The staff felt that Diane should work on her controls and that restraints would only reinforce the notion that she could not control her impulses. As this conflict in treatment philosophies escalated, Diane became more angry and accused various members of the staff of deliberately mistreating her and triggering even more flashbacks of abuse. In one interaction with her therapist, she angrily recited a litany of complaints and accused the therapist and staff of malpractice and abuse. The therapist felt uncomfortable and defensive, but also noticed that the patient was staring at the floor and seemed caught in a somewhat unreal scripted scenario. She said, "It feels to me as though you are talking *at* me as though I were an audience and not *to* me. I wonder if you can remember that I have tried very hard to listen to you and to resolve our differences, and that I am not at all interested in hurting you." Diane stopped talking abruptly, turned and looked at the therapist, and said, "Oh! That's right. I keep forgetting that you have actually been very helpful to me."

In the chronically disempowered world of the patient, change is not possible—neither internal change that helps the patient better adapt to the world nor change in the nature of abuse-related relationships. Hence, the patient and therapist are caught in a conundrum: The therapist attempts to promote change, while the patient cannot conceive of positive change and resists any change at all. This profound resistance to change may be the key characteristic of patients that appear impossible. Chronically disempowered patients are unable to ally with others and to use their support to reach new understandings and solutions. Instead, the scenarios of childhood abuse are reenacted in displacement without substantial change in their scripts. Although much tension, despair, and rage are vented, little is changed in patients' views of themselves or the world.

ANGER AND ENMESHMENT

Reenactments of past abusive relationships frequently involve interpersonal enmeshment (Pearlman & Saakvitne, 1995a). In the treatment of patients who have been profoundly mistreated, therapists may need to be active and involved in a way that fosters trust and attachment. However, this type of necessary involvement has the potential for intense dependency and enmeshment. Moreover, chronically disempowered patients approach the therapeutic relationship not only with deep mistrust, but with idealized hope as well. The therapist is seen not only as a potential abuser but as a potential rescuer (Davies & Frawley, 1994). To the extent that the therapist initially is able to respond to the patient in a helpful or gratifying manner, the patient develops a deep dependency on the therapist.

Patients' dependency combined with the angry and paranoid transferences that inevitably derive from past abuse often lead to intensely painful interpersonal struggles as the therapeutic relationship becomes an arena for acting out hostile dependency. Patients may find themselves repeatedly testing and challenging the therapists to determine if they can be trusted. Repetitive and excessive efforts of therapists to reassure patients can lead to escalation of a struggle that becomes a reenactment of abusive relationships, as in the following clinical example:

> Marilyn, a young woman with a history of abandonment, neglect, and abuse, repeatedly told her therapist that she was terrified that the therapist would abandon her. She also acted out this conflict in many ways. On many occasions (such as the therapist's vacation, change in appointment times, the therapist being late to appointments, misinterpretation of the therapist's comments) Marilyn would panic about being abandoned by the therapist; she would isolate herself, refusing contact with the therapist or friends. Overwhelmed with anger, self-blame, and despair, Marilyn would act self-destructively, drinking heavily, taking overdoses of medication, and engaging in risky behavior. The therapist redoubled his efforts to reassure Marilyn, and on several occasions promised never to leave her. These promises failed to reassure her and she engaged in increasingly serious self-destructive acts, almost as if to challenge the sincerity of the therapist's commitment. Finally, the therapist, feeling exhausted, frustrated, and overwhelmed, sought consultation. In a series of interactions with Marilyn, the therapist explained that he would continue to be committed to her, but only if the therapy was helpful. The therapist made it

clear that he did not feel it was helpful to conduct therapy in a way that recapitulated the enmeshed and abusive relationships of her childhood. The therapist emphasized that Marilyn had control over the relationship and could
ensure an ongoing relationship by learning to take care of herself.

In working with chronically disempowered patients, the management of
the therapeutic relationship may be the most difficult part of the therapy.
Many of these patients have grown up being targets of hostile projection or
profound neglect and they may have little concept of normal patterns of relating. Explicit attention to the therapeutic relationship must be a priority
throughout the course of the treatment. Most chronically disempowered patients have no understanding or expectation of being able to change their
patterns of relating. Rather than change, their primary goals in relationships
are to hold on to important nurturing relationships (particularly the relationship with the therapist), to discharge intolerable feelings such as anger,
and to obtain comfort. The following clinical illustration demonstrates how
some of these motivations become complex, painful, and repetitive scenarios:

> Carol, a 31-year-old woman with a 15-year history of psychiatric treatment
> and impairment, began work with her fifth therapist. Work with previous
> therapists had ended when she had overstepped boundaries, attempted sui-
> cide, or, in one case, when a therapist had moved out of town (because, Carol
> implied, the work with her was too stressful). Carol had a history of extensive
> neglect and abuse over the course of her childhood. She had been briefly mar-
> ried and had a child, who was in the custody of the state social services de-
> partment. She was on disability insurance. In addition to the diagnosis of
> PTSD, Carol had been thought to have DID, and she frequently referred to
> herself as "we." She had many medical difficulties, including migraine
> headaches, chronic fatigue syndrome, irritable bowel syndrome, and asthma.
> Because of Carol's history of intrusiveness, the therapist set firm guidelines
> about the nature of the therapy, appointment times, and her availability. Over
> the first 2 weeks of treatment, all seemed to go well. Carol seemed surpris-
> ingly workable, and the therapist wondered if prior treatments had gone
> poorly simply because of a poor treatment frame and clashes in personalities.
> As the therapy continued, Carol began bringing in small gifts for the therapist.
> Although the therapist first accepted the gifts (a collage and a small bouquet
> of wildflowers), she became uncomfortable when Carol gave her a Valentine's
> Day card. She attempted to discuss the meaning of this card with Carol, who
> reacted with surprise, wounded innocence, anger, and then shame and guilt.
> The therapist emphasized the importance of boundaries, and Carol apolo-
> gized for her behavior. A similar pattern emerged concerning telephone calls.
> The therapist initially agreed to talk to Carol in emergencies outside the office
> only once a week, although Carol was permitted to leave messages on the
> therapist's answering machine. Initial calls were intermittent and benign, but
> Carol soon began to leave numerous messages, some of which were so long as
> to exhaust the message capacity of the answering machine. Finally, Carol
> called the therapist in panic several times in one week because it was "really
> important." When the therapist brought up the issue of boundaries, Carol

seemed again surprised and ashamed. She later left a note of apology on the windshield of the therapist's car. Following this incident, the treatment seemed to progress reasonably well until the therapist announced that she was going on vacation. During the session just before the vacation, Carol asked if the therapist was going away with her husband. When the therapist asked why Carol assumed that she was married, Carol initially was silent, but eventually confessed that she had driven by the therapist's house, opened the mailbox, and looked at some letters she had found. In the shocked silence that followed, Carol hastened to add, "But I didn't open and read anything!"

When working with chronically disempowered patients, even many experienced therapists find that they have more difficulty maintaining usual boundaries and setting limits. Some of this difficulty has to do with the intensity of the therapeutic relationship and the patient's conviction that only the therapist can provide relief and solve interpersonal problems. Patients who feel tormented by their uncertainty about relationships may seek reassurance by asking therapists to blur boundaries, maintain dual relationships, and provide constant soothing. Particularly in times of crisis, it may seem reasonable for therapists to extend themselves to an extraordinary degree. However, any significant alteration of the normal structure of therapy should be made with caution. Blurred boundaries and lack of limits will almost certainly result in the recapitulation of the lack of boundaries and limits in the patient's abusive family-of-origin. It is a necessary and integral part of the early stages of treatment for disempowered patients to learn to collaborate in treatment and to work with therapists to respect and maintain the structure of the treatment.

CONTROL AND MANIPULATION

Lacking the ability to engage with others in a collaborative way, chronically disempowered patients continue to rely on control and manipulation as ways of meeting their needs. It should be stressed that from the patient's viewpoint, this interactive style is familiar and adaptive: Because it feels impossible to trust enough to do things *with* others, the only alternative is to do things *to* others. Although these ways of relating are understandable, they are nonetheless often extremely painful for caregivers. At times the demands on therapists may be infused with anger, such as with the patient who says, "You can't terminate with me and I can't leave you; I'm stuck with you because no one else would be willing to see me," or "You better do what I say, because if you don't I'll kill myself." One such coercive scenario became so extreme that a patient carried a deadly poison on her person at all times as evidence that she was willing to execute her threat. No such way of relating is therapeutically workable, and limits must be set while pursuing whatever measures are necessary to protect both the patient and the therapist. Extreme control and manipulation often result in termination of the therapeutic relationship.

Therapists' responses may also be molded in subtler ways. One common pattern of interaction occurs when patients react by feeling victimized whenever they do not receive a response that gratifies them. Even when empathically confronted or pushed toward therapeutic goals, chronically disempowered patients feel misunderstood, blamed, angry, and hurt. This kind of response can then lead to therapists avoiding necessary interventions or retreating from crucial therapeutic stances. This type of control and manipulation through chronic victimization is both common and remarkably effective, as in the following clinical illustration:

> Lorraine, a 30-year-old lesbian woman, began a vocational program that was designed as a transition from disability to paid employment, with a 3-month limit to participation in the program. After 2½ months, Lorraine had made little progress. She met with her case worker, who tried to question her about her future prospects. When the case worker asked why she was not ready to leave the program, she reacted strongly: "Are you saying that I've done something wrong? I'm sorry. I'm sorry. I'm sorry." The case worker apologized for having upset her with his demanding inquiries and approved an additional 3-month stay in the program. Three months later, when again Lorraine failed to obtain employment, the case worker approached her with trepidation and anxiety. Lorraine responded by saying, "I know I've been a failure in this program. I'm sure you have all been talking about me and how I haven't been able to get a job. I know you think I'm stupid and lazy, and you probably hate me because I'm gay. I'll leave and won't bother you again." The case worker hastened to offer another 3-month extension in the vocational program.

This example is not meant to imply that patients with childhood abuse always deliberately seek to manipulate others. Rather, the ingrained responses of these patients who feel repetitively victimized are infectious, perpetuating the patterns of victimization and chronic disempowerment.

FIXATION ON THE TRAUMA

In recent years, a consensus has emerged which suggests that the therapy of survivors of childhood abuse should proceed in stages (Chu, 1992c; Herman, 1992; Lebowitz, Harvey, & Herman, 1993). In general, abreactive work should only take place following a period of stabilization and containment. Herman, for example, advocated a phase of establishing safety prior to proceeding with abreaction (1992). Given chronically disempowered patients' tendency toward reenactment and revictimization, early work on safety is indeed important. As in work with abused children, dismantling defenses erected against past abuse is appropriate only when the current environment is safe. For adult patients to reexperience past abuse and to be able to distinguish it from current reality, the current environment must be safe from both internal and external threat, including the trauma of self-perpetuated abuse.

Some chronically disempowered patients appear to be fixated on exploring the trauma, regardless of the lack of safety and ongoing chaos in their lives. Having no sense of their own ability to gain control of their experience, these patients see abreaction as a panacea for their difficulties—a cathartic process from which they will emerge somehow changed. Unfortunately, however, this kind of premature abreaction is not only overwhelming, but self-perpetuating. The intense affect of past abuse is poorly tolerated, and patients retreat to self-harming behaviors. In addition, the dissociative barriers, which previously kept traumatic memories from flooding into consciousness, are weakened. Chronically disempowered patients lack the skills to have a sense of control over these memories, and they are vulnerable to repeated intrusions of unwanted and intolerable memories and experiences.

Although some patients with good ego strength may embark on abreactive work relatively early in treatment, most chronically disempowered patients require a long period of preliminary work prior to active focus on past trauma. In some patients, the extended focus of treatment must remain on these basic issues for many *years*. The following case illustrates some of these issues:

> An experienced therapist sought consultation for a patient he had been treating for more than 12 years. Although the treatment seemed to be going smoothly, the therapist was concerned about its pace. In describing the patient and the therapy, he noted, "About 2 years ago, she started telling me about memories of sexual abuse that she had hidden until then, and about 6 months ago, she started talking about a sense of having other 'people' inside of her, which sounds like multiple personalities. Do you think I really missed the boat?" After hearing about the extraordinary chaos of the patient's life, and the long, stabilizing, and ego-supportive therapy, the consultant concluded that although the therapist might have suspected the role of trauma and presence of dissociative symptoms earlier, the treatment probably had gone in the right direction. It seemed as though this patient needed a lengthy period of growth and stabilization before accessing traumatic material. This sense of the patient was confirmed subsequently as the patient began to reveal a long history of intentional and malevolent sadistic abuse. It was only her well-learned coping mechanisms and her strong relational bonds with her therapist and friends that kept her from decompensation and disorganization.

A primary identity as a trauma survivor may have deleterious effects on chronically disempowered patients. Such an identity may have the unintended consequences of patients' acceptance of their helplessness and victimization. More disturbingly, such patients may even develop a sense of entitlement: Having been victimized, they may feel that they deserve reparations. They may come to feel that they do not have to meet societal expectations of functioning and may expect that they are due some kind of compensation for their maltreatment. Because these kind of reparations are not forthcoming from the original perpetrators of abuse, they may expect that others, or society as a whole, should compensate them for their traumatic experiences. Although such expectations may be understandable, they are rarely realistic or fulfilled.

TREATMENT IMPLICATIONS

The principles and clinical practice used to treat patients with complex posttraumatic and dissociative disorder that are described elsewhere in this volume are critically important in treating chronically disempowered patients. Some particularly relevant elements of treatment are essential in treating these most vulnerable patients.

CLARIFICATION OF THE THERAPEUTIC AGENDA

In the treatment of chronically disempowered survivors of childhood abuse, therapists' understanding of the nature of therapy may differ considerably from patients' assumptions about therapy. For example, therapists may place a high value on patients gaining a sense of mastery over their lives through learning better self-care, gaining control over their feelings and impulses, and understanding how their lives have been affected by experience. In contrast, chronically disempowered patients may not be able to conceive of developing a sense of mastery over their lives. Patients may assume that the therapy will simply help them to feel better, and that their therapists should do whatever is necessary to care for them and to deal with their feelings and impulses. Given patients' assumptions about themselves as chronically victimized and powerless, it is not surprising that they assume that there must be some external locus of control in their lives.

Differences in assumptions about the agenda of therapy are common in the treatment of disempowered patients. Even experienced therapists repeatedly make the mistake of assuming that there are shared goals of the treatment. When there is not a mutually agreed upon agenda for the therapy, impasses inevitably arise, particularly around issues such as being taken care of versus learning self-care, and impulsive tension-release versus learning to cope with dysphoric affect. It is the therapist's responsibility to provide explicit explanation and teaching to patients about the process of therapy. Furthermore, given the chronic disempowerment that patients experience, therapists must provide such psychoeducation at the beginning of the treatment and then again throughout the course of the treatment. The following clinical example illustrates some common issues concerning the treatment process:

> Judy, a 32-year-old married woman, had a long history of depression and had been treated for years with psychotherpy and medication. She was on disability and had few demands on her life, but reported feeling overwhelmed by her family responsibilities. She began a new therapy, and it soon became clear to the therapist that Judy had problems related to many experiences of childhood abuse, that included intense devaluation and physical abuse. Both outside the office (as described by the patient) and within the therapy sessions, Judy would seem to reenact being victimized. She would bitterly describe how she knew that others (including the therapist) thought of her as worthless, how helpless she was to change her life, and how suicidal she felt. She was convinced that it was her fate to be abandoned (despite a 12-year marriage) and felt that she was of no importance to anyone else. The therapist would gently try to comfort Judy, empathizing with her despair, but also expressing his conviction that she was indeed worthwhile. He would also remind her of her many accomplishments and her value to her family, helping her gain a better sense of perspective. As the therapy continued, Judy began making increasing numbers of emergency telephone calls to the therapist. Typically, she would feel panicky and overwhelmed and call the therapist, saying that she was about to kill herself. The therapist responded patiently at first, but soon became frustrated and worried at the increasing frequency of the telephone calls. Finally, following some consultation, the therapist began to talk to Judy about the need to limit emergency calls. She was furious and incredulous. "What am I supposed to do when I'm going to kill myself?" she demanded. The therapist responded, "I hoped that you would use the therapy to learn to soothe yourself and to know how to cope when you feel overwhelmed and unhappy." Judy replied with genuine confusion, "I thought that was *your* job!"

It is inevitable that in the course of treatment the therapist will provide support and comfort to traumatized patients. Such interventions may be differently understood by different patients. For example, patients with a greater sense of self-empowerment may implicitly understand that a therapist who provides support, validation, and caring is a model that the patient can internalize (e.g., "How can I learn to provide this for myself?"). Chronically disempowered patients, on the other hand, may see the therapist's interventions as a substitute for the often arduous work of learning self-regard, self-soothing, and self-care (e.g., "How can I get my therapist to do more of this for me?"). Moreover, because these patients may not have any sense of interpersonal relatedness, they see learning to care for themselves only as a lonely, impossible, and unwanted task. This dysfunctional, albeit understandable, outlook has enormous regressive potential: As more support is provided by the therapist, the patient becomes less competent. This impasse often results in an increasing intensity of the therapy and an associated deterioration of the patient's clinical condition.

Therapists must provide ongoing psychoeducation and support to help disempowered patients understand that they must learn about self-care and mutuality in relationships. Therapists must be empathic about the difficulties that disempowered patients have in facing these tasks and must be prepared to repeatedly encourage patients to take a stance that will help them gain an internal sense of control. It is only in this context that therapy is helpful, and therapists must not collude in perpetuating patients' disempowerment through endless cycles of regressive caretaking. The goal of any therapy is increased self-esteem and self-efficacy, and no therapist would knowingly participate in therapy that increased patients' disempowerment.

TREATMENT INTENSITY AND FUNCTIONING

The intensity of treatment with chronically disempowered patients should be closely monitored. There is a danger that treatment can become a substitute for coping with the real world, and that functioning can be abandoned in favor of an identity as an impaired psychiatric patient. In general, a session frequency of once or twice per week is optimal. More frequent sessions are generally regressive. Although frequent sessions encourage a sense of object constancy, they allow patients to surrender too much of their own control and coping mechanisms and engender an interpersonal intensity that is threatening and consuming for many patients. If more frequent contact with others is needed, it should be structured as part of a therapeutic program or activities, preferably not involving the primary therapist.

An emphasis on functioning is especially important with chronically disempowered patients. Even minimal completion of tasks contributes to a sense of accomplishment and self-efficacy. Such basic efforts as getting out of bed, showering, and taking care of personal needs can be the beginning of seeing oneself as having control over one's self and the environment. Such elementary efforts may progress toward structured activities, volunteer efforts, or even paid employment. A progressive ability to function— even if not initially perceived by the patient as important—may be one of the keys to growth beyond chronic disempowerment.

LEARNING RELATIONAL SKILLS AND AUTHENTICITY

As in the therapy of all severely traumatized patients, the essential interpersonal process for chronically disempowered patients is to help them establish mutual and collaborative patterns of relatedness. As patients repeatedly bring the reenactments of abusive interactions into the therapeutic arena, therapists must help them move toward respect and mutuality. Unfortunately, it is often a lengthy process of seemingly endless cycles of disconnection and reconnection before patients can begin to internalize a healthy model of interpersonal interactions. However, it is crucial in the treatment of chronically disempowered patients that therapists understand that corrective emotional experience involves patients learning to care for themselves in the context of supportive relationships, and not simply to be cared for by others.

Chronically disempowered patients adapt to the culture of the institutions of treatment. They become façile in the language of therapeutic settings and learn to talk about their "treatment," "working in therapy" and "safety." All these terms can be used in going through the motions of being in therapy and to obscure the underlying agenda of seeking attention and nurturing from caregivers. However, to truly make progress in treatment, patients must learn a new kind of authenticity, acknowledging their sense of helplessness and their wish for passive dependency and gratification. Only this kind of authenticity can allow patients to begin to grow and move from their disempowered positions. Therapists must be sensitive to patients' difficulty coming to terms with such brutal honesty. Patients' authenticity is only gradually achieved with therapists taking a nonjudgmental and empathic stance and helping them begin to grapple with difficult and painful realities.

A necessary trait for therapists who treat impossible and chronically disempowered patients is endless patience. Therapists must learn how to empathically set limits over and over, being aware that cycles of dysfunctional behavior rarely abate quickly and that only small incremental changes can be expected. However, lapses with regression to old behaviors or minor violations of the therapeutic contract should be tolerated only if there is progress over time toward the agreed-upon goals of treatment. The therapist is in the best position to provide productive treatment by being clear that the therapy is not only about sustaining the therapeutic relationship, but that incremental change is a prerequisite for continuing the treatment. Persistent absence of any perceived benefits in treatment or major violations of the therapeutic agreement should prompt therapists to consider whether the therapy is worthwhile, workable, or tolerable, and whether alternative management is indicated.

The treatment of chronically disempowered patients represents a significant challenge to individual clinicians and to the mental health profession. Many of these patients have been so egregiously abused that they have no belief in their own self-efficacy and little ability to relate to others in ways that might help them. As a result, clinicians must exercise sensitivity and skill to find ways to engage them and to work with them to maximize the possibilities for their growth and minimize regression.

In our era of limited health care resources, the treatment of chronically disempowered and traumatized patients must be closely examined. The frequency and intensity of outpatient treatment must be carefully balanced to provide both opportunities for growth and limits to the regressive potential of excessive caretaking. Alternatives to individual treatment, such as group treatment, should be considered. The utilization and nature of inpatient hospitalization must also be carefully evaluated. Although inpatient hospitalization is clearly indicated when patients are seriously at risk, inpatient treatment must emphasize stabilization and containment rather than exploration and abreaction. The inpatient settings must not become an arena for flight from impasses in outpatient therapy or for reenactment of abuse, or a substitute for learning to live in the world. Partial hospitalization may be an attractive alternative treatment modality for some patients with a more long-term course, but much must still be learned about the optimal mix of structure and programming needed to work with these challenging patients.

Clinicians must be patient and respectful of chronically disempowered survivors of abuse and the psychological prisons in which they live. Even at best, the objectives of the treatment seem formidable to most patients, and the process of therapy is long and arduous. However, therapists must also insist that these patients begin to share an agenda that will help them truly take control of their lives, even in small increments. Therapists must refuse to collude in interactions that result in reenactments of abuse or revictimization. The ultimate prognosis of many chronically disempowered patients is uncertain. Although many improve steadily with skillful treatment, others may have more long-term disability. In either case, therapists will provide good treatment if they approach therapeutic work with compassion, patience, and skill, as well as a commitment to growth and to do no harm.

CHAPTER 14

Controversies in the Treatment of Dissociation*

EVER SINCE the introduction of dissociative identity disorder (DID; then called multiple personality disorder) into the *DSM-III* (American Psychiatric Association, 1980) controversy has swirled around the nature and the validity of this diagnosis. Since the first comprehensive descriptions of DID began to appear in contemporary psychiatric literature (Bliss, 1980; Coons, 1980; Greaves, 1980), there has been a rapid growth in attention to this disorder, with the number of reported cases growing exponentially (Greaves, 1993; Ross, 1996). The public has also been heavily exposed to information about DID through the entertainment media, most notably the book *Sybil* (Schreiber, 1973), which was later made into a widely viewed motion picture. A flurry of interest in dissociation and DID ensued, in part due to the heightening public awareness of issues concerning child abuse and prevention. In many ways, because the concepts of dissociation and DID are inherently tied in with childhood traumatization, they have also been targeted in the backlash against naïve acceptance of all reports of childhood abuse. Some prominent professionals have attacked the diagnosis of DID and have characterized it as hysterical in nature, not naturalistically occurring, and a "psychiatric misadventure" (McHugh, 1992; Merskey, 1992). Unfortunately, there has been little consensus among those who hold extreme views concerning trauma and dissociation, and acrimony has continued to reign, fueled by the litigious and demagogic attacks by some critics, notably those promoted by the False Memory Syndrome Foundation.

Despite some defensiveness about dissociative disorders and the validity of reports of recovered memory of childhood abuse, professionals in the

---

*Portions of the section "Factitious and Malingered DID" are adapted from the article "The simulation of multiple personalities: A case report" (Brick & Chu, 1991).

trauma and dissociation field have reexamined their understanding of basic concepts related to childhood traumatization. As the dust begins to settle, there is ample evidence of the validity of dissociation and dissociative disorders. Moreover, the link between dissociative pathology and childhood trauma is clear (see Chapter 3). However, there is also evidence of a variety of alternative mechanisms that can explain some cases of dissociation and related symptoms, such as amnesia and recovered memory. Even professionals who accept trauma-related dissociation must also understand that some dissociative presentations may derive from etiologies other than trauma. Although a detailed examination of each of these alternative etiologies is beyond the scope of this volume, some of the critical issues are discussed here.

PSEUDODISSOCIATION

Dissociative phenomena exist on a continuum, and a range of dissociative symptoms are found in psychiatric patients (Bernstein & Putnam, 1986). Not all dissociation is DID, and, in fact, only approximately 20% of patients with clinically significant levels of dissociative symptoms appear to have DID (Chu & Dill, 1990; Ross, Anderson, Fleisher, & Norton, 1991). Hence, it is important *not* to treat patients with lesser levels of dissociation as though they have DID. In general, there is no clear evidence that authentic DID can be iatrogenically created *de novo* in adult persons who do not have some preexisting dissociative capacity or history of trauma (Braun, 1984, 1989; Ross, Norton, & Fraser, 1989). However, patients with lesser degrees of dissociation can be pushed into DID-like presentation by naïve or overzealous therapists (Chu, 1991a; Kluft, 1996). Or pseudodissociation can result from poor therapeutic practices, as in the following clinical illustration:

> Michelle, a 19-year-old college student, sought treatment for depression in a program for the treatment of women's issues and personality disorders. After approximately 2 months of treatment, she was seen in consultation to evaluate the possibility of a dissociative disorder. To the consultant's surprise, Michelle spoke easily of her various alters, naming and describing many of them. Upon being asked how she knew she had these alters, Michelle replied, "I know this program is about personality disorders and I figured I must have multiple personalities. I was up several nights just finding my personalities and naming them!" When the consultant carefully asked about the possibility of childhood abuse, Michelle said, "I know I wasn't treated very nice when I was a kid, but I don't remember being sexually abused. However, my therapist says that I must have amnesia for the abuse and that my sexual abuse is the reason I am so afraid of men and sex."

Although this kind of suggestive clinical practice is far from the norm, some misguided therapists seem to be fixated on finding sexual abuse and evidence of dissociation. In particular, there is no evidence that past sexual abuse can be presumed (especially in the absence of memories of the abuse) if patients endorse specific symptom checklists (e.g., anxiety in response to sexual experiences, certain somatic symptoms, nightmares about sexual abuse). Treatment must be carefully directed toward evaluating what is known about the patient and moving the patient toward reducing internal fragmentation and dissociation. Therapists must be cautious about conjectures of presumed abuse and any activities or interventions that tend to reinforce or elaborate internal states.

Frequent difficulties with pseudodissociation appear to arise in patients who come to believe that they have DID. Some of these patients appear to have some level of dissociative experiences, and some have trauma in their backgrounds. Others seem to suffer primarily from severe personality disorders with intense identity diffusion and internal emptiness. For many of these patients, the DID diagnosis appears to become a focus for their lives. Even in the initial stages of treatment, they embrace the diagnosis and often speak of themselves as "we" and refer to their alters. Some patients arrive at the conclusion that they have DID because the description of different internal self-states resonates best with their own experience. Others seem to assume the diagnosis to explain why their impulses or behaviors are out of their control, and point to their multiplicity as a way of disavowing responsibility for their actions. In either case, the DID diagnosis is inappropriate and detrimental to treatment. To the extent to which patients cling to their DID identity, the treatment of the underlying difficulties is not possible. Furthermore, any use of the DID diagnosis to disavow out-of-control impulses makes change in behavior unlikely. The clinical implications of these pseudo-DID presentations are varied. For patients who have *some* dissociation, acceptance of their internal experience of separateness is important, and treatment can then be directed in a way that helps patients reduce both the fragmentation and the emphasis on the DID. However, for patients who have other disorders that are masquerading as DID, gentle but direct confrontation may be necessary. As painful as this process may be for both patient and therapist, the therapist must not collude with a false diagnosis and work on issues that are unrelated to the central problems.

Some psychologically healthier persons appear to use DID as a metaphor. That is, they can identify internal parts of themselves that feel poorly integrated with their primary identities, for example, an "inner child." For the most part, these patients are able to recognize that indeed all internal parts are components of a single self, and they readily assume responsibility for their inner selves and their behavior. Although efforts to clarify the patients' sense of self are important, there is rarely a need to confront or change the way they understand themselves. For the most part, such patients move easily into internal empathy, cooperation, and self-care, and the identity of self as multiple is given up when it no longer serves a useful purpose. The following clinical example illustrates the use of DID as a metaphor:

> Nancy, a 35-year-old married nurse, was aware of having grown up in a family that routinely victimized her. She recalled her childhood as a painful period in which she was treated as the family maid and nanny, caring for her parents and younger siblings. Her mother viewed her with contempt and her alcoholic and psychotic father regularly brutalized her. During the course of treatment, Nancy also uncovered clear memories of near murderous abuse, including being thrown out a window, which explained current radiologic evidence of old fractures of her arm, ribs, and skull. Although understanding that she had been abused, Nancy had difficulty believing and understanding that she had not brought on the abuse by bad behavior or inadequate completion of her assigned tasks, and she was able to have little compassion for herself. However, as the therapy progressed, she began to be aware of a young part of herself that continued to experience intense pain related to her childhood abuse. She named this part "Little Nancy" and began to talk about and relate to this part of herself almost as if it were a separate self. She began to have increasing compassion for her younger self, particularly after a brief hypnotic session in which "Big Nancy" visualized "Little Nancy" as physically bowed under the weight of adult responsibilities and overwhelming shame and humiliation. This intervention marked the turning point in Nancy's being able to accept herself as a whole; she let down her stoic defenses, understood her childhood experiences, and was better able to care for herself.

Neurologic presentations that resemble DID are uncommon, but not rare. Some investigators have linked dissociative phenomena to neurologic abnormalities such as temporal lobe or complex partial seizures (Mesulam, 1981; Schenk & Bear, 1981). Although soft or nonspecific findings on neurologic examination and EEG are present in many psychiatric patients, patients with neurologically based dissociation may have clearer positive findings, particularly on neuropsychological testing. Of particular note in these presentations is long-standing pervasive depersonalization and derealization. Amnesia, when present, is usually attributable to chronic difficulties in concentration, focus, and information processing, rather than extensive periods of time loss. A known history of abuse or traumatization is often not present. A clinical example follows:

> Stephanie, a 27-year-old college graduate, was admitted to a trauma program because of long-standing difficulties with dissociative symptoms. She had struggled with a severe learning disability for most of her life, but was able to complete college through much work and self-discipline. However, she continued to suffer chronic depersonalization and derealization, and she had difficulty retaining information. A therapist had questioned the possibility of DID, and although there was no known history of trauma, Stephanie had begun to have dreams of some kind of sexual abuse. A neurologic evaluation and an awake EEG failed to reveal any abnormalities, but neuropsychological

testing showed findings consistent with right-brain dysfunction, and an MRI of the brain revealed a 1 centimeter cyst in the right temporal lobe. Stephanie was advised to seek treatment that would address her style of learning and processing information and would help her become grounded in states that minimized the depersonalization and derealization.

FACTITIOUS AND MALINGERED DID

As with any other diagnosis that captures public and professional attention, DID may be simulated. Information about DID is widespread, and as noted by forensic psychologist Nicholas Spanos and colleagues (Spanos, Weekes, & Lorne, 1985)

> When given the appropriate inducements, enacting the multiple personality role is a relatively easy task. . . . Following the rules for being a multiple means remembering which experiences, behavior, and preferences go with Identity A and which go with Identity B. (p. 372)

The deliberate simulation of this disorder, while not common, is far from rare. Such a possibility should be carefully considered in the differential diagnosis of possible DID patients, both as malingering in forensic settings (Coons, 1991) and as factitious disorder in clinical settings (Brick & Chu, 1991; Kluft, 1987c).

How can a clinician approach the task of sorting through potential fiction? In addition to the careful examination of presenting features, psychiatrist Richard Kluft (1987c) suggested other areas of differences between true DID patients and malingerers:

Malingerers generally were unable to manifest consistent alternate personalities over time in terms of memory, affect, and personal characteristics.

Malingerers were generally unconvincing about any evidence of dividedness in the distant past.

Malingerers did not have histories of prior unsuccessful treatments.

Malingerers tended to have stereotyped good/bad personalities, while true DID cases commonly showed a "tetrad configuration of depleted host, persecutors, traumatized alters, and protectors."

True DID patients rarely "played up" their symptoms and tended to "minimize public manifestations of their disorder."

A somewhat more complicated presentation of factitious DID appears to be a form of Munchausen's Disease in which the patient seems to be deliberately fabricating medical and/or psychiatric symptoms, with the motivation of remaining in a patient role. A related syndrome, Munchausen's-By-Proxy, is manifested by the patient's seeming to mold others (often the patient's children) into having medical or psychiatric difficulties. The underlying psychiatric disorder is almost always a severe personality disorder with borderline and narcissistic features, often based on a history of pervasive childhood deprivation. Often there are both psychological and physical symptoms, as in the following clinical illustration:

> Dottie, a 42-year-old nurse and mother of two, was being treated for a number of psychiatric and medical difficulties. She had a known history of childhood trauma and at various times had been given the diagnoses of PTSD, DID, major depression, and bipolar disorder. Over years she had alternated between periods of reasonable functioning and other periods when she required either medical or psychiatric hospitalization. Dottie had received many kinds of treatment, including intensive individual psychotherapy, medication, and electroconvulsive treatment. No interventions seemed to bring about lasting improvement. During one hospitalization for depression, she appeared almost cheerful, but intimated that she knew her alters were planning to kill her. Indeed, the presumed alters did talk with her therapist about their rage at being suppressed and their homicidal plans, precipitating a series of suicide precautions. One morning, Dottie appeared very ill, and an intensive work-up revealed a severe urinary tract infection; Dottie was transported to a medical unit for treatment. While packing Dottie's clothes, an alert member of the nursing staff spotted a urinary catheter. When confronted by hospital staff, Dottie was evasive, but did not deny that she had used the catheter to introduce contaminated material into her bladder. She later told the staff on the medical ward that she had multiple personalities and that one of her alters was trying to kill her through this method. Dottie also reported that her children had serious problems. Taking one of the nurses into her confidence, she reported that her 14-year-old daughter had DID and that her 10-year-old son was suicidal.

One final twist concerning factitious DID has been seen in the forensic arena. In some situations, patients convince their therapists and other treaters that they have DID, but later recant the DID and the associated history of abuse. Subsequently, they move on to situations that fail to give them sufficient attention, and then go on to accuse their treaters of malpractice—of having implanted false memories of abuse and convincing them they had DID. It is sadly ironic that these patients accuse others of having believed the very behaviors that they so diligently tried to portray, and that the accusations prolong the attention on them that they pathologically crave.

THE RITUAL ABUSE CONTROVERSY

Ritual abuse, that is, the systematic and malevolent abuse of children by organized groups of perpetrators sometimes involved in cult activities, emerged as an issue in the late 1980s. Many patients, especially those with DID, reported extensive childhood victimization in satanic cults and even adult involvement in such activities. Many clinicians came to believe, based on the reports of their patients, in an organized international underground network of cult participants, many of whom were involved in satanism. These persons were believed to have practiced ritual sexual abuse, murder, cannibalism, and other atrocities, and to have perpetuated their activities through intergenerational cycles. Members of the cult were said to have infiltrated all normal spheres of life, from schools and religious organizations to police and government agencies. Although such activities are now not seen as widespread or pervasive, the genesis of the ritual abuse stories is still unclear (Greaves, 1992). The origins and nature of ritual abuse beliefs have been the subject of several lengthy and detailed accounts (e.g., Sakheim & Devine, 1992; Victor, 1993). One theory suggests that the stories have their basis in some actual occurrences, perhaps deliberately distorted by abusers (e.g., the simulated killing and dismemberment of a doll being understood by a young child as actual murder). Other theories point to contagion effects, particularly noting that ritual abuse stories began to proliferate following the publication of a sensationalistic and religious account of satanic abuse titled *Michelle Remembers* (Smith & Pazder, 1980). Cultural phenomena and collective unconscious human fantasies have also been suspected as the genesis of ritual abuse memories. Most cultures have dark stories of witches and even cannibalism, such as those found in fairy tales (e.g., "Hansel and Gretel") that fascinate, thrill, and horrify children.

Some patients with apparent pseudodissociation falsely embrace having been "ritually abused." Others seem to have actually experienced organized and deliberate abuse. Despite the shift to skepticism about the validity of accounts of satanic ritual abuse, psychologist David Sakheim (1996) pointed out that organized, sadistic, and malevolent abuse is known to occur and is not rare. This view is consistent with clinical experience that a substantial number of patients seem to have severe and persistent PTSD and complex dissociative disorders based on systematic and deliberate traumatization. Although the groups of perpetrators may be home grown rather than part of a widespread conspiracy, the victimization of children in gangs, sex rings, and even occult groups results in massive devastation of the self and in ongoing florid and disabling dissociative symptomatology. Rather than suggesting the need for specialized interventions (e.g., deprogramming), this level of serious psychiatric symptomatology and disability requires even more careful and conservative treatment. Patients who have undergone truly malevolent abuse are the most shattered, vulnerable, and precarious, and the injunction to do no harm has priority.

THE EVALUATION OF THE VALIDITY
OF DISSOCIATION AND MEMORY

Clinical experience with many patients who have been traumatized suggests that the validity of their traumatization is not an issue in most cases.

However, for a substantial minority of patients there is considerable question about their reports of dissociation and recovered memory (see Chapter 5). The discussion of these issues is not simply academic because the health and future of patients depends on understanding and assessment of their true difficulties. Some characteristics seem to distinguish those with true dissociation and traumatic histories from those whose histories are less authentic. No single characteristic is universally present in patients with severe PTSD and dissociative disorders, and it is usually a comprehensive assessment of a variety of characteristics that leads the best understanding of the nature of patients' difficulties.

Patients with severe dissociative disorders such as DID generally have intense ambivalence about their disorder, often moving through cycles of acceptance and denial. Only late in treatment can they sustain an ongoing understanding of their difficulties and consistently tolerate thinking of themselves as being fragmented. In contrast, even early in treatment, patients with a variety of inauthentic dissociative symptoms appear to focus on their multiplicity and repeatedly point out how their dissociation affects their behavior. Similarly, victims of childhood abuse are universally ambivalent about the abuse and are usually ashamed and reluctant to discuss their traumatization, particularly early in treatment. They vacillate between acknowledging the abuse and denying its existence or importance. In contrast, patients with less credible accounts of abuse consistently assert their belief in having been abused. They tend to become fixated on having their therapists validate their accounts of victimization.

For the most part, the level of current post-traumatic and dissociative symptoms should be proportional to the history of past dissociative symptoms and traumatization. There is a general equivalence to traumatization and the development of trauma-related symptoms in most patients: The greater the past traumatization, the greater the current post-traumatic and dissociative symptomatology. For example, most patients with true DID have extensive evidence of early childhood abuse, as well as childhood and current episodes of amnesia. Most also have long-standing experiences of severe dissociative symptoms, including amnesia and the sense of internal fragmentation (e.g., different selves or voices heard from inside the head). Most have a history of recurrent PTSD. Without a background of such symptomatology, true DID is unlikely. The onset of true DID in adulthood is rare and has been observed only when a highly stressful event triggers the expression of latent post-traumatic and dissociative symptoms related to severe childhood traumatization.

The recovery of memories of childhood abuse in patients who had heretofore been unaware of such events is relatively uncommon. Although this clinical picture has been described and is sometimes observed for bona fide abuse, the more common experience is for patients to have at least some idea that they had been victimized as children or to realize that events they considered normal were actually abusive. However, it is common for patients who have always known about some abuse to recall or recover more details about the abuse or other incidents of abuse. The memories of patients who have no recollection of abuse and who suddenly recover memories certainly should not be dismissed out-of-hand, but their overall validity should be carefully evaluated using other criteria.

Many persons who have survived severe childhood abuse deny the centrality of these experiences in their lives, attempting to distance or block out the overwhelming impact of the abuse. Patients with less valid abuse reports seem to focus on their traumatization as their primary identity. True survivors of abuse tend to minimize the nature and extent of their traumatization, whereas persons with hysteria-driven, embellished, or factitious abuse seem to produce ever more outlandish, bizarre, and graphic accounts of victimization and torture (often including satanic ritual abuse). Ironically, they sometimes seem to be conveying an indirect challenge to their credulous therapists to believe ever less credible accounts of their abuse.

Some characteristics of therapists may also have a role in the accurate understanding of dissociative disorders and memories of childhood abuse. In general, better professional training and an in-depth training in at least one major school of psychotherapy is helpful and makes therapists less likely to naïvely accept or even promote inauthentic accounts of patients' experiences. In the evaluation of dissociative symptoms and memory, it is also helpful for therapists to maintain professional neutrality, good boundaries, and role definition. Therapists must also be aware of their own fear of confronting patients or making them feel angry, disappointed, or abandoned. It is more helpful for therapists to engage patients in a mutual exploration of sensitive issues early in treatment than to be stuck in the impasse of continually trying to avoid conflict or placate angry patients.

Therapists must know their own limits. They should not use modalities in which they have little expertise (e.g., hypnosis, guided imagery, expressive therapies) because in incompetent hands many interventions can foster a blurring between reality and fantasy. Therapists must also be willing to ask for help and consultation from colleagues and personal supports because isolation can sometimes lead to extreme distortions in the intense patient–therapist dyad. Finally, therapists must practice sound psychotherapy. Meticulous attention to the fundamental concepts of traditional psychotherapy and the principles of treating severely traumatized patients facilitates the best possibility of clinical improvement, personal growth, and the chance to rebuild shattered lives.

INTEGRATING MULTIPLE VIEWS
OF DISSOCIATION

This book began by tracing the pendulum swings of societal and professional belief in the existence and effects of childhood abuse. However, even with an acceptance of traumatically based disorders, it is unwise to assume that all dissociative presentations derive from childhood abuse. It seems a fitting but ironic end to this volume to note that there is no single way of understanding the nature of DID and dissociative symptoms. Those of us who study and treat DID and pathological dissociation have developed a healthy respect for the complexities of these difficulties. We have learned that severe dissociative presentations and reports of abuse can result from a variety of circumstances. Certainly, trauma-related cases of DID and dissociation are prevalent in patient populations, and our understanding of the relationship between childhood trauma and adult dissociation is now based on both empirical research and theoretical models. However, we must also acknowledge that apparent DID and dissociative symptoms may sometimes emerge from different circumstances. Those of us who treat and study trauma-related disorders must now integrate multiple views of dissociation.

Some wise mental health professionals have passionately argued about DID, reminiscent of John Godfrey Saxe's satirical poem titled "The Blind Men and Elephant" (1851), his version of an Indian fable, possibly attributable to Mualana Jalaluddin Rumi, a thirteenth-century Afghani mystic. In this fable, six learned blind men of Indostan went to study the elephant. Each felt only a part of the elephant and concluded that the elephant must be like the part he touched—that is, like a wall (the elephant's side), spear (tusk), snake (trunk), tree (leg), fan (ear), and rope (tail). Each blind man was convinced that he was correct and persisted in his views. This fable has its analogy in our current-day controversy over the nature of dissociative phenomena. Although views of traumatically based dissociative phenomena may have more general validity, we are like the learned but foolish blind men of Indostan if we understand our initial ideas and our own early experiences to be the *only* valid interpretation of all that we observe. This verse (Chu, 1997a), adapted from Saxes's satirical poem, perhaps may serve as a reminder that the important and serious work with traumatized patients requires honesty, flexibility, integrity, and humor:

Six men who had great expertise
In the human mind,
Went to see some Multiples,
To see if they could find
What circumstances might have led
To the symptoms of this kind.

The First, a learned specialist
In trauma most abstruse,
Saw clearly that traumatic pasts
Of patients was no ruse.
Cried he, "It's clear that Multiples
Have always had abuse!"

The Second, an able therapist
Of noted mastery,
Hearing tales of devilish doings,
Said, "It's no mystery
That Multiples have likely had
A cult-ish history!"

The Third, a scholar of repute,
Said, "Multiples conform
To their treaters' expectations
And the cultural norm.
They're grand hysterics who conceal
Their conflicts 'neath a storm!"

The Fourth, a famed psychiatrist
Who knew biology
Said, "What these Multiples are like
Is mighty clear to me.
I don't acknowledge that they are
Occurring naturally."

The Fifth, a teacher of renown,
Was skeptical at best:
"These Multiples are feigning woe
To see if they can wrest
Attention from their therapists;
Impairment is their quest!"

The Sixth, a legal-minded sage
Saw a conspiracy
'Tween therapists and Multiples
To form false memory:
"They think that their 'abuse' should have
A legal remedy!"

And so these men of mental health
Disputed loud and long,
Each in his own opinion
Exceeding stiff and strong.
And each was partly in the right,
And all in part were wrong. (pp. 2–3)

Epilogue

WHY WE DO THIS WORK

THE CHALLENGES involved in clinical work with traumatized and dissociative patients are sometimes all too clear. Many of us who treat survivors of childhood abuse find our practices flooded with persons who have suffered devastating victimization and who present for treatment with a nightmarish mix of problems that may include out-of-control dissociative and post-traumatic symptoms, depression, chronic anxiety, self-mutilation, continuous suicidal impulses, substance abuse and eating disorders, self-hate, intense aloneness, and pervasive mistrust of others. Furthermore, having grown up in abusive environments, our patients almost inevitably reenact with us the interpersonal battlegrounds of their family relationships. They re-create scenarios of victimization, betrayal, and abandonment, sometimes through unpleasant mechanisms including control, manipulation, and exploitation that mirror their childhood experiences. Perhaps the most dysphoric experience of working with our patients concerns the empathy and involvement that is necessary for their treatment. To be effective, we must often feel the unbearable and explosive torment that comprises the daily experience of those we seek to help.

Many of us entered the field of mental health with considerable naïveté. We wanted to help others by involving ourselves in their lives. We felt that if we could only be good enough for our patients through exercising kind and thoughtful care, they would respond with positive growth and healing. Moreover (although we may not have admitted this), we hoped that patients would see us as compassionate, sensitive, and supportive, and would reward us with their respect, appreciation, and gratitude. Confronted with the reality of clinical practice, we soon learned that none of this was likely to occur quickly, and most of us developed strong skills in delaying gratification. We learned that the paths we follow with our patients are often long,

painful, and out of our control. Some of these paths are exceedingly difficult, and it is only through patience and endurance that patients are able to
perceive that their fleeting moments of peace and happiness are beginning
to mesh into a stable fabric of true recovery.

Why, then, do we do this work? Undoubtedly, some reasons are personal. Many of us have had our own painful experiences of feeling lost, victimized, or disenfranchised. We identify with our patients (hopefully not
too strongly) and we use our own experiences (hopefully not too promi-
nently) in our work. And, of course, there is the element of voyeurism—the
all-too-human trait that underlies our fascination with stories of appalling
human misfortune. However, many of us who survive and even thrive in
this field rely on three areas of gratification. The first is skill. We learn to
help those who are terribly damaged by their experiences. We are forced to
examine the essential elements of what actually helps persons heal from victimization. We learn how to help patients cope with uncontrollable and
overwhelming symptoms. We develop the skills around changing profoundly negative personal beliefs and assisting patients in building a new
sense of identity. We learn (often the hard way) about maintaining therapeutic perspective and therapeutic neutrality, limits and boundaries, and
the structure of treatment. We develop a high level of interpersonal skills in
negotiating complicated and painful interactions with patients, learning
how to combine empathy with confrontation, and providing both understanding and the imperative to change. We justifiably can take pride in having the ability to treat those whom others see as too difficult and too
damaged to help.

The second area of gratification is personal growth and widsom. We are
changed from our work with traumatized patients. We learn some vital
truths about human beings—many negative traits certainly, but also about
the indomitable human spirit and the ability to struggle against extraordinary odds to achieve fulfillment. We learn how we all depend on our connections with others and the value of a sense of community. We are tested
to find meaning where there seems to be none, and learn about the value of
patience, introspection, and perseverance. Through our work we are exposed to our own intense and uncomfortable feelings such as helplessness,
panic, and isolation, and even anger, hatred, and sadism. In integrating
these feelings we learn self-acceptance. We achieve some widsom about
what we can do and what we cannot do, and in the process come to a better
self-understanding of our own strengths and limitations.

The third area from which we derive gratification is the pleasure and sat-
isfaction of having some of our patients actually get better—eventually.
They develop a healthy and positive sense of themselves, and they become
more skilled in dealing with their lives. Having been able to acknowledge
their past traumatization and having found ways to engage with others de-

spite having been victimized, some of our patients achieve a striking depth of character that has been forged through overcoming adversity. We are an essential part of this process of healing from trauma. One patient described this well: "It has been an incredibly long journey. I'm a different person than I used to be. When I was young and in such pain, I didn't know there was any other world. I thought I knew everything, but I didn't know anything. I only knew my pain. It has taken so many years to dismantle the negative and destructive structures of my life so that I could have the chance to rebuild my life on a solid foundation. I now know that I'm a good and decent person. I like myself and other people, and I know how to deal with the world—perhaps even better than people who haven't had to go through what I've gone through. I not only *exist* in life, but I actually *live* my life. I know you will say that I have been primarily responsible for getting better. I agree, but I am certain that I couldn't have done it without you. You believed in me, you listened to me, you put up with me, and you stood by me. Your being there for me has helped me become someone I never dreamed I could become. You will always be a part of me and I will always carry you with me."

That is why we do this work.

James A. Chu, M.D.
Belmont, Massachusetts

APPENDIX

The Dissociative Experiences Scale

I N THE LATE 1980s Drs. Eve Bernstein Carlson and Frank W. Putnam (1986) of the National Institutes of Mental Health introduced a scale called the Dissociative Experiences Scale (DES), which made it possible to begin to quantify the level of dissociative symptoms in individual patients. The levels of these symptoms were elevated in patients with trauma-related disorders such as PTSD and dissociative disorders, but were not substantially elevated in patients with other psychiatric disorders (including temporal lobe epilepsy, in which depersonalization and derealization are markedly elevated, but with only small elevations in pervasive amnesia). The DES consists of 28 items that describe common dissociative experiences. It is a simple tool that persons can complete in a few minutes. Each individual item asks about the percentage of time (from 0% to 100%) that a particular dissociative symptoms is experienced. The overall DES score is the average of all the individual scores. Although the DES was designed as a research instrument, it is an excellent source for clinical inquiries concerning dissociative symptoms and a good clinical screening tool for determining the possible presence of trauma-related disorders. Scores of 20 or more are consistent with various kinds of post-traumatic or dissociative disorders. Median DES scores for subjects in the original study were:

	N	Percentage
Subjects scoring at or above the median scores for		
Normals (4.38)	81	83%
Agoraphobia (7.38)	71	72%
Schizophrenia (20.63)	32	33%
PTSD (31.3)	24	24%
MPD (DID) (57.1)	6	6%

Two versions of the DES exist, one using slash marks on a 100 mm. line (the score for each item is the nearest 5 mm point (e.g., 0, 5, 10), and one using percentage numbers as the scale. Both versions appear on the following pages.

Dissociative Experiences Scale I

This questionnaire consists of 28 questions about experiences you have had in your daily life. We are interested in how often you have had these experiences. It is important, however, that your answers show how often these experiences happen to you when you are *not under the influence of alcohol or drugs*. To answer the questions, please determine to what degree the experience described in the question applies to you and mark the line with a vertical slash at the appropriate place, as shown in the example below:

Example: 0%_____/_____100%

1. Some people have the experience of driving a car and suddenly realizing that they don't remember what has happened during all or part of the trip. Mark the line to show what percentage of the time this happens to you.

   0% _____100%

2. Some people find that sometimes they are listening to someone talk and they suddenly realize that they did not hear part or all of what was just said. Mark the line to show what percentage of the time this happens to you.

   0% _____100%

3. Some people have the experience of finding themselves in a place and having no idea how they got there. Mark the line to show what percentage of the time this happens to you.

   0% _____100%

4. Some people have the experience of finding themselves dressed in clothes that they don't remember putting on. Mark the line to show what percentage of the time this happens to you.

   0% _____100%

5. Some people have the experience of finding new things among their belongings that they do not remember buying. Mark the line to show what percentage of the time this happens to you.

   0% _____100%

6. Some people sometimes find that they are approached by people that they do not know who call them by another name or insist that they have met them before. Mark the line to show what percentage of the time this happens to you.

   0% _____100%

7. Some people sometimes have the experience of feeling as though they are standing next to themselves or watching themselves do something and they actually see themselves as though they were looking at another person. Mark the line to show what percentage of the time this happens to you.

   0% _____100%

8. Some people are told that they sometimes do not recognize friends or family members. Mark the line to show what percentage of the time this happens to you.

   0% _____100%

9. Some people find that they have no memory for some important events in their lives (for example, a wedding or graduation). Mark the line to show what percentage of the important events in your life you have no memory for.

   0% _____100%

10. Some people have the experience of being accused of lying when they do not think that they have lied. Mark the line to show what percentage of the time this happens to you.

    0% _____100%

11. Some people have the experience of looking in a mirror and not recognizing themselves. Mark the line to show what percentage of the time this happens to you.

    0% _____100%

12. Some people sometimes have the experience of feeling that other people, objects, and the world around them are not real. Mark the line to show what percentage of the time this happens to you.

    0% _____100%

13. Some people sometimes have the experience of feeling that their body does not seem to belong to them. Mark the line to show what percentage of the time this happens to you.

    0% _____100%

14. Some people have the experience of sometimes remembering a past event so vividly that they feel as if they were reliving that event. Mark the line to show what percentage of the time this happens to you.

0% _____100%

15. Some people have the experience of not being sure whether things that they remember happening really did happen or whether they just dreamed them. Mark the line to show what percentage of the time this happens to you.

0% _____100%

16. Some people have the experience of being in a familiar place but finding it strange and unfamiliar. Mark the line to show what percentage of the time this happens to you.

0% _____100%

17. Some people find that when they are watching television or a movie they become so absorbed in the story that they are unaware of other events happening around them. Mark the line to show what percentage of the time this happens to you.

0% _____100%

18. Some people sometimes find that they become so involved in a fantasy or daydream that it feels as though it were really happening to them. Mark the line to show what percentage of the time this happens to you.

0% _____100%

19. Some people find that they sometimes are able to ignore pain. Mark the line to show what percentage of the time this happens to you.

0% _____100%

20. Some people find that they sometimes sit staring off into space, thinking of nothing, and are not aware of the passage of time. Mark the line to show what percentage of the time this happens to you.

0% _____100%

21. Some people sometimes find that when they are alone they talk out loud to themselves. Mark the line to show what percentage of the time this happens to you.

0% _____100%

22. Some people find that in one situation they may act so differently compared to another situation that they feel almost as if they were two different people. Mark the line to show what percentage of the time this happens to you.

0% _____100%

23. Some people sometimes find that in certain situations they are able to do things with amazing case and spontaneity that would usually be difficult for them (for example, sports, work, social interactions, etc.). Mark the line to show what percentage of the time this happens to you.

0% _____100%

24. Some people sometimes find that they cannot remember whether they have done something or have just thought about doing that thing (for example, not knowing whether they have just mailed a letter or have just thought about mailing it). Mark the line to show what percentage of the time this happens to you.

0% _____100%

25. Some people sometimes find evidence that they have done things that they do not remember doing. Mark the line to show what percentage of the time this happens to you.

0% _____100%

26. Some people sometimes find writings, drawings, or notes among their belongings that they must have done but cannot remember doing. Mark the line to show what percentage of the time this happens to you.

0% _____100%

27. Some people sometimes find that they hear voices inside their head which tell them to do things or comment on things that they are doing. Mark the line to show what percentage of the time this happens to you.

0% _____100%

28. Some people sometimes feel as if they are looking at the world through a fog so that people and objects appear far away or unclear. Mark the line to show what percentage of the time this happens to you.

0% _____100%

Dissociative Experiences Scale II

This questionnaire consists of 28 questions about experiences you have had in your daily life. We are interested in how often you have had these experiences. It is important, however, that your answers show how often these experiences happen to you when you are *not under the influence of alcohol or drugs.* To answer the questions, please determine to what degree the experience described in the question applies to you and circle the appropriate number to show what percentage of the time you have had the experience.

Example: 0%   10   20   30   40   50   60   70   80   90   100%

1. Some people have the experience of driving a car and suddenly realizing that they don't remember what has happened during all or part of the trip. Circle a number to show what percentage of the time this happens to you.

   0%   10   20   30   40   50   60   70   80   90   100%

2. Some people find that sometimes they are listening to someone talk and they suddenly realize that they did not hear part or all of what was just said. Circle a number to show what percentage of the time this happens to you.

   0%   10   20   30   40   50   60   70   80   90   100%

3. Some people have the experience of finding themselves in a place and having no idea how they got there. Circle a number to show what percentage of the time this happens to you.

   0%   10   20   30   40   50   60   70   80   90   100%

4. Some people have the experience of finding themselves dressed in clothes that they don't remember putting on. Circle a number to show what percentage of the time this happens to you.

   0%   10   20   30   40   50   60   70   80   90   100%

5. Some people have the experience of finding new things among their belongings that they do not remember buying. Circle a number to show what percentage of the time this happens to you.

   0%   10   20   30   40   50   60   70   80   90   100%

6. Some people sometimes find that they are approached by people that they do not know who call them by another name or insist that they have met them before. Circle a number to show what percentage of the time this happens to you.

   0%   10   20   30   40   50   60   70   80   90   100%

7. Some people sometimes have the experience of feeling as though they are standing next to themselves or watching themselves do something and they actually see themselves as though they were looking at another person. Circle a number to show what percentage of the time this happens to you.

0%   10   20   30   40   50   60   70   80   90   100%

8. Some people are told that they sometimes do not recognize friends or family members. Circle a number to show what percentage of the time this happens to you.

0%   10   20   30   40   50   60   70   80   90   100%

9. Some people find that they have no memory for some important events in their lives (for example, a wedding or graduation). Circle a number to show what percentage of the important events in your life you have no memory for.

0%   10   20   30   40   50   60   70   80   90   100%

10. Some people have the experience of being accused of lying when they do not think that they have lied. Circle a number to show what percentage of the time this happens to you.

0%   10   20   30   40   50   60   70   80   90   100%

11. Some people have the experience of looking in a mirror and not recognizing themselves. Circle a number to show what percentage of the time this happens to you.

0%   10   20   30   40   50   60   70   80   90   100%

12. Some people sometimes have the experience of feeling that other people, objects, and the world around them are not real. Circle a number to show what percentage of the time this happens to you.

0%   10   20   30   40   50   60   70   80   90   100%

13. Some people sometimes have the experience of feeling that their body does not seem to belong to them. Circle a number to show what percentage of the time this happens to you.

0%   10   20   30   40   50   60   70   80   90   100%

14. Some people have the experience of sometimes remembering a past event so vividly that they feel as if they were reliving that event. Circle a number to show what percentage of the time this happens to you.

0%   10   20   30   40   50   60   70   80   90   100%

15. Some people have the experience of not being sure whether things that they remember happening really did happen or whether they just dreamed them. Circle a number to show what percentage of the time this happens to you.

0%   10   20   30   40   50   60   70   80   90   100%

16. Some people have the experience of being in a familiar place but finding it strange and unfamiliar. Circle a number to show what percentage of the time this happens to you.

0%   10   20   30   40   50   60   70   80   90   100%

17. Some people find that when they are watching television or a movie they become so absorbed in the story that they are unaware of other events happening around them. Circle a number to show what percentage of the time this happens to you.

0%   10   20   30   40   50   60   70   80   90   100%

18. Some people sometimes find that they become so involved in a fantasy or daydream that it feels as though it were really happening to them. Circle a number to show what percentage of the time this happens to you.

0%   10   20   30   40   50   60   70   80   90   100%

19. Some people find that they sometimes are able to ignore pain. Circle a number to show what percentage of the time this happens to you.

0%   10   20   30   40   50   60   70   80   90   100%

20. Some people find that they sometimes sit staring off into space, thinking of nothing, and are not aware of the passage of time. Circle a number to show what percentage of the time this happens to you.

0%   10   20   30   40   50   60   70   80   90   100%

21. Some people sometimes find that when they are alone they talk out loud to themselves. Circle a number to show what percentage of the time this happens to you.

0%   10   20   30   40   50   60   70   80   90   100%

22. Some people find that in one situation they may act so differently compared to another situation that they feel almost as if they were two different people. Circle a number to show what percentage of the time this happens to you.

0%   10   20   30   40   50   60   70   80   90   100%

23. Some people sometimes find that in certain situations they are able to do things with amazing ease and spontaneity that would usually be difficult for them (for example, sports, work, social interactions). Circle a number to show what percentage of the time this happens to you.

    0%   10   20   30   40   50   60   70   80   90   100%

24. Some people sometimes find that they cannot remember whether they have done something or have just thought about doing that thing (for example, not knowing whether they have just mailed a letter or have just thought about mailing it). Circle a number to show what percentage of the time this happens to you.

    0%   10   20   30   40   50   60   70   80   90   100%

25. Some people sometimes find evidence that they have done things that they do not remember doing. Circle a number to show what percentage of the time this happens to you.

    0%   10   20   30   40   50   60   70   80   90   100%

26. Some people sometimes find writings, drawings, or notes among their belongings that they must have done but cannot remember doing. Mark the line to show what percentage of the time this happens to you.

    0%   10   20   30   40   50   60   70   80   90   100%

27. Some people sometimes find that they hear voices inside their head which tell them to do things or comment on things that they are doing. Circle a number to show what percentage of the time this happens to you.

    0%   10   20   30   40   50   60   70   80   90   100%

28. Some people sometimes feel as if they are looking at the world through a fog so that people and objects appear far away or unclear. Circle a number to show what percentage of the time this happens to you.

    0%   10   20   30   40   50   60   70   80   90   100%

References

Adler, G. (1985). *Borderline psychopathology and its treatment.* New York: Jason Aronson.

Adler, G., & Buie, D. (1972). The misuses of confrontation in the treatment of borderline personality. *International Journal of Psychoanalytic Psychotherapy, 1*(3), 109–120.

Albach, F., Moorman, P. P., & Bermond, B. (1996). Memory recovery of childhood sexual abuse. *Dissociation.*

American Psychiatric Association. (1980). *Diagnostic and statistical manual of mental disorders* (3rd ed.). Washington, DC: Author.

American Psychiatric Association. (1994). *Diagnostic and statistical manual of mental disorders* (4th ed.). Washington, DC: Author.

Appelbaum, P. S., Uyehara, L. A., & Elin, M. R. (Eds.). (1997). *Trauma and memory: Clinical and legal controversies.* New York: Oxford University Press.

Barsky, A. J. (1996). Hypochondriasis: Medical management and psychiatric treatment. *Psychosomatics, 37,* 48–56.

Barsky, A. J., Wool, C., Barnett, M. C., & Cleary, P. D. (1994). Histories of childhood trauma in adult hypochondriacal patients. *American Journal of Psychiatry, 151,* 397–401.

Benham, E. (1995). Coping strategies: A psychoeducational approach to post-traumatic symptomatology. *American Journal of Psychosocial Nursing, 33*(6), 30–35.

Bernstein, E. M., & Putnam, F. W. (1986). Development, reliability, and validity of a dissociation scale. *Journal of Nervous and Mental Disease, 174,* 727–734.

Bliss, E. L. (1980). Multiple personalities. *Archives of General Psychiatry, 37,* 1388–1397.

Bowlby, J. (1984). Violence in the family as a disorder of the attachment and caregiving systems. *American Journal of Psychoanalysis, 44,* 9–27.

Brandchaft, B., & Stolorow, R. D. (1987). The borderline concept: An intersubjective viewpoint. In J. Grotstein, M. F. Solomon, & J. A. Long, (Eds.), *The borderline patient* (pp. 103–126). New Jersey: The Analytic Press.

Braun, B. G. (1984). Hypnosis creates multiple personalities: Myth or reality? *International Journal of Clinical and Experimental Hypnosis, 32,* 191–197.

Braun, B. G. (1986). Issues in the psychotherapy of multiple personality disorder. In B. G. Braun (Ed.), *Treatment of multiple personality disorder* (pp. 1–28). Washington, DC: American Psychiatric Press.

Braun, B. G. (1988). The BASK model of dissociation. *Dissociation, 1*(1), 4–23.

Braun, B. G. (1989). Iatrophilia and iatrophobia in the diagnosis and treatment of MPD. *Dissociation, 2,* 66–69.

Braun, B. G. (1990). Dissociative disorders as sequelae to incest. In R. P. Kluft (Ed.), *Incest-related syndromes of adult psychopathology* (pp. 227–246). Washington, DC: American Psychiatric Press.

Braun, B. G. (1993). Aids to the treatment of multiple personality disorder on a general psychiatric unit. In R. P. Kluft & C. G. Fine (Eds.), *Clinical perspectives on multiple personality disorder* (pp. 155–175). Washington, DC: American Psychiatric Press.

Braun, B. G., & Sachs, R. G. (1985). The development of multiple personality disorder: Predisposing, precipitating, and perpetuating factors. In R. P. Kluft (Ed.), *Childhood antecedents of multiple personality disorder* (pp. 37–64). Washington, DC: American Psychiatric Press.

Bremner, J. D., Randall, P., Vermetten, E., Staib, L., Bronen, R. A., Mazure, C., Capelli, S., McCarthy, G., Innis, R. B., & Charney, D. S. (1997). MRI-based measurements of hippocampal volume in posttraumatic stress disorder related to childhood physical and sexual abuse. *Biologic Psychiatry, 41,* 23–32.

Bremner, J. D., Randall, P. R., Scott, T. M., Bronen, R. A., Delaney, R. C., Seibyl, J. P., Southwick, S. M., McCarthy, G., Charney, D. S., & Innis, R. B. (1995). MRI-based measurement of hippocampal volume in posttraumatic stress disorder. *American Journal of Psychiatry, 152,* 973–981.

Breslau, N., Davis, G. C., Andreski, P., & Peterson, E. (1991). Traumatic events and posttraumatic stress disorder in an urban population of young adults. *Archives of General Psychiatry, 48,* 216–222.

Brick, S. S., & Chu, J. A. (1991). The simulation of multiple personalities: A case report. *Psychotherapy, 28,* 267–272.

Briere, J. (1992). *Child abuse trauma: Theory and treatment of the lasting effects.* New York: Sage Publications.

Briere, J., & Conte, J. (1993). Self-reported amnesia for abuse in adults molested as children. *Journal of Traumatic Stress, 6,* 21–31.

Briere, J., & Runtz, M. (1987). Post sexual abuse trauma: Data and implications for clinical practice. *Journal of Interpersonal Violence, 2,* 367–379.

Briere, J., & Runtz, M. (1988). Symptomatology associated with childhood sexual victimization in a non-clinical adult sample. *Child Abuse and Neglect, 12,* 331–341.

Brown, D. (1995). Pseudomemories: The standard of science and the standard of care in trauma treatment. *American Journal of Clinical Hypnosis, 37*(3), 1–24.

Brown, D., Scheflin, A. W., & Hammond, D. C. (1997). *Memory, trauma treatment and law.* New York: W. W. Norton & Co.

Brown, R., & Kulick, J. (1977). Flashbulb memories. *Cognition, 5,* 73–99.

Browne, A., & Finkelhor, D. (1985). The traumatic impact of child sexual abuse: A conceptualization. *American Journal of Orthopsychiatry, 55,* 530–541.

Browne, A., & Finkelhor, D. (1986). Impact of child sexual abuse: A review of the research. *Psychology Bulletin, 99,* 66–77.

Browning, D. H., & Boatman, B. (1977). Incest: Children at risk. *American Journal of Psychiatry, 134,* 69–72.

Bryer, J. B., Nelson, B. A., Miller, J. B., & Krol, P. A. (1987). Childhood sexual and physical abuse as factors in adult psychiatric illness. *American Journal of Psychiatry, 144,* 1426–1430.

Buie, D., & Adler, G. (1972). The uses of confrontation in the treatment of borderline personality. *International Journal of Psychoanalytic Psychotherapy, 1*(3), 90–108.

Burgess, A. W., Groth, A. N., Holmstrom, L. L., & Sgroi, S. M. (1978). *Sexual Assault of Children and Adolescents.* Lexington, MA: Lexington Books.

Cahill, L., Prins, B., Weber, M., & McGaugh, J. L. (1994). β-adrenergic activation and memory for emotional events. *Nature, 371,* 702–704.

Cameron, C. (1994). Women survivors confronting their abusers: Issues, decisions and outcomes. *Journal of Child Sexual Abuse, 3,* 7–35.

Carmen, E. H., & Rieker, P. P. (1989). A psychosocial model of the victim-to-patient process: Implications for treatment. *Psychiatric Clinics of North America, 12,* 431–444.

Carmen, E. H., Rieker, P. P., & Mills, T. (1984). Victims of violence and psychiatric illness. *American Journal of Psychiatry, 141,* 378–383.

Caul, D. (1978). *Treatment philosophies in the management of multiple personality.* Paper presented at the 131st meeting of the American Psychiatric Association, Atlanta, GA.

Ceci, S. J., & Huffman, M. L. C. (1997). How suggestible are preschool children? Cognitive and social factors. *Journal of the American Academy of Child and Adolescent Psychiatry, 36,* 948–958.

Ceci, S. J., Huffman, M. L. C., Smith, E., & Loftus, E. W. (1994). Repeatedly thinking about non-events: Source misattributions among preschoolers. *Consciousness and Cognition, 3,* 388–407.

Charney, D. S., Deutch, A. Y., Krystal, J. H., Southwick, S. M., & Davis, M. (1993). Psychobiologic mechanisms of posttraumatic stress disorder. *Archives of General Psychiatry, 50,* 294–305.

Christianson, S.-Å., & Loftus, E. (1987). Memory for traumatic events. *Applied Cognitive Psychology, 1,* 225–239.

Christianson, S.-Å., & Loftus, E. (1991). Remembering emotional events: The fate of detailed information. *Memory and Cognition, 5,* 81–108.

Chu, J. A. (1988). Ten traps for therapists in the treatment of trauma survivors. *Dissociation, 1*(4), 24–32.

Chu, J. A. (1991a). On the misdiagnosis of multiple personality disorder. *Dissociation, 4,* 200–204.

Chu, J. A. (1991b). The repetition compulsion revisited: Reliving dissociated trauma. *Psychotherapy, 28,* 327–332.

Chu, J. A. (1992a). Empathic confrontation in the treatment of childhood abuse survivors, including a tribute to the legacy of Dr. David Caul. *Dissociation, 5,* 98–103.

Chu, J. A. (1992b). The revictimization of adult women with histories of childhood abuse. *Journal of Psychotherapy Practice and Research, 1,* 259–269.

Chu, J. A. (1992c). The therapeutic roller coaster: Dilemmas in the treatment of childhood abuse survivors. *Journal of Psychotherapy Practice and Research, 1,* 351–370.

Chu, J. A. (1994). The rational treatment of multiple personality disorder. *Psychotherapy, 31,* 94–100.

Chu, J. A. (1997a). The president's message, March, 1997. *The International Society for the Study of Dissociation News, 15*(2), 2–3.

Chu, J. A. (1997b). Trauma and dissociative disorders. In L. I. Sederer & A. J. Rothschild (Eds.), *Acute care psychiatry: Diagnosis and treatment* (pp. 195–220). New York: Williams and Wilkins.

Chu, J. A., & Dill, D. L. (1990). Dissociative symptoms in relation to childhood physical and sexual abuse. *American Journal of Psychiatry, 147,* 887–892.

Chu, J. A., Dill, D. L., & Murphy, D. E. Depressive and post-traumatic symptomatology in adults with histories of childhood abuse. Unpublished manuscript.

Chu, J. A., Frey, L. M., Ganzel, B., & Matthews, J. A. Memories of childhood abuse: Amnesia, dissociation, and corroboration. Unpublished manuscript.

Chu, J. A., Matthews, J. A., Frey, L. M., & Ganzel, B. (1996). The nature of traumatic memories of childhood abuse. *Dissociation, 9,* 2–17.

Chu, J. A., & Terk, K. (in press). Inpatient treatment of dissociative identity disorder: An overview. In B. M. Cohen & J. A. Turkus (Eds.), *Dissociative identity disorder: Continuum of care.* New York: Jason Aronson.

Cohen, N. J., & Squire, L. R. (1980). Preserved learning and retention of pattern analyzing skill in amnesiacs: Dissociation of knowing how and knowing that. *Science, 210,* 207–210.

Comstock, C. M. (1991). Counter-transference and the suicidal multiple personality patient. *Dissociation, 4*, 25–35.

Coons, P. M. (1980). Multiple personality: Diagnostic considerations. *Journal of Clinical Psychiatry, 41*, 300–336.

Coons, P. M. (1991). Multiple personality and homicide defendants. *Psychiatric Clinics of North America, 14*, 757–768.

Coons, P. M., Cole, C., Pellow, T., & Milstein, V. (1990). Symptoms of posttraumatic stress and dissociation in women victims of abuse. In R. P. Kluft (Ed.), *Incest-related syndromes of adult psychopathology* (pp. 205–225). Washington, DC: American Psychiatric Press.

Courtois, C. A. (1979). The incest experience and its aftermath. *Victimology, 4*, 337–347.

Courtois, C. A. (1988). *Healing the incest wound: Adult survivors in therapy.* New York: W. W. Norton & Co.

Crabtree, A. (1992). Dissociation and memory: A two hundred year perspective. *Dissociation, 5*, 150–154.

Daum, I., Channon, S., & Canavar, A. (1989). Classical conditioning in patients with severe memory problems. *Journal of Abnormal Psychology, 93*, 98–105.

Davidson, J. R. T., Hughes, D., Blazer, D., & George, L. K. (1991). Posttraumatic stress disorder in the community: An epidemiological study. *Psychological Medicine, 21*, 1–19.

Davidson, J. R. T., Kudler, H. S., Saunders, W. B., Erickson, L., Smith, R. D., Stein, R. M., Lipper, S., Hammett, E. B., Mahoney, S. L., & Cavenar, J. O. (1993). Predicting response to amitriptyline in posttraumatic stress disorder. *American Journal of Psychiatry, 150*, 1024–1029.

Davidson, J. R. T., Kudler, H. S., Smith, R., Mahoney, S. L., Lipper, S., Hammett, E., Saunders, W. B., & Cavenar, J. (1990). Treatment of posttraumatic stress disorder with amitriptyline and placebo. *Archives of General Psychiatry, 47*, 259–266.

Davidson, J. R. T., Roth, S., & Newman, E. (1991). Fluoxitine in post-traumatic stress disorder. *Journal of Traumatic Stress, 4*, 418–423.

Davies, J. M., & Frawley, M. G. (1994). *Treating the adult survivors of childhood sexual abuse*. New York: Basic Books.

Davis, M. (1992). The role of the amygdala in fear and anxiety. *Annual Review of Neuroscience, 15*, 353–375.

de Yong, M. (1982). Self-injurious behavior in incest victims: A research note. *Child Welfare, 61*, 577–584.

DiClemente, R. J., Ponton, L. E., & Hartley, D. (1991). Prevalence and correlates of cutting behavior: Risk for HIV transmission. *Journal of the American Academy of Child and Adolescent Psychiatry, 30*, 735–739.

Donaldson, M. A., & Gardner, R. (1985). Diagnosis and treatment of traumatic stress among women after childhood incest. In C. Figley (Ed.), *Trauma and its wake* (pp. 356–377). New York: Brunner/Mazel.

Dutton, D., & Painter, S. L. (1981). Traumatic bonding: The development of emotional attachments in battered women and other relationships of intermittent abuse. *Victimology, 6*, 139–155.

Dutton, M. A., Burghardt, K. J., Perrin, S. G., Chrestman, K. R., & Halle, P. M. (1994). Battered women's cognitive schemata. *Journal of Traumatic Stress, 7*, 237–255.

Eich, J. E., & Metcalfe, J. (1989). Mood dependent learning for internal versus external events. *Journal of Experimental Psychology: Learning, Memory and Cognition, 15*, 443–455.

Elliott, D. M., & Briere, J. (1995). Posttraumatic stress associated with delayed recall of sexual abuse: A general population study. *Journal of Traumatic Stress, 8*, 629–647.

Ensink, B. J. (1992). *Confusing realities: A study of child sexual abuse and psychiatric symptoms.* Amsterdam: VU University Press.

Erdelyi, M. H. (1985). *Psychoanalysis: Freud's cognitive psychology.* New York: Free Press.

Erdelyi, M. H. (1990). Repression, reconstruction, and defense: History and integration of the psychoanalytic and experimental frameworks. In J. Singer (Ed.), *Repression and dissociation: Implications for personality theory, psychopathology, and health* (pp. 1–31). Chicago: University of Chicago Press.

Erickson, E. (1968). *Identity, youth and crisis.* New York: W. W. Norton & Co.

Eriksen, C. (1952). Defense against ego threat in memory and perception. *Journal of Abnormal and Social Psychology, 3*, 253–256.

Eriksen, C. (1953). Individual differences in defensive forgetting. *Journal of Experimental Psychology, 44*, 442–443.

Famularo, R., Kinscherff, R., & Fenton, T. (1988). Propranolol treatment for childhood posttraumatic stress disorder. *American Journal of Diseases of Children, 142*, 1244–1247.

Favazza, A., DeRosario, L., & Conteiro, K. (1989). Self-mutilation and eating disorders. *Suicide and Life-Threatening Behavior, 19*, 352–361.

Feldman-Summers, S., & Jones, G. (1984). Psychological impacts of sexual contact between therapists and other health care professionals and their clients. *Journal of Consulting and Clinical Psychology, 52*, 1054–1061.

Feldman-Summers, S., & Pope, K. S. (1994). The experience of "forgetting" childhood abuse: A national survey of psychologists. *Journal of Consulting and Clinical Psychology, 62*, 636–639.

Fesler, F. A. (1991). Valproate in combat-related posttraumatic stress disorder. *Journal of Clinical Psychiatry, 52*, 361–364.

Fine, C. G. (1989). Treatment errors and iatrogenesis across therapeutic modalities in MPD and allied dissociative disorders. *Dissociation, 2*, 77–82.

Finkelhor, D. (1984). *Child sexual abuse: New theory and research.* New York: Free Press.

Finkelhor, D., & Browne, A. (1985). The traumatic impact of child sexual abuse: A conceptualization. *American Journal of Orthopsychiatry, 55*, 530–541.

Finkelhor, D., Hotaling, G., Lewis, I. A., & Smith, C. (1990). Sexual abuse in a national survey of adult men and women: Prevalence, characteristics and risk factors. *Child Abuse and Neglect, 14*, 19–28.

Foa, E. B., Steketee, G., & Rothbaum, B. O. (1989). Behavioral/cognitive conceptualizations of post-traumatic stress disorder. *Behavior Therapy, 20*, 155–176.

Follette, V. M., Polusny, M. A., Bechtle, A. E., & Naugle, A. E. (1996). Cumulative trauma: The impact of child sexual abuse, adult sexual abuse, and spouse abuse. *Journal of Traumatic Stress, 9*, 25–35.

Fresh Air with Terri Gross. (November 1989). *Interview with Julia Child.* Winter Garden, FL: North Light Productions.

Freud, S. (1953). The interpretation of dreams. In J. Strachey (Ed.), *The standard edition of the complete psychological works of Sigmund Freud* (Vols. 4 & 5). London: Hogarth Press. (Original work published 1900)

Freud, S. (1955a). Beyond the pleasure principle. In J. Strachey (Ed.), *The standard edition of the complete psychological works of Sigmund Freud* (Vol. 18, pp. 7–64). London: Hogarth Press. (Original work published 1920)

Freud, S. (1955b). Studies on hysteria. In J. Strachey (Ed.), *The standard edition of the complete psychological works of Sigmund Freud* (Vol. 2). London: Hogarth Press. (Original work published 1893–1895)

Freud, S. (1962). The aetiology of hysteria. In J. Strachey (Ed.), *The standard edition of the complete psychological works of Sigmund Freud* (Vol. 3, pp. 191–221). London: Hogarth Press. (Original work published 1896)

Gelinas, D. J. (1983). The persisting negative effects of incest. *Psychiatry, 46*, 312–332.

Gold, S. N., Hughes, D., & Hohnecker, L. (1994). Degrees of repression of sexual abuse memories. *American Psychologist, 49*, 441–442.

Goldman, S. J., D'Angelo, E. J., DeMaso, D. R., & Mezzacappa, E. (1992). Physical and sexual abuse among children with borderline personality disorder. *American Journal of Psychiatry, 149*, 1723–1726.

Goodwin, J. (Ed.). (1982). *Sexual abuse: Incest victims and their families.* Littleton, MA: PSG Publishing.

Graf, P., Mandler, G., & Haden, P. (1982). Stimulating amnesia symptoms in normal subjects. *Science, 218*, 1243–1244.

Graf, P., & Schacter, D. L. (1985). Implicit and explicit memory for new associations in normal and amnesic subjects. *Journal of Experimental Psychology: Learning, Memory and Cognition, 11*, 501–518.

Greaves, G. B. (1980). Multiple personality. *Journal of Nervous and Mental Disease, 168*, 577–596.

Greaves, G. B. (1988). Common errors in the treatment of multiple personality disorder. *Dissociation, 1*(1), 61–66.

Greaves, G. (1992). Alternative hypotheses regarding claims of satanic cult activity: A critical analysis. In D. K. Sakheim & S. E. Devine (Eds.), *Out of darkness: Exploring satanism and ritual abuse* (pp. 45–72). New York: Lexington Books.

Greaves, G. B. (1993). A history of multiple personality disorder. In R. P. Kluft & C. G. Fine (Eds.), *Clinical perspectives on multiple personality disorder* (pp. 355–380). Washington, DC: American Psychiatric Press.

Greenson, R. (1967). *The technique and practice of psychoanalysis.* New York: International Universities Press.

Grinker, R. R., Werble, B., & Drye, R. (1968). *The borderline syndrome: A behavioral study of ego functions.* New York: Basic Books.

Grunebaum, H. U., & Klerman, G. L. (1967). Wrist slashing. *American Journal of Psychiatry, 124,* 527–534.

Gunderson, J., Frank, A., Ronningstam, E. R., Wachter, S., Lynch, F., & Wolf, P. J. (1989). Early discontinuance of borderline patients from psychotherapy. *Journal of Nervous and Mental Disease, 177,* 38–42.

Gunderson, J. G., & Chu, J. A. (1993). Treatment implications of past trauma in borderline personality disorder. *Harvard Review of Psychiatry, 1,* 75–81.

Gunderson, J. G., & Singer, M. T. (1975). Defining borderline patients: An overview. *American Journal of Psychiatry, 132,* 1–10.

Gutheil, T. G. (1989). Borderline personality disorder: Boundary violations, and patient–therapist sex: Medicolegal pitfalls. *American Journal of Psychiatry, 146,* 597–602.

Hall, R. C. W., Tice, L., Beresford, T. P., Wooley, B., & Hall, A. K. (1986). Sexual abuse in patients with anorexia and bulimia. *Psychosomatics, 30,* 73–79.

Helzer, J. E., Robins, L. N., & McEvoy, L. (1987). Post-traumatic distress in the general population. *New England Journal of Medicine, 317,* 1630–1634.

Hemingway, R. B., & Reigle, T. G. (1987). The involvement of endogenous opiate systems in learned helplessness and stress-induced analgesia. *Psychopharmacology, 93,* 353–357.

Herman, J. L. (1981). *Father–daughter incest.* Cambridge, MA: Harvard University Press.

Herman, J. L. (1992). *Trauma and recovery.* New York: Basic Books.

Herman, J. L., Perry, J. C., & van der Kolk, B. A. (1989). Childhood trauma in borderline personality disorder. *American Journal of Psychiatry, 146,* 490–495.

Herman, J. L., Russell, D., & Trocki, K. (1986). Long-term effects of incestuous abuse in childhood. *American Journal of Psychiatry, 143,* 1293–1296.

Herman, J. L., & Schatzhow, E. (1987). Recovery and verification of memories of childhood sexual trauma. *Psychoanalytic Psychology, 4*(1), 1–14.

Herman, J. L., & van der Kolk, B. A. (1987). Traumatic antecedents of borderline personality disorder. In B. A. van der Kolk (Ed.), *Psychological trauma* (pp. 111–127). Washington, DC: American Psychiatric Press.

Himber, J. (1994). Blood rituals: Self-cutting in female psychiatric patients. *Psychotherapy, 31*, 620–631.

Hoch, P., & Cattel, J. (1959). The diagnosis of pseudoneurotic schizophrenia. *Psychiatric Quarterly, 33*, 17–43.

Holmes, D. (1974). Investigation of repression: Differential recall of material experimentally or naturally associated with ego threat. *Psychological Bulletin, 81*, 632–653.

Holmes, D. S. (1990). Evidence for repression: An examination of 60 years of research. In J. Singer (Ed.), *Repression and dissociation: Implications for personality theory, psychopathology, and health* (pp. 85–102). Chicago: University of Chicago Press.

Horovitz, R. P., & Braun, B. G. (1984). Are multiple personalities borderline? *Psychiatric Clinics of North America, 7*, 69–88.

Hyman, I. E., & Pentland, J. (1996). The role of mental imagery in the creation of false childhood memories. *Journal of Memory and Language, 35*, 101–117.

Hyman, I. E., Troy, T. H., & Billings, F. J. (1995). False memories of childhood experiences. *Applied Cognitive Psychology, 9*, 181–197.

Jacoby, L. L., Lindsay, S., & Toth, J. P. (1992). Unconscious influences revealed. *American Psychologist, 47*, 802–809.

Jacoby, L. L., & Witherspoon, D. (1982). Remembering without awareness. *Canadian Journal of Psychology, 36*, 300–324.

James, J., & Meyerding, J. (1977). Early sexual experience and prostitution. *American Journal of Psychiatry, 134*, 1381–1385.

Janet, P. (1907). *The major symptoms of hysteria.* New York: Macmillan.

Janoff-Bulman, R. (1992). *Shattered assumptions: Towards a new psychology of trauma.* New York: Free Press.

Jordan, J. V., Kaplan, A. G., Miller, J. B., Stiver, I. P., & Surrey, J. L. (Eds.). (1991). *Women's growth in connection.* New York: Guilford Press.

Keane, T. M., Fairbank, J. A., Caddell, J. M., & Zimering, R. T. (1989). Implosive (flooding) therapy reduces symptoms of PTSD in Vietnam combat veterans. *Behavior Therapy, 20*, 245–260.

Kernberg, O. (1967). Borderline personality disorder. *Journal of the American Psychoanalytic Association, 15*, 641–685.

Kernberg, O. F. (1968). The treatment of patients with borderline personality organization. *International Journal of Psychoanalysis, 49*, 600–619.

Kernberg, O. F. (1970). A psychoanalytic classification of character pathology. *Journal of the American Psychoanalytic Association, 18*, 800–822.

Kernberg, O. F. (1984). *Severe personality disorders: Psychotherapeutic strategies.* New Haven, CT: Yale University Press.

Kessler, R. C., Sonnega, A., Bromet, E., Hughes, M., & Nelson, C. B. (1995). Posttraumatic stress disorder in the National Comorbidity Study. *Archives of General Psychiatry, 52*, 1048–1060.

Kihlstrom, J. F., & Hoyt, I. (1990). Repression, dissociation, and hypnosis. In J. L. Singer (Ed.), *Repression and dissociation: Implications for personality theory, psychopathology, and health* (pp. 181–208). Chicago: University of Chicago Press.

Kinzie, J. D., & Leung, P. (1989). Clonidine in Cambodian patients with posttraumatic stress disorder. *Journal of Nervous and Mental Disease, 177,* 546–550.

Kirby, J. S., Chu, J. A., & Dill, D. L. (1993). Severity, frequency, and age of onset of physical and sexual abuse as factors in the development of dissociative symptoms. *Comprehensive Psychiatry, 34,* 258–263.

Klein, N. A. (1994). Sertraline efficacy in depressed combat veterans with posttraumatic stress disorder. *American Journal of Psychiatry, 151,* 621.

Kluft, R. P. (1984a). Aspects of treatment of multiple personality disorder. *Psychiatric Annals, 14,* 51–55.

Kluft, R. P. (1984b). Treatment of multiple personality disorder: A study of 33 cases. *Psychiatric Clinics of North America, 7,* 9–29.

Kluft, R. P. (1987a). First-rank symptoms as a diagnostic clue to multiple personality disorder. *American Journal of Psychiatry, 144,* 293–298.

Kluft, R. P. (1987b). The parental fitness of mothers with multiple personality disorder: A preliminary study. *Child Abuse and Neglect, 11,* 273–280.

Kluft, R. P. (1987c). The simulation and dissimulation of multiple personality disorder. *American Journal of Clinical Hypnosis, 30,* 104–118.

Kluft, R. P. (1988). On giving consultations to therapists treating multiple personality disorder: Fifteen years' experience—Part I (Diagnosis and treatment). *Dissociation, 1* (3), 23–29.

Kluft, R. P. (1989a). Iatrogenic creation of new alter personalities. *Dissociation, 2,* 83–91.

Kluft, R. P. (1989b). The rehabilitation of therapists overwhelmed by their work with multiple personality disorder patients. *Dissociation, 2,* 244–250.

Kluft, R. P. (1989c). Treating patients sexually exploited by a previous therapist. *Psychiatric Clinics of North America, 12,* 483–500.

Kluft, R. P. (1990). Incest and subsequent revictimization: The case of therapist–patient sexual exploitation, with a description of the sitting duck syndrome. In R. P. Kluft (Ed.), *Incest-related syndromes of adult psychopathology* (pp. 263–287). Washington, DC: American Psychiatric Press.

Kluft, R. P. (1991). The hospital treatment of multiple personality disorder. *Psychiatric Clinics of North America, 14,* 695–719.

Kluft, R. P. (1995). The confirmation and disconfirmation of memories of abuse in dissociative identity disorder patients: A naturalistic study. *Dissociation, 8,* 253–258.

Kluft, R. P. (1996). Dissociative identity disorder. In L. K. Michelson & W. J. Ray (Eds.), *Handbook of dissociation: Theoretical, empirical, and clinical perspectives* (pp. 337–366). New York: Plenum Press.

Kluft, R. P., & Fine, C. G. (Eds.). (1993). *Clinical approaches to the integration of personalities*. Washington, DC: American Psychiatric Press.

Knight, R. (1958). Borderline states. *Bulletin of the Menninger Clinic, 17*, 1–12.

Kolb, J. E., & Gunderson, J. G. (1990). Review of Kernberg, O. F., Selzer, M. A., Koenisberg, H. W., Carr, A. C., Appelbaum, A. H. (1989). Psychodynamic psychotherapy of borderline patients. *International Review of Psychoanalysis, 17*, 513–516.

Kolb, L. C. (1987). A neuropsychological hypothesis explaining posttraumatic stress disorders. *American Journal of Psychiatry, 144*, 989–995.

Kolb, L. C., Burris, B., & Griffiths, S. (1984). Propranolol and clonidine in the treatment of chronic posttraumatic stress of war. In B. A. van der Kolk (Ed.), *Posttraumatic stress disorder: Psychological and biological sequelae* (pp. 97–107). Washington, DC: American Psychiatric Press.

Kosten, T. R. (1992). Alexithymia as a predictor of treatment response in PTSD. *Journal of Traumatic Stress, 5*, 563–573.

Kramer, T. H., Buckhout, R., Fox, P., Widman, E., & Tusche, B. (1991). Effects of stress on recall. *Applied Cognitive Psychology, 5*, 483–488.

Krystal, J. H., Kosten, T. R., Southwick, S., Mason, J. W., Perry, B. D., & Giller, E. L. (1989). Neurobiological aspects of PTSD: Review of clinical and preclinical studies. *Behavior Therapy, 20*, 177–198.

Kulka, R. A., Schlenger, W. E., Fairbank, J. A., Hough, R. L., Jordan, B. K., Marmer, C. R., & Weiss, D. S. (1990). *Trauma and the Vietnam War generation*. New York: Brunner/Mazel.

Lebowitz, L., Harvey, M. R., & Herman, J. L. (1993). A stage-by-dimension model of recovery from sexual trauma. *Interpersonal Violence, 8*, 378–391.

Le Doux, J. E. (1992). Emotion as memory: Anatomical systems underlying indelible neural traces. In S.-Å. Christianson (Ed.), *The handbook of emotion and memory* (pp. 269–287). Hillsdale, NJ: Erlbaum.

Lewin, R. A. (1991). Preliminary thoughts on milieu treatment of patients with multiple personality disorder. *The Psychiatric Hospital, 22*, 161–163.

Lipper, S., Davidson, J. R. T., Grady, T. A., Edinger, J. D., Hammett, E. B., Mahorny, S. L., & Cavenar, J. O. (1986). Preliminary study of carbamazepine in posttraumatic stress disorder. *Psychosomatics, 27*, 849–854.

Loewenstein, R. J. (1990). Somatoform disorders in victims of child abuse. In R. P. Kluft (Ed.), *Incest-related syndromes of adult psychopathology* (pp. 75–112). Washington, DC: American Psychiatric Press.

Loewenstein, R. J., Hornstein, N., & Farber, B. (1988). Open trial of clonazepam in the treatment of post-traumatic stress symptoms in multiple personality disorder. *Dissociation, 1*(3), 3–12.

Loftus, E. (1979). Reacting to blatantly contradictory information. *Memory and Cognition, 7*, 368–374.

Loftus, E. F. (1993). The reality of repressed memories. *American Psychologist, 48*, 518–537.

Loftus, E. F., Korf, N. L., & Schooler, J. W. (1989). Misguided memories: Sincere distortions of reality. In J. C. Yuille (Ed.), *Credibility assessment* (pp. 155–173). Norwell, MA: Kluwer Academic Publishers.

Loftus, E. F., Polonsky, S., & Fullilove, M. T. (1994). Memories of childhood sexual abuse. *Psychology of Women Quarterly, 18,* 64–84.

Ludolph, P. S., Westen, D., Misle, B., Jackson, A., Wixon, J., & Wiss, F. C. (1990). The borderline diagnosis in adolescents: Symptoms and developmental history. *American Journal of Psychiatry, 147,* 470–476.

MacFarlane, K., & Korbin, J. (1983). Confronting the incest secret long after the fact: A family study of multiple victimization with strategies for intervention. *Child Abuse and Neglect, 7,* 225–240.

Mahler, M. S. (1971). A study of the separation-individuation process and its possible application to borderline phenomena in the psychoanalytic situation. *Psychoanalytic Study of the Child, 26,* 403–424.

Mahler, M. S. (1972). Rapprochement subphase of the separation-individuation process. *Psychoanalytic Quarterly, 41,* 487–506.

Mann, J. (1973). Confrontation as a mode of teaching. In G. Adler & P. G. Myerson (Eds.), *Confrontation in psychotherapy* (pp. 39–48). New York: Science House.

Masson, J. M. (1984). The assault on truth: Freud's suppression of the seduction theory. New York: Farrar, Straus & Giroux.

Masterson, J. (1972). *Treatment of the borderline adolescent: A developmental approach.* New York: Wiley-Interscience.

Matthews, J. A., & Chu, J. A. (1997). Psychodynamic therapy for patients with early childhood trauma. In P. S. Appelbaum, L. A. Uyehara, & M. R. Elin (Eds.), *Trauma and memory: Clinical and legal controversies* (pp. 316–343). New York: Oxford University Press.

McFall, M. E., Murburg, M. M., Roszell, D. K., & Veith, R. C. (1989). Psychophysiologic and neuroendocrine findings in posttraumatic stress disorder: A review of theory and research. *Journal of Anxiety Disorders, 3,* 243–257.

McGaugh, J. L. (1989). Involvement of hormonal and neuromodulatory systems in the regulation of memory storage. *Annual Review of Neuroscience, 12,* 255–287.

McGaugh, J. L. (1992). Affect, neuromodulatory systems and memory storage. In S.-Å. Christianson (Ed.), *The handbook of emotion and memory* (pp. 245–267). Hillsdale, NJ: Lawrence Erlbaum Associates.

McGaugh, J. L., Introini, I. B., & Castellano, C. (1993). Involvement of opioid peptides in learning and memory. In A. Herz (Ed.), *Opioids II* (pp. 429–447). New York: Springer-Verlag.

McHugh, P. R. (1992). Psychiatric misadventures. *The American Scholar, 61,* 497–510.

Meiselman, K. (1978). *Incest.* San Francisco: Jossey-Bass.

Merskey, H. (1992). The manufacture of personalities: The production of multiple personality disorder. *British Journal of Psychiatry, 160,* 327–340.

Mesulam, M. M. (1981). Dissociative states with abnormal temporal lobe EEG: Multiple personality and the illusion of possession. *Archives of Neurology, 38,* 178–181.

Meyer-Williams, L. (1994). Recall of childhood trauma: A prospective study of women's memories of child sexual abuse. *Journal of Consulting and Clinical Psychology, 62,* 1167–1176.

Meyer-Williams, L., & Banyard, V. L. (1997). Perspectives on adult memories of childhood sexual abuse: A research review. In L. J. Dickstein, M. B. Riba, & J. M. Oldham (Eds.), *American Psychiatric Press review of psychiatry* (Vol. 16, pp. 123–151). Washington, DC: American Psychiatric Press.

Miller, R. (1979). Development from one to two years: Language acquisition. In J. Noshpitz (Ed.), *Basic handbook of child psychiatry* (pp. 127–144). New York: Basic Books.

Morrison, J. (1989). Childhood sexual histories of women with somatization disorder. *American Journal of Psychiatry, 146,* 239–241.

Myerson, P. G. (1973). The meanings of confrontation. In G. Adler & P. G. Myerson (Eds.), *Confrontation in psychotherapy* (pp. 21–38). New York: Science House.

Nagy, L. M., Morgan, C. A., Southwick, S. M., & Charney, D. S. (1993). Open prospective trial of fluoxetine for posttraumatic stress disorder. *Journal of Clinical Psychopharmacology, 13,* 107–114.

National Public Radio Morning Edition. (February 1996). *Recovered memory debate still incites disagreement.* Washington, DC: Author.

National Victim Center, Crime Victims Research and Treatment Center. (1992). *Rape in America: A report to the nation.* Arlington, VA: Author.

Neisser, U., & Harsch, N. (1992). Phantom flashbulb: False recollections of hearing news about the *Challenger.* In E. Winograd & U. Neisser (Eds.), *Affect and accuracy in recall* (pp. 9–31). New York: Cambridge University Press.

Ofshe, R. J. (1992). Inadvertent hypnosis during interrogation: False confession due to dissociative state, misidentified multiple personality and the satanic cult hypothesis. *International Journal of Clinical and Experimental Hypnosis, 40,* 125–126.

Ofshe, R. J., & Singer, M. T. (1994). Recovered-memory therapy and robust repression: Influence and pseudomemories. *International Journal of Clinical and Experimental Hypnosis, 42,* 391–410.

Ogata, S. N., Silk, K. R., Goodrich, S., Lohr, N. E., Westen, D., & Hill, E. M. (1990). Childhood sexual and physical abuse in adult patients with borderline personality disorder. *American Journal of Psychiatry, 147,* 1008–1013.

Pearlman, L. A., & Saakvitne, K. W. (1995a). Psychoanalytic theory and psychological trauma: History and critical review. In L. A. Pearlman & K. W.

Saakvitne (Eds.), *Trauma and the therapist: Countertransference and vicarious traumatization in psychotherapy with incest survivors* (pp. 35–54). New York: W. W. Norton & Co.

Pearlman, L. A., & Saakvitne, K. W. (1995b). *Trauma and the therapist: Countertransference and vicarious traumatization in psychotherapy with incest survivors*. New York: W. W. Norton & Co.

Peterson, R. G. (1994). Comment on Loftus. *American Psychologist, 49*, 443.

Piaget, J. (1962). *Plays, dreams and imitation in childhood*. New York: W. W. Norton & Co.

Pitman, R. K., van der Kolk, B. A., Orr, S. P., & Greenberg, M. S. (1990). Naloxone-reversible analgesic response to combat related stimuli in posttraumatic stress disorder. *Archives of General Psychiatry, 47*, 541–547.

Polster, M. R., Nadel, L., & Schacter, D. L. (1991). Cognitive neuroscience analyses of memory: A historical perspective. *Journal of Cognitive Neuroscience, 3*, 95–116.

Pope, H. G., & Hudson, J. I. (1995). Can memories of child sexual abuse be repressed? *Psychological Medicine, 25*, 121–126.

Pribor, E. F., & Dinwiddie, S. H. (1992). Psychiatric correlates of incest in childhood. *American Journal of Psychiatry, 149*, 53–56.

Pribor, E. F., Yutzy, S. H., Dean, T., & Wetzel, R. D. (1993). Briquet's syndrome, dissociation, and abuse. *American Journal of Psychiatry, 150*, 1507–1511.

Putnam, F. W. (1985). Dissociation as a response to extreme trauma. In R. P. Kluft (Ed.), *Childhood antecedents of multiple personality* (pp. 65–97). Washington, DC: American Psychiatric Press.

Putnam, F. W. (1989). *The diagnosis and treatment of multiple personality disorder*. New York: Guilford Press.

Putnam, F. W., Carlson, E. B., Ross, C. A., Anderson, G., Clark, P., Torem, M., Bowman, E. S., Coons, P. M., Chu, J. A., Dill, D. L., Loewenstein, R. J., & Braun, B. G. (1996). Patterns of dissociation in clinical and non-clinical samples. *Journal of Nervous and Mental Disease, 184*, 673–979.

Putnam, F. W., Guroff, J. J., Silberman, E. K., Barban, L., & Post, R. M. (1986). The clinical phenomenology of multiple personality disorder: A review of 100 cases. *Journal of Clinical Psychiatry, 47*, 258–293.

Rainey, J. M., Aleem, A., Ortiz, A., Yeragani, V., Pohl, R., & Berchou, R. (1987). A laboratory procedure for the induction of flashbacks. *American Journal of Psychiatry, 144*, 1317–1319.

Reist, C., Kaufmann, C. D., Haier, R. J., Sangdahl, C., de Mer, E. M., Chicz-DeMet, A., & Nelson, J. M. (1989). A controlled trial of desipramine in 18 men with posttraumatic stress disorder. *American Journal of Psychiatry, 149*, 513–516.

Resnick, H. S., Kilpatrick, D. G., Dansky, B. S., Saunders, B. E., & Best, C. L. (1993). Prevalence of civilian trauma and posttraumatic stress disorder in a representative national sample of women. *Journal of Consulting and Clinical Psychology, 61*, 984–991.

Ross, C. A. (1989). *Multiple personality disorder: Diagnosis, clinical features and treatment.* New York: Wiley.

Ross, C. A. (1996). History, phenomenology, and epidemiology of dissociation. In L. K. Michelson & W. J. Ray (Eds.), *Handbook of dissociation: Theoretical, empirical, and clinical perspectives* (pp. 3–24). New York: Plenum Press.

Ross, C. A., Anderson, G., Fleisher, W. P., & Norton, G. R. (1991). The frequency of multiple personality disorder among psychiatric inpatients. *American Journal of Psychiatry, 148*, 1717–1720.

Ross, C. A., Miller, S. D., Reagor, P., Bjornson, L., Fraser, G. A., & Anderson, G. (1990). Structured interview data on 102 cases of multiple personality disorder from four centers. *American Journal of Psychiatry, 147*, 596–601.

Ross, C. A., Norton, G. R., & Fraser, G. A. (1989). Evidence against the iatrogenesis of multiple personality disorder. *Dissociation, 2*, 61–64.

Russell, D. E. H. (1986). *The secret trauma: Incest in the lives of girls and women.* New York: Basic Books.

Russell, P. *The theory of the crunch.* Unpublished manuscript.

Rutter, M. (1987). Psychosocial resilience and protective mechanisms. *American Journal of Orthopsychiatry, 57*, 316–331.

Sakheim, D. K. (1996). Clinical aspects of sadistic ritual abuse. In L. K. Michelson & W. J. Ray (Eds.), *Handbook of dissociation: Theoretical, empirical, and clinical perspectives* (pp. 569–594). New York: Plenum Press.

Sakheim, D. K., & Devine, S. E. (Eds.). (1992). *Out of darkness: Exploring satanism and ritual abuse.* New York: Lexington Books.

Sakheim, D. K., Hess, E. P., & Chivas, A. (1988). General principles for short-term inpatient work with multiple personality disorder patients. *Psychotherapy, 25*, 117–124.

Salkovskis, P. M. (1989). Somatic problems. In K. Hawkin, P. M. Salkovskis, & J. W. Kirk (Eds.), *Cognitive–behavioral approaches to adult psychiatric disorders* (pp. 235–276). Oxford, England: Oxford University Press.

Sapolsky, R. M. (1986). Glucocorticoid toxicity in the hippocampus: Reversal by supplementation with brain fuels. *Journal of Neuroscience, 6*, 2240–2244.

Sapolsky, R. M., Krey, L. C., & McEwen, B. S. (1986). The neuroendocrinology of stress and aging: The glucocorticoid cascade hypothesis. *Endocrine Review, 7*, 284–301.

Sapolsky, R. M., Uno, H., Rebert, C. S., & Finch, C. E. (1990). Hippocampal damage associated with prolonged glucocorticoid exposure in primates. *Journal of Neuroscience, 10*, 2897–2902.

Saporta, J. A., & Case, J. (1984). The role of medication in treating adult survivors of incest. In P. Paddison (Ed.), *Treating adult survivors of incest* (pp. 101–134). Washington, DC: American Psychiatric Press.

Sartori, G., Masterson, J., & Job, R. (1987). Direct-route reading and the locus of lexical decision. In M. Coltheart, G. Sartori, & R. Job (Eds.), *The cognitive neuropsychology of language* (pp. 59–78). London: Erlbaum.

Saunders, B., & Giolas, M. H. (1991). Dissociation and childhood trauma in psychologically disturbed adolescents. *American Journal of Psychiatry, 148,* 50–54.

Saunders, E. A., & Arnold, F. A. (1993). A critique of conceptual and treatment approaches to borderline psychopathology in light of findings about childhood abuse. *Psychiatry, 56,* 188–203.

Saxe, G. N., van der Kolk, B. A., Berkowitz, R., Chinman, G., Hall, K., Lieberg, G., & Schwartz, J. (1993). Dissociative disorders in psychiatric inpatients. *American Journal of Psychiatry, 150,* 1037–1042.

Saxe, J. G. (1851). *Poems by John Godfrey Saxe.* Boston: Ticknor, Reed, and Fields.

Schacter, D. L. (1985). Priming of old and new knowledge in amnesic patients and normal subjects. *Annals of the New York Academy of Science, 444,* 44–53.

Schacter, D. L. (1987). Implicit memory: History and current status. *Journal of Experimental Psychology: Learning, Memory and Cognition, 13,* 501–518.

Schacter, D. L. (1990). Implicit memory: Multiple perspectives. *Bulletin of the Psychonomic Society, 29,* 338–340.

Schacter, D. L. (1992). Priming and multiple memory systems: Perceptual mechanisms of implicit memory. *Journal of Cognitive Neuroscience, 4,* 244–256.

Schatzow, E., & Herman, J. L. (1989). Breaking secrecy: Adult survivors disclose to their families. *Psychiatric Clinics of North America, 12,* 337–350.

Scheflin, A. W., & Brown, D. (1996). Repressed memory or dissociative amnesia: What the science says. *Journal of Psychiatry & Law, 24,* 143–188.

Schenk, L., & Bear, D. (1981). Multiple personality and related dissociative phenomena in patients with temporal lobe epilepsy. *American Journal of Psychiatry, 138,* 1311–1315.

Schiffer, F., Teicher, M. H., & Papanicolaou, A. C. (1995). Evoked potential evidence for right brain activity during the recall of traumatic memories. *Journal of Neuropsychiatry and Clinical Neuroscience, 7,* 169–175.

Schoener, G., Milgrom, J., Gonsiorek, J., Luepker, E., & Conroe, R. (1990). *Psychotherapists' sexual involvement with clients.* Minneapolis, MN: Walk-In Counseling Center.

Schooler, J., Gerhard, E., & Loftus, E. (1986). Qualities of the unreal. *Journal of Experimental Psychology: Learning, Memory and Cognition, 12,* 171–181.

Schreiber, F. R. (1973). *Sybil.* Chicago: Henry Regnery.

Schumaker, J. F. (Ed.). (1991). *Human suggestibility: Advances in theory, research, and application.* New York: Routledge.

Sgroi, S. (Ed.). (1982). *Handbook of clinical intervention in child sexual abuse.* Lexington, MA: Lexington Books.

Shapiro, S. (1987). Self-mutilation and self-blame in incest victims. *American Journal of Psychotherapy, 41,* 46–54.

Shengold, L. (1979). Child abuse and deprivation: Soul murder. *Journal of the American Psychoanalytic Association, 27,* 533–599.

Shengold, L. (1989). *Soul murder.* New Haven, CT: Yale University Press.

Shore, J. H., Vollmer, W. M., & Tatum, E. I. (1989). Community patterns of posttraumatic stress disorder. *Journal of Nervous and Mental Disease, 177,* 681–685.

Silbert, M. H., & Pines, A. M. (1981). Sexual child abuse as an antecedent to prostitution. *Child Abuse and Neglect, 5,* 407–411.

Smith, M., & Pazder, L. (1980). *Michelle remembers.* New York: Congdon and Lattes.

Southwick, S. M., Krystal, J. H., Morgan, A., Johnson, D., Nagy, L., Nicolaou, A., Henninger, G. R., & Charney, D. S. (1993). Abnormal noradrenergic function in posttraumatic stress disorder. *Archives of General Psychiatry, 50,* 266–274.

Spanos, N. P., Weekes, J. R., & Lorne, D. B. (1985). Multiple personality: A social psychological perspective. *Journal of Abnormal Psychology, 94,* 362–367.

Spiegel, D. (1986). Dissociation, double binds, and posttraumatic stress in multiple personality disorder. In B. G. Braun (Ed.), *Treatment of multiple personality disorder.* Washington, DC: American Psychiatric Press.

Steinmeyer, S. M. (1991). Some hard-learned lessons in the milieu management of multiple personality disorder. *The Psychiatric Hospital, 22,* 1–4.

Summit, R. (1983). The child sexual abuse accommodation syndrome. *Child Abuse and Neglect, 7,* 177–193.

Surrey, J. L. Relationship and empowerment. In J. V. Jordan, A. G. Kaplan, J. B. Miller, I. P. Stiver, & J. L. Surrey (Eds.), *Women's growth in connection* (pp. 162–180). New York: Guilford Press.

Surrey, J. L., Michaels, A., Levin, S., & Swett, C. (1990). Reported history of physical and sexual abuse and severity of symptomatology in women psychiatric outpatients. *American Journal of Orthopsychiatry, 60,* 412–417.

Swanson, L., & Biaggo, M. K. (1985). Therapeutic perspectives on father–daughter incest. *American Journal of Psychiatry, 142,* 667–674.

Terr, L. (1979). Children of Chowchilla. *Psychoanalytic Study of the Child, 34,* 547–623.

Terr, L. (1983). Chowchilla revisited: The effects of psychic trauma four years after a school bus kidnapping. *American Journal of Psychiatry, 140,* 1543–1550.

Terr, L. (1985). Remembered images of psychic trauma. *Psychoanalytic Study of the Child, 40,* 493–533.

Terr, L. (1988). What happens to memories of early childhood trauma? *Journal of the American Academy of Child and Adolescent Psychiatry, 27,* 96–104.

Terr, L. C. (1991). Childhood traumas: An outline and overview. *American Journal of Psychiatry, 148*, 10–20.

Tobias, B. A., Kihlstrom, J. F., & Schacter, D. L. (1992). Emotion and implicit memory. In S.-Å. Christianson (Ed.), *The handbook of emotion and memory* (pp. 67–92). Hillsdale, NJ: Erlbaum.

Tudor, T. G., & Holmes, D. S. (1973). Differential recall of successes and failures. *Journal of Research in Personality, 7*, 208–224.

Tulving, E. (1972). Episodic and semantic memory. In E. Tulving & W. Donaldson (Eds.), *Organization of memory* (pp. 381–403). New York: Academic Press.

Tulving, E. (1983). *Elements of episodic memory*. Oxford: Clarendon Press.

Tulving, E., Schacter, D. L., & Stark, H. L. (1982). Priming effects in fragment completion are independent of recognition memory. *Journal of Experimental Psychology: Learning, Memory and Cognition, 8*, 336–342.

Ulman, R. B., & Brothers, D. (1988). *The shattered self*. Hillsdale, NJ: Analytic Press.

U.S. Department of Health and Human Services, Administration for Children and Families, National Center on Child Abuse and Neglect. (1981). *The first national incidence study of child abuse and neglect (1979)*. Washington, DC: U.S. Government Printing Office.

U.S. Department of Health and Human Services, Administration for Children and Families, National Center on Child Abuse and Neglect. (1988). *The second national incidence study of child abuse and neglect (1986)*. Washington, DC: U.S. Government Printing Office.

U.S. Department of Health and Human Services, Administration for Children and Families, National Center on Child Abuse and Neglect. (1996a). *Child maltreatment 1994: Reports from the states to the National Center on Child Abuse and Neglect*. Washington, DC: U.S. Government Printing Office.

U.S. Department of Health and Human Services, Administration for Children and Families, National Center on Child Abuse and Neglect. (1996b). *The third national incidence study of child abuse and neglect (1993)*. Washington, DC: U.S. Government Printing Office.

U.S. Department of Health and Human Services, Office of Human Development Services, U.S. Advisory Board on Child Abuse and Neglect. (1990). *Child abuse and neglect: Critical first steps in response to a national emergency*. Washington, DC: U.S. Government Printing Office.

Vaillant, G. E. (1992). The beginning of wisdom is never calling a patient borderline. *Journal of Psychotherapy Practice and Research, 1*, 117–134.

van der Kolk, B. A. (1987). The psychobiology of the trauma response: Hyperarousal, constriction and addiction to traumatic reexposure. In B. A. van der Kolk (Ed.), *Psychological trauma* (pp. 63–87). Washington, DC: American Psychiatric Press.

van der Kolk, B. A. (1993). Group psychotherapy with posttraumatic stress disorders. In H. I. Kaplan & B. J. Sadock (Eds.), *Comprehensive textbook of group psychotherapy* (pp. 550–560). Baltimore: Williams & Wilkins.

van der Kolk, B. A. (1994). The body keeps the score: Memory and the evolving psychobiology of posttraumatic stress. *Harvard Review of Psychiatry, 1,* 253–265.

van der Kolk, B. A., Dreyfuss, D., Michaels, M., Shera, D., Berkowitz, B., Fisler, R., & Saxe, G. (1994). Fluoxetine in posttraumatic stress disorder. *Journal of Clinical Psychiatry, 55,* 517–522.

van der Kolk, B. A., & Ducey, C. P. (1989). The psychological processing of traumatic experience: Rorschach patterns in PTSD. *Journal of Traumatic Stress, 2,* 259–274.

van der Kolk, B. A., Greenberg, M., Boyd, H., & Krystal, J. (1985). Inescapable shock, neurotransmitters and addition to trauma: Towards a psychobiology of post traumatic stress. *Biologic Psychiatry, 20,* 314–325.

van der Kolk, B. A., & Kadish, W. (1987). Amnesia, dissociation and the return of the repressed. In B. A. van der Kolk (Ed.), *Psychological trauma* (pp. 173–190). Washington, DC: American Psychiatric Press.

van der Kolk, B. A., Perry, J. C., & Herman, J. L. (1991). Childhood origins of self-destructive behavior. *American Journal of Psychiatry, 148,* 1665–1671.

van der Kolk, B. A., & Saporta, J. (1991). The biological response to psychic trauma: Mechanisms and treatment of intrusions and numbing. *Anxiety Research, 4,* 199–212.

van der Kolk, B. A., & van der Hart, O. (1991). The intrusive past: The flexibility of memory and the engraving of trauma. *American Imago, 48,* 425–454.

Victor, J. S. (1993). *Satanic panic: The creation of a contemporary legend.* Chicago: Open Court.

Waldinger, R., & Gunderson, J. (1987). *Effective psychotherapy with borderline patients.* Washington DC: American Psychiatric Press.

Wallerstein, R. S. (1986). *Forty-two lives in treatment.* New York: Guilford Press.

Warren, A. R., & Swartwood, J. N. (1992). Developmental issues in flashbulb memory research: Children recall the *Challenger* event. In E. Winograd & U. Neisser (Eds.), *Affect and accuracy in recall* (pp. 95–120). New York: Cambridge University Press.

Warrington, E. K., & Weiskrantz, L. (1982). New method of testing long-term retention with special reference to amnesic patients. *Nature, 217,* 972–974.

Warwick, H. M. C., & Marks, I. M. (1988). Behavioural treatment of illness phobia and hypochondriasis. *British Journal of Psychiatry, 152,* 239–241.

Watkins, J. G., & Watkins, H. H. (1989). The theory and practice of ego-state therapy. In H. Grayson (Ed.), *Short term approaches to psychotherapy* (pp. 176–220). New York: Human Sciences Press.

Welch, S. L., & Fairburn, C. G. (1994). Histories of childhood trauma in bulimia nervosa: Three integrated case controls. *American Journal of Psychiatry, 151*, 402–407.

Westen, D., Ludolph, P., Misle, B., Ruffins, S., & Block, M. J. (1990). Physical and sexual abuse in adolescent girls with borderline personality disorder. *American Journal of Orthopsychiatry, 60*, 55–66.

Widom, C. S. (1996). *Accuracy of adult reports of child abuse.* Unpublished manuscript: State University of New York at Albany.

Willer, J. C., Dehen, H., & Cambier, J. (1981). Stress-induced analgesia in humans: Endogenous opioids and naloxone-reversible depression of pain reflexes. *Science, 212*, 689–691.

Wise, M. L. (1989). Adult self-injury as a survival response in victim-survivors of childhood abuse. *Journal of Chemical Dependency Treatment, 3*, 185–201.

Wolf, M. E., Alavi, A., & Mosnaim, A. D. (1988). Posttraumatic stress disorder in Vietnam veterans: Clinical and EEG findings. *Biologic Psychiatry, 23*, 642–644.

Yehuda, R., Giller, E. L., Southwick, S. M., Lowy, M. T., & Mason, J. W. (1991). Hypothalamic-pituitary-adrenal dysfunction in posttraumatic stress disorder. *Biologic Psychiatry, 30*, 1031–1048.

Zanarini, M. C., Gunderson, J. G., & Marino, M. F. (1987). Childhood experiences of borderline patients. *Comprehensive Psychiatry, 30*, 18–25.

Zetzel, E., & Meissner, W. W. (1973). *Basic concepts of psychoanalytic psychiatry.* New York: Basic Books.

Author Index

Subject Index

AA (Alcoholics Anonymous)
    behavior modification use, 94
Abandonment. *See also* neglect;
        relational support
    cutting as reaction to feeling of, 96
    fear of, as borderline personality
        disorder trait, 46
    fears of abuse survivors, empathic
        confrontation strategies, 140
Abreaction
    acute care considerations, 171
    adult PTSD treatment, vs. childhood
        trauma treatment, 48
    critical nature of preparation for, 87,
        90
    flooding techniques, in treatment of
        adult PTSD, 48, 77
    as middle stage task, 86
    phases of, 87
    premature
        chronically disempowered
        patients fixation on need for,
        189
        empathic confrontation of
        demands for, 140
        handling DID patient demands
        for, 151
        negative effects of, 42, 49, 76
    as process not goal, 90
    symptom control skills as
        prerequisite to effective, 117
    term definition, 86

Abuse. *See also* child abuse; emotional
        abuse; neglect; physical abuse;
        sexual abuse all kinds, impact
        on psychological development
        of children, 12
    consequences. *See* borderline
        personality disorder; DID
        (Dissociative Identity Disorder);
        dissociation; PTSD; self-harming
    exacerbating factors, 13
    responsibility for
        child abuse survivors view that
        they have, 47
        distinguishing from
        responsibility for self-care, 51
    right brain activation, 40
Acceptance
    as abreaction phase, 87
    as product of middle stage work, 88
Acknowledgment of early trauma
        significance
    as early stage treatment task, 81–82
    as SAFER model component, 79, 151
ACTH (adrenal corticotrophic
        hormone)
    stress-related role, 55
Acting out. *See also* behavior;
        symptoms, control of
    cutting as form of, 96
    differential diagnosis issues, 166
    nonverbal experience as stimulus
        for, 40

12 struggle for acceptance, with love of capture